The Mastery Approach to Competency-Based Education

EDUCATIONAL PSYCHOLOGY

Allen J. Edwards, Series Editor
Department of Psychology
Southwest Missouri State University
Springfield, Missouri

Phillip S. Strain, Thomas P. Cooke, and Tony Apolloni. Teaching Exceptional Children: Assessing and Modifying Social Behavior

Donald E. P. Smith and others. A Technology of Reading and Writing (in four volumes).

> Vol. 1. *Learning to Read and Write: A Task Analysis (by Donald E. P. Smith)*
>
> Vol. 2. *Criterion-Referenced Tests for Reading and Writing (by Judith M. Smith, Donald E. P. Smith, and James R. Brink)*
>
> Vol. 3. *The Adaptive Classroom (by Donald E. P. Smith)*

Joel R. Levin and Vernon L. Allen (eds.). Cognitive Learning in Children: Theories and Strategies

Vernon L. Allen (ed.). Children as Teachers: Theory and Research on Tutoring

Gilbert R. Austin. Early Childhood Education: An International Perspective

António Simões (ed.). The Bilingual Child: Research and Analysis of Existing Educational Themes

Erness Bright Brody and Nathan Brody. Intelligence: Nature, Determinants, and Consequences

Samuel Ball (ed.). Motivation in Education

J. Nina Lieberman. Playfulness: Its Relationship to Imagination and Creativity

Harry L. Hom, Jr. and Paul A. Robinson (eds.). Psychological Processes in Early Education

Donald J. Treffinger, J. Kent Davis, and Richard E. Ripple (eds.). Handbook on Teaching Educational Psychology

Harvey Lesser. Television and the Preschool Child: A Psychological Theory of Instruction and Curriculum Development

Kay Pomerance Torshen. The Mastery Approach to Competency-Based Education

In preparation:

Donald E. P. Smith and others. A Technology of Reading and Writing (in four volumes).

> Vol. 4. *Preparing Instructional Tasks (by Judith M. Smith)*

Thomas R. Kratochwill. Strategies to Evaluate Changes, in the Single Subject

The Mastery Approach to Competency-Based Education

KAY POMERANCE TORSHEN

Department of Psychology
University of Illinois at Chicago Circle
Chicago, Illinois

ACADEMIC PRESS New York San Francisco London 1977

A Subsidiary of Harcourt Brace Jovanovich, Publishers

Permission from the publisher, Science Research Associates, Inc., to reprint excerpts and figures appearing on the following pages is gratefully acknowledged.

Pages	Source
58	From *SRA Mathematics Learning System, 1972–74 Field Verification Study* by Arlene M. Suchaniak and Vernon S. Larsen. © 1975, SRA, Inc.
145	From *Distar™ Arithmetic I, II, Behavioral Objectives, Developmental Edition.* © 1971, SRA, Inc.
146	From *Distar™ Arithmetic II* by Siegfried Engelmann and Doug Carnine. © 1970, SRA, Inc.
150–151, 154–155, 155–156, 156–157, 158	From *SRA Mathematics Learning Systems, Teacher's Guide, Level 4* by M. DeVault, H. Frehmeyer, H. J. Greenberg, and S. J. Bezuska. © 1974, SRA, Inc.
152–153, 159, 160, 161	From *SRA Mathematics Learning Systems, Resource Box B* by M. DeVault, H. Frehmeyer, H. J. Greenberg, and S. J. Bezuska. © 1974, SRA, Inc.
165, 166, 167	From *SRA Criterion-Referenced Measurement Program: An Evaluation Tool, The Guide to Mastery.* © 1975, 1974, The Regents of the University of California.
168	From *SRA Learning Cycle Guide, Reading K–3.* © 1976, SRA, Inc.

ACADEMIC PRESS, INC.
111 Fifth Avenue, New York, New York 10003

United Kingdom Edition published by
ACADEMIC PRESS, INC. (LONDON) LTD.
24/28 Oval Road, London NW1

Library of Congress Cataloging in Publication Data

Torshen, Kay Pomerance.
    The mastery approach to competency-based education.

    (Educational psychology)
    Bibliography: p.
    1.   Educational psychology.   2.   Individualized
instruction.   3.   Grading and marking (Students)
I.   Title.
LB1051.T655   370'.732   76-55972
ISBN 0–12–696050–X

PRINTED IN THE UNITED STATES OF AMERICA

Contents

Preface   ix

I   INTRODUCTION TO COMPETENCY-BASED EDUCATION AND MASTERY

1   Introduction   3

2   Average-Based Education   9
Widespread Use of Average   9
Instructional Level Inappropriate for Many Students   13
Measures Supply Insufficient Information   13
Averaging Produces Labels   14

3   Competency-Based Education   19
Program Goals   19
Planning   20
Advantages   24
Potential Implementation Problems   24

4   Domains of Competence   29
Domains of the "Humane Curriculum"   30
The Arts of Learning   34
Conclusion   36

II   MASTERY: THEORY AND RESEARCH

5   The Mastery Model   41
The Mastery Components   41

When Is Mastery Appropriate?   44
Derivation of the Mastery Model   46

6   Mastery Model Implementation: Cognitive Consequences   55

Objective-Referenced Postassessment Performance   57
Norm-Referenced Standardized Achievement Tests   67
Retention   71
Reduction in Extent to Which Cognitive Entry Characteristics
    Determine Postassessment Performance   72
Conclusion   73

7   Mastery Model Implementation: Affective Consequences   75

Teachers' Perceptions   76
Parents' Perceptions of Curricula Structured according to
    the Mastery Model   79
Students' Perceptions   80
Affective Consequences of Instructional Conditions
    Created by Mastery Model Implementation   84

8   Research Relevant to Specific Mastery Model Components   103

Objectives   103
Preassessment   106
Sequencing of Objectives and Instructional Activities   107
Instruction   112
Diagnostic Assessment   122
Prescription   126
Postassessment   134

                                        III   PRACTICAL CONCERNS

9   Implementation Examples and Evaluation   143

Competencies   143
Objectives   145
Samples of Curricula Which Implement the Six Mastery Components   147
A Sample Unit in the University of Illinois College of
    Medicine Curriculum   148
A Sample Multiplication Unit in the Mathematics
    Learning System (SRA, 1974)   149
Unit Objectives   150
Preassessment   151
Sample Learning Activities (Desired Student Response)   155
Diagnostic Assessment   157
Prescription   159
Postassessment   159
Science Research Associates Assessment Instruments   162
Formative and Summative Mastery Model Curriculum Evaluation   170

10   Problems and Potential   179
    Administrative Problems   179
    Technical Problems   183
    Advantages of Mastery   188

Bibliography   193

Index   225

Preface

The goal of this volume is to provide practitioners, professors, and advanced students with a synthesis and critical evaluation of the theory, research, and practical experience derived from investigations of competency-based education throughout the twentieth century. No one denies that the goal of teaching is to foster learning. Yet, to date, there have been relatively few successful systematic attempts to determine the effectiveness of specific teaching methods or to design methods that maximize positive and minimize negative results.

As is evident from only cursory review of mass media publications, the effectiveness and value of our formal educational structure is increasingly questioned. This is as it should be in a society where so large an amount of limited resources is allocated to the training of the populace. However, criticisms offered repeatedly and in good faith by diverse factions of the population highlight those goals and expectations that are not being satisfied by the educational systems. In recent years, criticism has often been directed to deficits in mastery of basic skills. In current national and local surveys, approximately 90% of recent high school graduates recommended that schools provide more instruction in reading and mathematics (NAEP, 1973; Chicago Board of Education, 1976).

If educational systems are to continue in their highly favored position in our society, they need to be responsive to such criticism. This volume explores methods of satisfying these expectations with regard to education by causing the educative process to attain the results that we rightly expect.

The first section of the book focuses upon issues and problems relevant to implementation of competency-based educational programs covering a wide range of subject matter areas and student age levels, from preschool through graduate and professional training. The remaining two sections contain an in-depth consideration of the mastery model for curriculum structure that continues to be widely used in competency-based educational programs at all academic levels, as well as in business and industrial training programs. This model is given considerable attention herein because it can be implemented efficiently and has demonstrated effectiveness in developing basic student competencies.

Though competency-based educational programs are widely implemented by practitioners and investigated by researchers, examples of these implementations and results of this research are usually presented in fragmented fashion, classified by age of the students, subject matter of the program, or a single component of the curriculum structure, such as the objectives or the evaluation methods. The general objective of this book is to synthesize the results of the vast range of investigations and implementations conducted throughout the twentieth century in order to illuminate for practitioners the paths to follow and pitfalls to avoid, to highlight for researchers the crucial questions in need of further investigation, and to provide the advanced student with a telescopic view into the state of this particular art. The book is designed as a professional level and reference work for researchers, practitioners, and university professors involved in designing and implementing competency-based instruction and training programs or in developing the competencies of teachers and trainers. It can also serve as a text for advanced undergraduate and graduate students in education, instructional design, and industrial psychology courses.

This book could not have been completed without the generous assistance and counsel of colleagues, research assistants, students, and friends working in the areas of corporate training, professional and graduate training, and preschool through university teaching. I acknowledge with thanks the support, encouragement, and helpful suggestions made by so many individuals, too numerous to mention here, though the work of some is cited throughout this volume. Lastly, and most importantly, I wish to acknowledge the wise counsel as well as the perserverance and encouragement provided by my husband, Jerome H. Torshen, and my children, Jonathan Zachary and Jacqueline Joy.

Introduction to Competency-Based Education and Mastery

1

Introduction

At this very moment, thousands of students at every educational level and in all types of educational facilities are working on school projects that will, in due course, be labeled "unsatisfactory," "poor," or "failure." Students fail so often and so universally that some people are convinced that failure is an essential and inevitable aspect of the educational process.

However, failure often produces harmful consequences that work against the goals of education. Many dedicated teachers have doubted their own professional abilities when they could find no alternative other than giving a failing grade or flunking a student. And many students who received repeated and consistent evidence that their work was unsatisfactory have been convinced that school was a place where they could not succeed. When sincere attempts to teach and to learn meet with repeated negative responses, the instructional process can actually eliminate those activities that are essential to productive education.

The instruction available in many classrooms is inappropriate for the levels at which many of the students are functioning. Many students lack the basic skills and knowledge needed to learn from the instruction presented to them.

Moreover, the procedures often used to measure and grade students' work limit the number of students who can earn positive evaluations. In effect, these procedures prescribe less than positive evaluations for many students in a class, regardless of the level at which the students are performing. For them, school can be both unpleasant and inefficient.

These instructional and evaluation procedures can be detrimental to students' intellectual, social, and emotional development. Students do not learn efficiently when the level of the instruction is inappropriate for them. Valuable instructional resources and learning time are wasted, and students may fail to acquire essential skills and knowledge.

Furthermore, students need to receive evidence that they are producing good work. However, widely used evaluation procedures deprive many students of these positive evaluations. When students do not earn positive evaluations for their academic performance, they may not develop positive concepts of themselves in academic areas, expectations of future performance commensurate with their ability, or motivation to perform well on academic tasks.

The results of national and multinational studies of instructional variables related to educational achievement suggest that large segments of the student population require considerably more instruction in basic skills than they are currently receiving in their respective schools. One study was conducted by the International Association for the Evaluation of Education Achievement (IEA), an organization of 22 national research centers, one in each of 22 countries. During the past 15 years, these research centers have related measures of student achievement and attitudes to instructional, social, and economic factors in each nation. The results of this investigation showed that, in each country, the students' achievement in language and literature, mathematics and science was strongly related to their reading comprehension and word knowledge. Those students who had difficulty understanding teachers' explanations and instructions were at a significant disadvantage. Development of verbal ability (word knowledge and reading comprehension) appeared to be essential if the student was to succeed in the school (Bloom, 1974b).

The IEA research demonstrated that the top 5% of the students in the United States and in other developed nations performed at roughly comparable high achievement levels, in spite of differences in curriculum, instructional procedures, and social and cultural variations. Typically, these high achievers had high levels of verbal ability and came from homes in which parents were highly educated. The students appeared to learn almost spontaneously, even when the quality of their formal education was far from ideal. Stephens (1967) used the term "spontaneous schooling" to describe this phenomenon in which a small percentage of the student population achieves at very high levels, regardless of the quality of the formal education they receive. However, the educational achievement of most of the student population was dependent upon the quality of formal schooling they received.

A national study of school achievement in the United States (Coleman *et al.*, 1966) also showed that students' verbal ability was a significant determinant of their success in school. Students who did not develop adequate vocabulary and reading comprehension skills in the early grades were often severely handicapped.

Few of the 22 countries surveyed by the IEA provided adequate education for the 90% of the student population who achieved below the highest levels. The education provided for the lower 50% of the students was particularly inadequate. Those students who were not able to develop prerequisite skills, particularly verbal skills, during their early school years were frequently unable to perform adequately during their remaining years in school. For many of these students, formal schooling provided frequent and consistent evidence that their educational achievement was far less than adequate.

The performance of many students may be inadequate because they lack the verbal skills to benefit from the instruction they receive. The evidence reported here suggests that present school curricula do not contain enough of the type of instruction needed to provide most students with the verbal skills essential to success in school. Those students who fail to acquire the high levels of verbal skills needed to achieve well in school are doomed to spend the remainder of their academic careers in environments in which evidence that they have performed successfully comes infrequently, if at all.

If students are to earn positive evaluations and to experience success in the classroom, they must demonstrate competent academic performance, including mastery of educational tasks. When students fail to demonstrate performance that is competent and is recognized as such, they fail to produce work that is worthy of reward.

Each student needs access to instruction appropriate for his own level if he is to obtain maximum benefit from the time he spends in school. Instruction in basic skills and knowledge should continue until he has developed adequate competence.

When the student does produce good work, he needs to receive some evidence that his performance is good. Such evidence indicates to the student, to his teacher and parents, and to his classmates that this student is capable of performing well in school. Receiving positive evaluations for good work encourages the student to develop self-confidence and realistic, positive expectations concerning future performance. These positive evaluations may also reinforce the efforts the student puts forth to produce the academic work and may motivate the student to continue these efforts.

The student who does not earn positive evaluations for his academic work may lack evidence that he can perform well in academic areas. When his efforts to perform well and the work he produces do not earn favorable evaluations, he may not remain motivated to continue trying to do well on academic tasks.

Nevertheless, many of the methods used to evaluate students' academic performances provide positive evaluations only to those students who perform better than their peers. These methods evaluate a student's work by comparing his performance with the average performance produced by his classmates or by students in his grade or age group.

If the performance of students who achieve "below grade level" is judged to be less than successful, then up to 50% of the student population might receive evidence that their performance is not up to par. Even if every student in a group produced competent work, many of the students might not receive favorable evaluations. By definition, everyone cannot perform above average.

During the time that he is in school, a student needs to attain mastery of essential learning tasks (Erikson, 1959), to see himself as a competent student and to receive evaluations that indicate to him and to those who are important to him that his performance has been successful (Kelly, 1971; Skinner, 1968; White, 1960). If he fails to attain mastery or to achieve the status of one who is competent and successful, his chances for healthy development can be substantially reduced.

Yet, teachers are often given a homogeneous set of achievement standards that all students are expected to master at the same time. Individual differences are usually accounted for by ranking the students in the classroom on a single set of achievement criteria. Students who learn most or all of what is expected of them receive high ranks, and students who do not, receive low ranks. The ranks are often expressed in number or letter grades. These are general statements of the student's achievement status among his peers. Often the student is not clear about the specific aspects of his performance used to determine his status (Boehm & White, 1967). The grade in itself does not designate what or how much the student has learned or how he can correct his mistakes and improve his performance.

When the student's rank among his classmates is a primary method of evaluating his academic achievement, the students in each classroom whose measured achievement is average or below average may be told that their achievement ranges from mediocre to poor (Bloom, 1968). These evaluations do not encourage the students to develop views of themselves as competent learners. In fact, evaluating a student's academic work as either mediocre or poor encourages the student, his parents, his teachers, and his friends to view him as an inadequate learner of academic subjects.

Initially, most children want to do well in school (Entwisle, 1973). But the student who has experienced consistent failure in the classroom tends to lower his own expectations concerning school success. He may direct his energy outside the classroom to athletics or youth gangs or to other areas where he can experience the satisfaction of success. The student who has been negatively evaluated in the classroom rationalizes that school is not important to him because he believes it is impossible for him to succeed there (Lewis, 1974). If a student is to continue to expect to do well in school, he needs to receive some positive evaluations for his academic performance. If an individual is to develop a positive concept of himself as a student, he needs to perform competently and to receive evaluations that he interprets to be positive within his own frame of reference (Torshen, 1969, 1973).

When the student is perceived as a less than competent learner, forces are set in motion that reduce the chances that his potential will be developed to its fullest extent in school. The other students and his teachers may come to view him as having less potential than he really has. The academic goals he sets for himself and those that are set for him by his well-intentioned teachers may not sufficiently challenge his true abilities (Brophy & Good, 1974). A student may divert his own personal resources to nonacademic areas because he believes that success in academic subjects is not open to him. If he does not apply his maximum efforts to learning school subjects, he may fail to acquire some of the skills and knowledge he needs as a basis for further learning. School tasks, in general, and test taking, in particular, may generate feelings of fear and anxiety that are additional stumbling blocks in his learning process. All of these factors can interfere with his academic learning in school, decreasing the chances that his academic performance will be commensurate with his academic abilities. If the quality of the student's academic achievement remains below his potential, the lowered evaluations he receives for that performance may serve to reinforce his lowered estimate of his own ability. Once this pattern of interactions has been firmly established, the cycle can be hard to break.

Students in almost every class differ in their goals, aptitudes and interests, values, heredity and home environment, experiences prior to entering school, and experiences both in and out of the classroom during their educational careers. They also differ in the speed with which they learn, the educational methods that efficiently and effectively produce mastery, and the way they use the time devoted to learning. The teacher faced with the job of creating an environment in which each student can develop his potential and attain competence is confronted with a monumental task.

This task may be impossible unless the teacher can employ the varied instructional methods and materials sufficiently appropriate for each student to enable him to master the basics of the curriculum. Each student needs access to instruction at the level appropriate for him. Flexible scheduling is needed to allocate the amount of time each student needs to attain mastery. Students with diverse interests and goals need instructional objectives appropriate for them. And evaluation methods must provide positive evaluations to each student when his performance is competent, even if his peers also produce work that is competent. Though these conditions appear reasonable, they are lacking in many classrooms at the present time.

The next chapter considers why instructional procedures that are *not* efficient means of helping each student acquire competence in basic skills and knowledge are, nevertheless, widely used today. Then, the focus shifts to competency-based education, the process designed with the aim that each student acquire skills, knowledge, attitudes, and values essential for competence.

2

Average-Based Education

Criticisms of schools as places where students fail, where students learn to believe that they are stupid and to dislike learning itself are common in contemporary professional and popular literature. The problems that have been raised here are familiar to all those concerned about education, though practical solutions have remained elusive.

Widespread overdependence upon the average in implementing instructional and evaluation procedures in classrooms is a major cause of the educational problems that have drawn recent criticism. School personnel have the power and capacity to correct this misuse of the average in the educational process. Procedures for doing so are the focus of subsequent chapters.

Widespread Use of Average

Educational processes based on the average have been used extensively in the United States since the late nineteenth century. At the end of the nineteenth century, only about 5% of the student population remained in school through age 18. Most students dropped out of school after a few years, since employment for unskilled and semiskilled laborers was readily available. Selection processes were

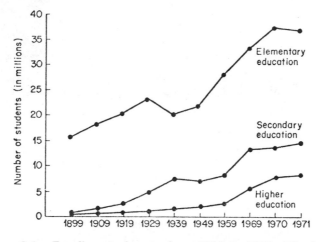

Figure 2.1. *Enrollment changes from 1899 to 1975. (The information on which this is based was abstracted from* The Digest of Educational Statistics *by Kenneth A. Simon and W. Vance Grant, U. S. Department of Health, Education and Welfare, National Center for Educational Statistics, 1971.)*

needed to identify the very small percentage of students who were most qualified for advanced education.

Until recently, selecting the 5% of the student population who would proceed beyond elementary school was one primary purpose of educational evaluation. In 1899, 17 million students were enrolled in all of the schools in the United States. Of these students, 95% attended elementary schools; 4% were enrolled in grades 9 through 12, and an additional 1% were enrolled in all institutions of higher education (see Figure 2.1).

If good students were to be retained after elementary school, their abilities had to be recognized before they left school (usually by the end of eighth grade) and entered the job market. For most families, having a child in secondary school meant substantial financial sacrifice. Three-quarters of the labor force in the United States was engaged in agricultural and in nonfarm unskilled labor. Elementary school taught reading, writing, and arithmetic; most vocational training was acquired on the job.

Early in the twentieth century, educators were faced with the tremendous task of adapting school curricula to the enormous influx of students from various socioeconomic backgrounds. Standards for mass education had to be established quickly. Some school systems employed criterion-referenced standards, but most shifted quickly to normative standards.

For example, in 1916, the Boston public school teachers were required to compose lists of words that all students had to spell by eighth grade. In addition, requirements for English were stated very precisely, and each student had to complete each requirement in order to graduate. However, when the English and spelling tests were given to a large number of students, the percentage of students in a class passing each item or task came to serve as a "standard by which [the teacher] could judge whether her class [was] above or below the general standard for the city [Tyler & Wolf, 1974, p. 75]." Thus, emphasis shifted from criterion-referenced assessments, which specified fixed achievement levels that each student was expected to attain, to norm-referenced evaluation, which compared the performance of students in a class with the average performance of students in the city.

The students' average performance levels were used to establish "reasonable" standards, so that the students would not be asked to perform tasks for which they were thought not to have the ability. Additionally, teachers would not be severely criticized if the students' performance was less than that of previous classes.

This premise was incorporated into the writings of many of the prominent educators of the time, including Charles H. Judd. Judd contended that widespread use of normative achievement measures was beneficial because these measures demonstrated that the schools could *not* produce students who attained either uniform or perfect levels of achievement:

> Indeed, the measures which have been made up to this time have more than justified their costs in efforts and money, because they have dispelled forever the idea that schools should produce a uniform product or one that is perfect in its attainment. . . . With the theoretical ideal of perfection overthrown, there is now an opportunity to set up rational demands. We can venture to tell parents with assurance that their children in the fifth grade are as good as the average if they misspell 50% of a certain list of words. We know this just as well as we know that a certain automobile engine cannot draw a ton of weight up a certain hill. No one has a right to make an unscientific demand of the automobile or of a school [Judd, 1918, p. 152; 160].

In essence, Judd stated that most students could not be brought to a given level of performance in skill subjects such as spelling. This position was based on the belief, widely held at the time, that innate limitations in the ability of students born of the recent immigrants and poor environmental backgrounds precluded their performing at high levels. Therefore, relative rather than absolute standards were applied to students' performance. Even though the original rationale has been seriously questioned, the use of relative standards remained prominent. Today, almost all commercially available standardized tests are norm-referenced (Tyler & Wolf, 1974).

In the nineteenth century, evaluation procedures that were norm-but not criterion-referenced provided an efficient method of selecting the elite students whose outstanding academic abilities qualified them for further education. As the United States became more industrialized, fewer jobs were available for the unskilled and semi-skilled workers. More managerial and professional jobs became available. To qualify for these jobs, people needed more than an elementary school education. Changes in student retention rates (percentage of the student population who stayed in school) between 1924 and 1962 are illustrated in Figure 2.2.

In those 38 years, the student dropout rate decreased radically. About 70% of the 1924 fifth graders entered eighth grade, whereas more than 70% of the 1962 fifth graders graduated from high school. About 50% of the 1924 fifth graders entered tenth grade, and 50% of the 1962 fifth graders entered college. By 1962, the elementary school teacher could predict that over 95% of his students would enter high school and over 50% would enter college.

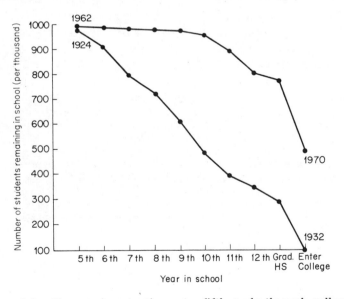

Figure 2.2. *Changes in retention rate, fifth grade through college. Retention rate refers to the number of students who stay in school. (The information on which this figure is based was obtained from* The Digest of Educational Statistics *by Kenneth A. Simon and W. Vance Grant, U. S. Department of Health, Education, and Welfare, National Center for Educational Statistics, 1971.)*

Today, in the United States, 75% of the student population remains in school until the age of 18. Jobs for unskilled and semi-skilled labor are scarce. Vocations and professions that could be learned through apprenticeship in the last century now require formal education. An adult's social status and his job opportunities are increasingly dependent upon how well he has learned what was taught in school. Though selecting a small elite group in the first few years of school is no longer a primary function of formal education, many of the procedures used for this purpose continue in widespread use (Westbury, 1972).

Instructional Level Inappropriate for Many Students

The students in any class often learn at different rates. Some may have learned the prerequisites needed to succeed in the course, while others have failed to learn some basic skill. The students may differ in the extent to which they can understand and benefit from one form of instruction. When all of the students in the class are given approximately the same instruction and approximately the same time to learn, their level of achievement attained upon completion of the course often varies extensively (Carroll, 1963a; 1973).

A survey of typical curriculum and instructional procedures disclosed that almost all of the students were exposed to one form of instruction, one text, and one set of lectures and recitations. Most of the teachers surveyed attempted to adjust the level of instruction to the students' individual differences by aiming the instruction at a level they estimated to be appropriate for some middle group of the students (Westbury, 1972). In addition, the majority of texts and other instructional materials were designed for the average level of the average age student in a particular grade. But this instruction was not equally appropriate for students performing considerably higher or lower than average. The instructional level may have been incorrect for these students because teachers lacked the information about each student's achievement needed to design and present appropriate instruction.

Measures Supply Insufficient Information

When a student's achievement is evaluated using norm-referenced standards exclusively, these evaluations alone cannot be used to determine what an individual student has learned and what he has not learned. Norm-referenced measures are not required to provide information about how much a student has learned or what skills he has acquired (Glaser, 1963). Information about the nature of the achievement that is actually being measured by the test and the relevance of that achievement is also difficult to obtain.

The National Assessment of Educational Progress measured students' learning in various curricular areas and age levels. As part of this assessment, widely used standardized achievement tests were analyzed. In general, those tests were found to be inappropriate for assessing what many students had actually learned in various education programs and at various age levels.

> A large part of the questions in the final form of a standard test are those that 40 to 60% of the children were able to answer. There are very few questions that represent the things being learned either by the slower learners or the more advanced ones. If a less advanced student is actually making progress in his learning, the typical standardized test furnishes so few questions that represent what he has been learning that it will not afford a dependable measure for him. The same holds true for advanced learners [Tyler, 1970].

When a standardized, norm-referenced achievement test is used to assess the progress of the student who performs considerably below average for his age, the level of the test he will take is usually determined by the student's age, not by the level at which he is performing. The test measures a range of performance, but the student may be performing at a level below the range. In that case, the test totally fails to measure the student's performance—let alone his progress. The same problem occurs for the student who performs above the range of performance measured by a test he takes. Yet, these test results continue to be highly valued and widely publicized, often as the sole indicators of the effectiveness of entire schools or educational programs.

Averaging Produces Labels

Another set of problems arises when the educational process is average-based. When the performance of a group of students is ranked and the average performance is determined, some students are judged to perform above average, some are judged to perform at approximately the group average, and some are judged to perform below average. An artificial set of labels is created, by the definition of "average," and these labels attach to students and their work.

But many of the total groups to which averaging procedures are applied do not contain a representative range of performance. For example, Torshen (1969, 1973) investigated schools in which students typically achieved 2 years above the national average for their age group as measured by norm-referenced standardized achievement tests. The academic evaluations having the strongest and most direct impact upon the students in those schools were derived by comparing each student's performance with the average performance of the students in his classroom. Those students who performed lower than their classmates were labeled "below average" even though they performed significantly above the national average for their age group. The labels attached to students' performance in their own classrooms related significantly to their self-concepts and mental health, even though those labels had little meaning outside of their own school (Torshen, 1973).

The IEA research strongly supported the conclusion that schools generally failed to rearrange the ordering of performance which children bring to them, based on class, background, and early experience (Purves & Levine, 1975). The student's status in school, established in the early school years, remained quite stable throughout his school career.

Once a student's status among his peers has been established and labeled, the student himself and the people who are important to him are influenced by his label. If the student's label is accepted as accurate, regardless of whether it is accurate, it serves as a basis for establishing achievement goals for the student and selecting the level of instruction he will receive. The student who is often told his work is below average may come to expect that he will continue to work below the average level of his classmates. He may have tried hard to do good work at some point in his educational career. If he earned about the same grades when he worked hard as when he did not, he may have come to believe that he could not do work that was considered good regardless of how hard he tried. Repeated evidence that his work was below average may have led to the belief that this student was not capable of doing very good work in school. The labeling process may have caused that student to limit his horizons and his personal goals.

The student who is consistently labeled as above average may set his expectations and expand his horizons accordingly. If he has received predominantly positive evaluations and if negative evaluations for his academic performance have been extremely infrequent, he may become convinced that he can do anything well with very little effort. Should he be confronted with a task that is difficult for him or should he receive evaluations that are not completely positive, he may have great difficulty in mobilizing his personal resources to deal with this less-than-positive evaluation.

If the labels assigned to students are not based on standards relevant to their long-range goals, the students may establish their concepts of their own ability and set their goals for themselves according to criteria that are inaccurate or inappropriate. In the schools included in the IEA investigation, students' verbal ability determined a significant proportion of their status among their classmates. If verbal ability is less relevant in nonacademic endeavors, then the importance of verbal ability is being overemphasized. Should students whose talents lie in other equally important areas become convinced that they are not capable of learning well in school, there is great risk that their natural talents may not develop properly and that their tremendous resource potential will be lost.

If average-based measures were accurate assessments of students' potential and were strongly related to their job performance or other criteria of success after school, continued use of these measures might be warranted. In fact, numerous research studies investigated relationships of students' academic status determined by average-based measures and their performance on the job after their schooling has been completed. More than 50 well-designed studies found absolutely no relationship between students' grades in school (these grades were determined by the process of averaging and, thus, represent the students' ranks among their classmates) and their success in their chosen occupation or profession (Hodgkinson, 1976). For example, prospective teachers' high school and college grade-point-averages failed to predict their eventual success in teaching in 97% of the cases investigated (Anderson, 1931; Barr, 1961). Students' grades were no more efficient in predicting success in other professions. College grades showed no statistically significant relationship to success in large business organizations (Kappell, 1962; Pallett, 1965), in the field of engineering (Martin, 1962), and in the medical profession. Success on the job was measured in various ways, including amount of salary earned, supervisors' judgments, judgments of members of the same profession, and amount of responsibility or promotions earned.

Even though norm-referenced assessments can contain considerable error and are far from perfect predictors of the student's future performance, they are a primary factor in determining educational and vocational opportunities. Norm-referenced procedures are often used as a basis for selecting students most likely to perform well in advanced academic programs. Colleges and universities often use students' high school grade-point-averages and their performance on norm-referenced standardized tests, such as the Scholastic Aptitude Test (SAT), as a basis for estimating how high school students will perform in college. However, these two measures failed to predict accurately a substantial portion of students' first-year college performance.

Only about 25% of students' freshman college grades could be accounted for by their high school grade-point-averages (Lewis, 1966; Hills, 1964). When the students' SAT performance was combined with their grade-point-average, about 40% of their freshman college grades were accurately predicted (Lewis, 1966; Hills, 1965). Well over half of the students' freshman college grades were determined by factors unrelated to their high school grade-point-averages and their SAT performance.

Even though a student's achievement level is above average when compared with that of his classmates or his age-mates, he may have failed to master some of the skills and knowledge essential to future success. Today's schools face the enormous task of providing students with the basic capabilities they will require to meet the diverse responsibilities they will face in an extremely complex world. As capacities for storage of information and for communication have increased, there have been corresponding increases in the amount of information available to the average citizen. Skills in reading, comprehension, reasoning, analysis, problem solving, and responding constructively to change are needed to deal intelligently with this vast amount of information. The student can reasonably expect that his success in his future job will be dependent upon the skills and knowledge he acquires in school. And he is likely to face further training and retraining during his occupational career as new methods continue to be discovered. A student's success in facing the challenges is becoming increasingly dependent on his mastery of basic academic skills.

Competency-based education, an approach to instruction that aims to teach each student the basic knowledge, skills, attitudes, and values essential to competence, is the subject of the next chapter. This approach begins by identifying the outcomes most important for students to attain. Then instructional programs appropriate for helping each student acquire the learning most relevant for him are designed. Each student in a class can learn from the same instruction, or varied types of instruction can be employed, depending upon the needs and preferences of the students and the resources available. Performance is evaluated by measuring whether the student reached each of the outcomes defined as essential for him.

3

Competency-Based Education

A competency-based education process begins by defining the outcomes each student is expected to attain. Then, the instructional program through which each student can arrive at these outcomes is designed.

A basic premise in the competency-based education process is that every student can arrive at the goals appropriate for him when he has access to appropriate instruction. Every student properly placed in an appropriate instructional program should learn the basic skills, knowledge, attitudes and/or values taught in the program.

Program Goals

The premise that every student can reach goals appropriate for him has been interpreted by some people to mean that competency-based education produces excessive homogeneity. This argument proposes that an effective competency-based educational program will produce students who are identical. Students who are products of this program will all have the same skills and knowledge and operate using the same procedures and methods (Cronbach, 1972). But sameness is not a necessary product of a competency-based educational program. In fact, products of a competency-based educa-

19

tional program will probably be considerably more diverse than those who are the products of average-based educational programs.

Goals that students reach in competency-based programs and the methods and materials used to reach those goals can be as diverse as the needs of the students and the resources available. Within any classroom, students can work toward many different goals using many different types of instruction. Or students in one class can work toward the same set of goals using similar instruction, if the goals and instruction are appropriate for each of the students in that class. Competency-based education is *not* based on the premise that all students should attain the same goals. Rather, the basic premise is that each student should attain the educational goals appropriate for him. All students should not learn the same things using the same methods. But each student should learn the basic skills and knowledge, attitudes and values he needs in order to be competent. The competency-based process focuses on selecting goals appropriate for each student and designing instruction that students use to reach these goals.

Planning

Three questions are basic to the planning of a competency-based educational program. The first question is, What outcomes should the student reach? This question focuses on the selection of the outcomes that the program will be designed to help students reach. The second question is, How can the students reach this destination? At issue here is the selection of the instruction most appropriate for helping the students arrive at these outcomes. The third question is, How will we know when the students have arrived at their destinations? This question deals with the evaluation of whether the students have reached the goals selected for the program.

The basic framework of a competency-based educational program is built upon the answers to these questions. Outcomes selected for a particular program define the goals that the students in the program are expected to attain. In the process of selecting these outcomes, the needs of the students and the needs of the society in which the program functions are assessed. The primary function of formal education is preparation for the future. This preparation can include a general education to prepare the child for adulthood. It can also include vocational or professional training to prepare the person for a specific job.

Goal Selection

In the process of selecting outcomes for a particular program, goals in each of the intellectual, emotional, social, and physical areas can be considered. One program can incorporate goals from each of these areas.

For example, when the members of the Children's Television Workshop selected goals for the children's educational program, "Sesame Street," they considered incorporating social, moral, and affective goals into the program. They decided to concentrate primarily on cognitive skills. When the show entered its sixth season, goals focusing on teaching children about behavior, emotions, and feelings were incorporated.

The following outcomes were selected for the sixth season of "Sesame Street": Children will develop the idea that a problem or situation may often be dealt with in many ways. Children will be aware of and will consider the emotions of others. Children will demonstrate feelings of pride in self-worth. Children will be conscious of various careers and will know that a person is primarily responsible for his or her own choice of career. Children will estimate properly their own abilities, resources and competencies toward coping with failure and getting along with social groups. Children will express feelings verbally and behaviorally (Banas, 1974, p. 13).

The goals selected for the "Sesame Street" program were intended to be appropriate for all of the students who watched the televised program and, thus, were exposed to the instruction. The designers of the program had little control over the students' exposure to the instruction because they could not control how much time any one student spent watching the televised lessons, nor could they control which students watched which lessons. As a result, goals for all of the students who might watch the program were selected.

There are some goals that are appropriate for every student who has the mental and physical capacity to attain them. For example, every student who can do so should be able to read and comprehend the daily newspaper, as a minimum skill level. Acquiring this reading skill is a priority goal for every student participating in the educational process. When this goal is selected as an outcome of a competency-based educational program, whatever instructional resources may be needed are allocated so that each student can reach this outcome. Students will continue receiving instruction in reading until they have learned to read at this level.

In average-based educational programs, some students who complete the regular reading instruction continue through years of formal instruction without acquiring basic reading skills. Often, no indication of their reading deficit is contained in their permanent record, and teachers in advanced subjects assume the students can read the high school texts without receiving any additional instruction in reading. If competency-based educational programs are effective, then each student should continue receiving formal instruction sufficient to reach the minimum level of competence in the basic skills before he completes the program. Competency-based education aims to produce students who are homogeneous to the extent that each student has acquired a minimum level of basic skills. In addition to learning basic skills, each student can progress toward whatever goals are appropriate for his needs, interests, and personal preferences.

Outcomes or goals of a competency-based educational program are often stated in terms of the performances that students are expected to demonstrate as evidence that they have acquired competence. For example, the faculty at the College of Medicine at the University of Illinois designed a competency-based curriculum for training doctors. The faculty defined the minimal professional competencies to be attained by all students graduating from the school (University of Illinois College of Medicine, 1973). The assumption was made that the medical student acquired the knowledge, skills, attitudes, and values that are prerequisites for becoming a competent doctor when he performed at or beyond the minimum levels of performance defined as the goals of this medical program.

Selection of Instruction and Resources

When the outcomes of a competency-based program are selected, the instruction and evaluation in that program are based on these outcomes. Instructional resources are allocated to maximize the likelihood that the students will reach the outcomes. Instructional methods and materials, teaching methods, and other services are selected and used in the program because they are judged to be efficient for helping students reach the outcomes.

Since students often learn at different rates and since one instructional method is not likely to be equally appropriate for every student, varied instruction may be needed if each student is to arrive at a specific outcome. If instruction is to be efficient and effective for this purpose, instructional time should be allocated according to the needs of the individual students in the program. Students should be allowed to continue receiving instruction until they have reached the outcomes specified in the program. And alternative instructional methods and materials should be available when needed.

Allocation of instructional resources for students who require large amounts of instruction in order to reach important outcomes should be determined by priorities placed on those outcomes. For example, reading skill may be judged to be a high priority outcome. In this case, whatever resources a student needs to acquire adequate skill in reading should be allocated. However, another outcome may be judged to be of less importance for the student to attain. For example, students in a swimming program may be expected to swim a mile by the end of the program. However, this goal may be judged to be of moderate importance for every student in the class. Each student can continue receiving swimming instruction throughout the duration of the program. If a student can only swim a half mile when the allotted instructional time has expired, he is not required to continue in the program. He may proceed to another program in which he receives instruction not dependent upon attaining the goal of the 1 mile swim. Thus, the amount of instructional resources allocated to a particular outcome is determined by the importance attached to that outcome.

Selection of Evaluation Procedures

Evaluation procedures in a competency-based program measure whether each student can perform at the levels defined in the program outcomes. In many competency-based programs, the outcomes are defined in terms of the levels of performance students are expected to demonstrate. In each performance area, a *minimum pass level* is defined. This level specifies the minimum performance level each student is to attain in order to perform acceptably in the program and to pass on to another program. The level of performance defined as adequate is the criterion used to determine whether student's performance is sufficient to "graduate" from this program.

Assessment of whether each student has attained the performance levels adequate for competence is crucial to a competency-based educational program. First, it is essential to determine whether each student has reached minimum pass levels. The student who performs at or beyond these levels should proceed to the next unit or sequence or graduate from the program. Second, it is important to identify students who have not yet attained one or more of the minimum pass levels. This information is used to prescribe instruc-

tion appropriate for helping the student reach each of the performance levels appropriate for him. Continued instruction is provided
until the student attains each minimum pass level.

Advantages

A primary advantage of the competency-based educational process is that it attempts to identify goals most relevant and important
for students to attain, to design and implement instruction that
maximizes the likelihood that students will attain those goals, and to
employ evaluation procedures that provide information about each
student's mastery of the goals prescribed for him. In a competency-
based program, the relevance of the program goals to the needs of
the students and the society can be considered extensively before the
actual instruction begins. Faculty, students, parents, instructional
design and evaluation specialists, persons employed in the vocation
or profession for which the program serves as preparation, prospective employees, community representatives, and other interested
persons can contribute input to the goal selection process. The actual
decisions about program goals are usually made at the state, local
district or local school levels.

When the performances students are expected to demonstrate are
identified, the validity of these proposed outcomes can be investigated using systematic research procedures. This research can examine the values students are expected to learn in the program. The
relevance of this learning to the competencies the program is designed to produce and to other postinstructional criteria can be
investigated.

Potential Implementation Problems

While competency-based education has many advantages, there
are several potential problems associated with implementation of a
competency-based program. In the typical traditional classroom, in
which competency-based educational procedures have not been implemented, a single text serves as the primary instructional material.
All of the students proceed through the instruction at the same pace,
which is set and led by the classroom teacher. All of the students
perform the same or similar learning activities on approximately the
same schedule. Examinations are given in each subject at regular

intervals, usually at the end of a chapter or unit in the text. Each examination is scored and returned to the student. Then the class proceeds to the next chapter of the text.

In order to shift from this classroom structure to a competency-based education program, changes in the curriculum, the staffing, the scheduling, and the reward system of the school are needed. In the area of curriculum, the outcomes that the instruction will be designed to produce must be identified. These outcomes are usually stated in the form of curriculum objectives. Agreement must be reached among faculty, and perhaps among students and community representatives, as to which objectives are most appropriate for a particular course. A system for determining whether the objectives are appropriate for each of the students who is participating in the course must be developed. High-priority objectives, the mastery of which is necessary for progress into the next sequence or for attainment of long-range goals, must be identified.

If the objectives selected for a particular program are actually trivial or irrelevant to the students' long-range goals, then the instruction will focus on trivial and irrelevant learning. At the present time, practitioners have few resources other than their own professional experience to help them in avoiding the selection of objectives that are trivial or irrelevant. To minimize this possibility, the objectives should be reexamined at regular intervals; annually, if possible. In addition, large-scale systematic research should be initiated to examine the long-term consequences of the objectives selected for specific instructional programs designed to teach basic skills.

Most of the texts available at present do not include enough instructional activities of sufficient quality and at the various levels necessary to enable all of the students in one classroom to attain mastery of a set of curriculum objectives. Of course, there are exceptions, such as the *Mathematics Learning System* (SRA, 1974) text series. However, most competency-based instructional programs will need to employ more than one text series and supplemental materials developed by several publishing companies, in addition to the instruction materials prepared by the classroom teachers and students. Location and coordination of the needed high quality material requires considerable professional time and commitment.

The evaluation measures that accompany most text series are not designed to help teachers locate their students at the appropriate point in the sequence of instruction, determine whether each student has mastered the most important skills and knowledge presented in a particular chapter or unit, or locate the source of a student's learning difficulties. Measures appropriate for this purpose often must be purchased separately. If these measures are not available for purchase, they can be constructed by evaluation specialists serving as consultants, curriculum specialists serving as full-time school staff, or the classroom teachers. Obviously, funds for purchase of supplemental materials or for payment for professional staff are needed.

The implementation of a competency-based educational program usually requires a modification in the number of faculty or in the responsibilities assigned to the faculty in a school. Most teachers will not accomplish the transition to competency-based education without help in identifying the objectives appropriate for their students, selecting and coordinating instructional materials, employing evaluation measures to place students at appropriate points in instructional sequence, and identifying students' learning difficulties that need remediation. At least in the initial stages, a curriculum specialist should visit each classroom weekly or biweekly to observe and evaluate each teacher's implementation of the competency-based curriculum and to provide recommendations for the improvement of instruction. In-service training and other consulting services should be provided to help teachers plan and implement classroom management and instructional procedures.

Flexible classroom scheduling is essential because students will learn at different rates and use a variety of instructional materials. Most classroom schedules in use at present do not contain many provisions for flexible time scheduling. Faculty will need assistance in designing and implementing flexible time schedules. In addition, many teachers may need assistance in planning and managing a classroom in which all of the students are not performing the same activities at the same time. The competency-based classroom is likely to be noisier than the traditional classroom, and both students and faculty must adjust to the increased noise level.

Finally, it is clear from this brief discussion of problems inherent in the implementation of competency-based education that considerable additional work and effort is required if this implementation is to be successful. The majority of the teachers cannot be expected to put forth the necessary effort unless they receive adequate support and encouragement from their superiors. Unless students recognize that mastery of the objectives is valuable to them and each student receives sufficient encouragement and assistance as well as recognition and positive evaluation when he does attain mastery, many students will not put forth the effort necessary to complete the competency-based program successfully. A competency-based program can only be successful in a climate in which mastery of the curriculum objectives is both valued and rewarded.

One of the primary factors which has interfered with the implementation of competency-based programs is the fear on the part of teachers and administrators that the specification of curriculum objectives and the measurement of students' mastery of these objectives will be politically and economically detrimental to the school faculty and the reputation of the school system. Faculties have proposed that specification of the curriculum objectives would cause severe criticism when some of their students failed to attain mastery of the objectives. By developing measures of students' academic progress, they would create additional weapons to be used by those who wish to criticize the schools. Furthermore, teachers and principals have been concerned that their classes and their schools would be ranked according to the percentage of students who demonstrated mastery of the curriculum objectives. Those classes and schools which fell below average in this race would receive unfavorable publicity and, perhaps, reduction of instructional resources. Faculty and administrators need assurances that the objectives and the evaluation procedures in the competency-based educational program will be used for the benefit of the students, and for no other purpose.

The next chapter examines various aspects of competence which can be developed in a competency-based educational program. Subsequent chapters deal with the mastery structure for planning and implementing competency-based educational programs.

4

Domains of Competence

Competency-based education can encompass the various domains of human traits and abilities. This chapter presents a general description of the diverse competencies that can be developed in educational programs.

The various facets of human competence have been classified into areas or categories, referred to as "domains." Each domain defines an aspect of human potential that can be developed through planned instructional activities. Each domain serves as a general category unit within which the needs and values of the students and of the society are addressed and goals of educational programs are defined. Specific aspects of a domain of competence are selected for development in a given competency-based educational program. These aspects of competence are the outcomes the program intends to produce. When the educational program is planned, the competencies are transformed into objectives, working definitions of the intended outcomes of the program.

The term "objective" represents a statement of the specific change in a learner's skills, knowledge, and/or abilities that the curriculum and instruction are designed to cause. This definition was popularized by Franklin Bobbit (1918), Ralph Tyler (1950), Robert Mager (1962), Fred Keller (1968) and others. In 1956, a classification system that categorized objectives into the cognitive, affective, and psychomotor domains was published in the *Taxonomy of Educational Objectives* (Bloom *et al.*, 1956). Although three domains were described, this work defined objectives in only one domain, the cognitive.

Subsequently, other taxonomies classifying domains of objectives have been published. The *Taxonomy of Educational Objectives: Handbook II: Affective Domain* (Krathwohl *et al.*, 1968) and *Taxonomy of the Psychomotor Domain* (Harrow, 1974) are two examples.

In this chapter, several classification systems for categorizing domains of competency are described. The *Taxonomies of Educational Objectives, Handbooks I and II* are perhaps the most widely known. In 1974, Arthur Foshay of Columbia University presented a classification system containing six domains, which are described herein. To illustrate the complexity of each, two approaches to defining objectives in the cognitive domain are then presented. Finally, competencies encompassing more than one domain are discussed.

The brief summary of various categories of competence is presented in this chapter to illustrate the complexity of the domains of competence issue and the ongoing controversy concerning categorization systems. Most educational programs conducted to date have focused on developing competencies in the cognitive domain. The emphasis on this domain reflects the current value attached to academic achievement in this area. However, competencies in other domains also need to be developed.

Domains of the "Humane Curriculum"

Arthur Foshay's six domains of competence, each considered essential for inclusion in a "humane curriculum," were presented in "decreasing order of our familiarity with them in schools [1974, p. 5]." These domains are:

1. the intellectual,
2. the emotional,
3. the social,
4. the physical,
5. the aesthetic,
6. the spiritual.

In presenting the six categories, Foshay stated: "All six, I will assert, are basic requirements for life; that is, if any one of them were wholly missing from one's *persona*, one would cease being human, and would destroy himself or be destroyed by others. They are, I repeat, requirements for survival [1974, p. 5]."

The first category, the intellectual, is similar to the cognitive domain described in the *Taxonomy of Educational Objectives* (Bloom *et al.*, 1956). Intellectual growth can be observed as children become sophisticated problem solvers. This domain concerns development of the higher mental processes that involve analysis, synthesis, and evaluation—all aspects of problem solving.

The second category, the emotional domain, involves the maturing capacity to know oneself and to be objective about oneself. This development includes the ability to examine and to rejoice in one's own feelings. Here, the ability to be aware of one's own feelings is crucial.

The third category, the domain of social development, includes developing abilities that enable one to function in social organizations. Included here is a progression from strict dependency on an authority figure to increasing social autonomy. This category also includes objectives that have been traditionally contained under character or moral development. Examples are the development of citizenship, the ability to adapt or to adjust to a given society, and the ability to be socially productive and to value others.

The fourth category, the domain of physical development, includes the growing realization of one's self as a physical being. This domain includes the examination of various perceptual systems and the building of increased perceptual discrimination. Here, students learn to see better, to hear better, to feel or touch with greater sensitivity, to taste with discrimination and pleasure, to become aware of movement.

The fifth domain, the aesthetic, focuses on the aesthetic response, which includes four aspects: the formal, the technical, the sensuous, and the expressive. The formal response is a response to form, a recognition of the purely formal qualities of the aesthetic object. The technical response involves recognition of the technique used in producing the aesthetic object. The sensuous response involves acknowledgment and awareness of the appeal to the senses of the aesthetic object, including color, texture, movement, order, and taste. The expressive response assesses the meaning of the experience. Here, the person interacts with the aesthetic experience and examines how it is part of himself.

The sixth domain, the spiritual, involves the search for meaning.

Questions such as, "What is the meaning of existence or of death?" "What is infinity?" which cannot be answered rationally, are confronted. The spiritual response involves experiences of wonder, of awe, and confrontation of questions that can be sublime or terrifying.

Each of the domains of human development in which the student is expected to become competent encompasses varied aspects of human behavior. The cognitive or intellectual domain has been the subject of the most extensive attempts to define the classes of behavior involved. The classes of behavior involved in the cognitive domain demonstrate the complex and diverse aspects of student behavior involved in each domain.

The Cognitive Domain

The *Taxonomy of Educational Objectives: Cognitive Domain* (Bloom *et al.*, 1956) described six classes of cognitive behavior. Ranging from least complex to most complex, they are: knowledge, comprehension, application, analysis, synthesis, and evaluation.

Knowledge involves the recall of specifics and universals, the recall of methods and processes, and the recall of pattern, structure, and setting. The knowledge category includes knowledge of specifics, of terminology, of specific facts, of ways and means of organizing and dealing with specifics, the knowledge of trends and conventions, knowledge of classifications of criteria and methodology. Also included are knowledge of the universals and abstractions of a field, of principles and generalizations, of theories and structures.

The remaining five classes of behavior are considered to be intellectual abilities and skills that include organized modes of operation and generalized techniques for dealing with materials and problems.

Comprehension is the lowest level of understanding. Comprehension includes the process of translation, interpretation, and extrapolation.

The next level of intellectual skills and abilities is application, which includes the use of abstraction in particular and concrete situations.

The third intellectual ability level is analysis, which includes the breakdown of a communication into its constituent elements or parts. Analysis of elements, of relationships, and of organizational principles fall within this category.

The fourth level of intellectual abilities is synthesis, which includes the putting together of elements and parts to form a whole.

This includes the production of a unique communication, the production of a plan or proposed set of operations, and the derivation of a set of abstract relationships.

Evaluation is considered to be the highest level of intellectual skills and abilities. Evaluation includes judgments about the value of materials and methods for given purposes, use of standards of appraisal, and qualitative and quantitative judgments regarding the extent to which material and methods satisfy criteria.

Assumptions Basic to Cognitive Domain Classifications

The premise that there are different types or levels of learning was used in differentiating the levels of cognitive development presented in the *Taxonomy of Educational Objectives* (Bloom *et al.*, 1956). Instruction designed to facilitate one level of cognitive development may or may not facilitate another type of learning. Considerable attention has been devoted to describing and categorizing various types of learning. To cite one example, Tiemann and Markle (1973) presented a model containing three general types of learning: psychomotor, memory, and complex cognitive learning.

Psychomotor learning usually involves making physical responses. For example, an American must learn to make a particular sound—the Spanish trilled *r*—when he is learning the Spanish language. Memory learning includes the recall and recognition categories of the *Taxonomy*. Memorizing of vocabulary, definitions, facts, associations, and sequences are included in this category. Complex cognitive learning involves learning of concepts, applying rules and principles, and using problem solving strategies.

Distinctions between memory learning and complex cognitive learning are essential to the educational process. The teaching of memory learning and the teaching of complex cognitive learning often require different instructional and assessment methods. For example, in a class studying the government of the United States, the students may be asked to memorize the names of the presidents and vice presidents and the senators and congressmen from their state. They may learn to associate these names with a democratic form of government. They may learn to sequence the names according to a hierarchy of authority. However, the students can memorize the names of the officials and their positions without understanding concepts of democracy such as the check-and-balance system.

On the other hand, students studying United States' government can learn the concepts and basic principles of democracy and use these concepts and principles to propose solutions to problems that arise in a democratic form of government. Instruction designed to produce this type of complex cognitive learning will probably take a different form from the instruction designed to guide students to memorize the names of the public officials.

The Tiemann–Markle model, based on the hierarchical model of learning developed by Gagné (1965), is only one example of a theoretical formulation designed to discriminate various types of learning. Other theoretical formulations that discriminate learning involving association from learning involving more complex processes have been described by Piaget (1952 a,b, 1954) and Hunt (1961).

All of these models of learning emphasize that there are distinct differences between the memory-association type of learning and more complex learning processes. Much of the learning evaluated by widely used standardized achievement tests consists of the recall and recognition type, which deals with memory and associative learning processes. Complex, cognitive processes are usually more difficult to teach. Also, students' learning of these processes is more difficult to evaluate than is the memory-association type of learning. For example, it is difficult to determine if a student understands the concept of "democracy." A question on an examination asking the student to present his understanding of the concept "democracy" may elicit a definition of the term. The student may have memorized this definition without really understanding the concept. The teacher may find that the student's definition corresponds to the real meaning of the concept, and it is easy to assume that the student understands the concept. However, if the student is presenting a definition memorized without understanding, his learning on the complex cognitive level has not been appropriately evaluated.

To this point in this chapter, six general areas or domains of competence have been discussed. The diverse types of learning that are included in the cognitive or intellectual domain were described in some detail as an illustration of the complexity of the learning included in each domain. There are some types of competence that students are expected to attain as a result of formal education that do not apply primarily to one of the above domains.

The Arts of Learning

The types of competence that are not domain-specific can be described as "the arts of learning." They are general skills associated with the learning process that should be learned through academic instruction. Foshay (1974) presented three general skills students should attain that are not specific to one domain. First, students should become fluent. Fluency includes recognition of the symbol system, the phenomena, the data, or the media that compose the subject matter. In reading, for example, students will reliably recognize words; in the arts, they will recognize the properties of the media; and in geography, they will be able to interpret maps and other data. The second general skill that students should attain is the ability to manipulate the data, or symbol systems, or phenomena in such a way as to extract meaning. Third, having learned to be fluent in a given field and to manipulate the data so as to make it meaningful, the students should persist in carrying on the activities of that field. Once the student has learned to read, it is hoped he will continue to read even after his formal instruction in reading has ended. Fluency, manipulation, and persistence are three general skills prescribed for the student who is to become competent.

Other "arts of learning" involve the ability to take the initiative and the ability to be creative. The ability to react constructively to challenge and to respond positively to change are additional desirable competences.

Joseph Schwab (1974) composed a catalog of competencies in which he described the arts of access, of the eclectic, and of deliberation that, in his view, are valid goals of a liberal education.

Schwab defined the arts of access: "These are the arts by which we know what questions to ask of a work—a scientific paper, a novel, a lecture, a lithograph, a sonata, a cinema—and the arts, in short, by which we gain access to sources of sense and sensibility and make them our own [1974, p. 14]."

Schwab described five arts of access. The first is access to at least one system of mathematics or one well-theorized facet of physics so that the student will experience elegance in learning. The second is access to sources of biological knowledge so that the student will understand his own body. The third is access to the continuing discoveries of the social sciences so that the student will understand how to protect his own privacy, to share in determining his destiny, and to distinguish what is cheap in the social sciences from what is valuable. The fourth involves access to two fine arts, one of them the fine art of the word, such as the novel, the drama, or the poem; and the second, a fine art that caresses a single sense. Access to a craft and to some skill in the art of communication, of speaking and listening with clarity and distinction, are included here. The student should also have access to at least one experience of sustained inquiry, such as a small piece of scientific research, the study of some persons or community, or of sustained inquiry into some philosophical issue or into a major piece of fine art.

Last, the student should attain a beginning mastery of the arts of the practical. This mastery should include what Schwab called "arts of eclectic," which involves the ability to use organized sources of information and to build temporary and tentative bridges among them for purpose of solving practical problems. Included in the arts of the practical are what Schwab called the "arts of deliberation." This includes the ability to weigh alternative formulations of a problem, to trace alternative actions to their consequences, and to appropriately terminate deliberation in the interest of action.

The third group of practical arts is composed of the arts of persuading and being persuaded, including the arts of being an effective member of a committee and of making a committee work. Also included are the arts of collaboration toward proximate goals on the part of the people whose ultimate goals may differ.

Conclusion

This chapter has presented the general and theoretical description of the diverse types of competencies that are the goals of formal education. The purpose of this discussion was to illuminate the complex and various dimensions of competence that may be produced in instructional programs. Competence involves human performance in intellectual, affective (the emotional and social), and physical areas. These abilities influence performance in each of the six domains of competence: the intellectual, the emotional, the social, the physical, the aesthetic, and the spiritual. Each domain encompasses a variety of types of learning. Educational processes must be specifically designed to teach each of the various categories of learning in each domain if the student's potential for learning is to be developed. In addition to considering each domain of competence, competence in the general arts of learning must be developed. These competencies include initiative, creativity, ability to deal with change, fluency, manipulation and persistence, and the arts of gaining access to learning, of bridging gaps among various subject areas, and of deliberation. Competency-based education can guide students in the development of these competencies.

The development of competence is a long-term, long-range operation, the result of many educational experiences that occur over a period of years. Since no two students will have the same experiences, each student can be expected to finish his educational career with a unique set of competencies. If his education has been successful, the student will have attained levels of performance adequate to prepare him to meet his future needs and responsibilities.

The next chapter presents the mastery model, a system for organizing the education curriculum to maximize the likelihood that each student will attain the levels of performance he needs in order to be competent. This model can be applied to instructional programs designed to produce competence in each of the six domains. The system can be used with individualized or group-based classroom structures.

Mastery:
Theory and Research

5
The Mastery Model

The success of any competency-based education program is dependent upon the student's success in attaining the levels of performance that are essential for competence. Mastery, the attainment of adequate levels of performance, is the goal of competency-based education.

Mastery is the name given to a model used to structure curricula. This structure is designed to maximize the likelihood that each student will reach the performance levels essential for competence. The mastery process operates on the proposition that almost every student can learn the basic skills and knowledge that are the core of the school curriculum when the instruction is of good quality and appropriate for him and when he spends adequate time in learning (Carroll, 1971; Bloom, 1971b).

The Mastery Components

The mastery model contains six components: objectives, preassessment, instruction, diagnostic assessment, prescription, and postassessment. A variety of instructional methods, ranging from lectures for an entire class to individual instruction, can be employed. The teachers and students determine the instructional methods and classroom management plan for the curriculum.

41

The mastery model is particularly useful for those aspects of the curriculum devoted to the teaching of basic skills, concepts, and facts. The skills, concepts, and facts taught in a curriculum designed according to the mastery model must be measurable with accuracy sufficient to distinguish students who have learned successfully from students who have not.

The basic ideas underlying the mastery structure are hundreds of years old. In the twentieth century, considerable attention has been drawn to these ideas through the writings of J. Franklin Bobbitt, from 1918 through 1941, Ralph Tyler, in 1950, and Benjamin Bloom, John Carroll, Fred Keller, Robert Mager, and others, beginning in the 1960s.

Each of the components of the mastery structure has an important function in helping students learn the basic skills, concepts, and facts of the curriculum. The components and their primary functions are described here as a general introduction to the model. Each of the components plays an important part in organizing the curriculum efficiently, ensuring that students enter at their own level and progress at their own pace, and giving each student the greatest possible exposure to the instruction most likely to help him reach his goals.

Objectives

Objectives are the first component of the mastery model. The objectives are specific statements of the outcomes or goals that students in the instructional program are expected to reach. These statements represent samples from the domains of competence discussed in the preceding chapter. They define the specific skills, the key concepts and ideas, or the specific facts that the student must learn in order to complete the program successfully.

Minimum Pass Levels

In each skill, concept, and fact area defined in the objectives, the minimum level of performance essential for each student to attain is identified. These performance levels are called *mastery levels* or *minimum pass levels*.

Preassessment

The preassessment component of the mastery model determines each student's starting point and the methods of instruction he will use in the program. This assessment identifies each student's present status relative to the outcomes he is expected to reach by the end of the program. The student's prior performance on achievement tests and ability tests, in prior courses and in previous units, and the observations and judgments of teachers and the student himself can supply the information incorporated into this assessment process.

Instruction

The third component is the *instruction*. In selecting the instruction for a program, the crucial question is: Can the student use this instruction to proceed from his initial status to mastery of the objectives? There is no restriction on the type of instruction that can be used in a mastery program. When more than one appropriate instructional method is available, then the teacher or the student can select the instructional option he prefers.

Diagnostic Assessment

The *diagnostic assessment* component provides information concerning how well the instructional program is working while the instruction is in progress. This assessment procedure measures what each student has learned and what he has failed to learn at regular intervals throughout the instructional program. The information is used to pace the student's learning and to improve upon those segments of the instruction that have not been effective. This component of the structure is crucial in adapting the instruction to the needs of the individual students.

Prescription

The *prescription* component of the mastery structure consists of the instructional activities recommended on the basis of the diagnostic assessment. When the diagnostic assessment shows that a student needs further instruction, the prescription is *remediation*. According to the diagnosis of the problem, the student is given additional instruction or alternative instruction, or he repeats the instruction he has just completed.

Relocation is prescribed for a student when the diagnostic assessment indicates that he does not have the prerequisites needed to perform successfully in this instruction or when it has become apparent that a different objective would be more appropriate. The student can proceed to another topic, or he can receive special instruction to develop his prerequisite skills before he continues in the program.

Enrichment materials and instruction are prescribed for the student when the diagnostic evaluation indicates that he has performed successfully and would benefit from continued instruction at this level in the program. Enrichment is composed of additional learning activities at approximately the same skill level as the instructional activity the student has just completed.

When remediation has been prescribed, students complete their remedial instruction and then an alternate form of the diagnostic assessment is administered. The student continues *recycling* through the remediation and diagnostic evaluation until he performs at the minimum pass level. Recycling should be continued until the student has mastered the crucial skills, or the student should be placed in another objective sequence.

If more than one objective is included in an instructional sequence, then the instruction and diagnostic evaluations for the other objectives in the sequence are completed in the manner described above. When the sequence has been completed, the final assessment procedure is administered.

Postassessment

The *postassessment*, the final component of the mastery model, measures whether each student has reached the outcomes identified in the objectives. Each student's mastery of each of the crucial skills, concepts, and facts defined in the objectives is measured. If a student has failed to master a crucial objective, the student is either recycled through the instructional program or additional instruction is prescribed for him as part of his next instructional program. That student continues to receive instruction until he reaches the minimum pass level.

A diagram of all of the components in the mastery structure is contained in Figure 5.1.

Sequences of instruction in mastery curricula are often divided into *units*, each covering approximately one to two weeks of instruction. The organization of the curriculum into units is optional.

When Is Mastery Appropriate?

The mastery structure is most appropriate for those aspects of the curriculum that involve the basic skills, concepts, facts, and

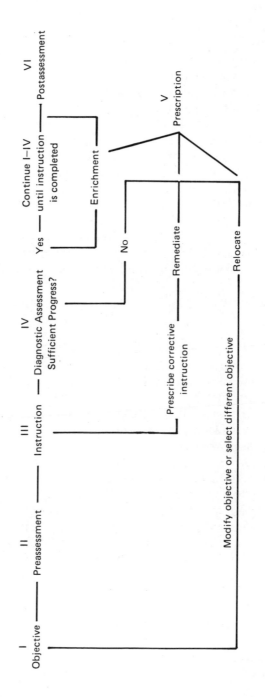

Figure 5.1. *Components of the mastery structure.*

45

attitudes that the student cannot afford not to learn. Most frequently, the mastery structure is used for the objectives that constitute the minimum core of the curriculum.

When the mastery structure is implemented, it is necessary to define indicators of the student's behavior that will be used to determine whether the students have attained the minimum pass levels. One must be able to measure the presence or absence of these behaviors with sufficient accuracy to distinguish between those who have attained mastery and those who have not. Furthermore, school personnel must be able to design and implement learning activities that bring students from nonmastery to mastery of the skills, concepts, facts, and attitudes defined in the objectives. The content of the objectives must be sufficiently basic to the curriculum that it is worth the allocation of effort and resources entailed in implementing the mastery structure. The mastery structure is appropriate for any subject matter or topic that meets these qualifications.

Derivation of the Mastery Model

Early in the twentieth century, two widely read and respected educators, J. Franklin Bobbitt and W. W. Charters, presented some of the concepts basic to the mastery model. Two of Bobbitt's books, *The Curriculum* (1918) and *How to Make a Curriculum* (1924) spelled out how to identify the major curriculum objectives and how to plan appropriate learning activities.

In *Curriculum Construction* (1923), Charters also focused on the use of objectives in designing a curriculum. In addition, Charters described what he called "analysis of activities." This analysis was conducted for the purpose of selecting the most appropriate activities for teaching the objectives and organizing the activities into hierarchical sequences. The activities analysis has continued to be important to curriculum in the twentieth century and has received considerable attention in the various taxonomies of objectives (see, for example, Bloom *et al.*, 1956) and in the writings on task analysis (see, for example, Gagné & Briggs, 1974).

In the 1920s, instructional programs based on mastery principles were implemented. In the Winnetka Plan (Washburne, 1922), the curriculum objectives were recorded on students' report cards, called "goal cards." The Winnetka goal cards still appear in texts on educational evaluation (see, for example, Gronlund, 1974). A second implementation occurred at the University of Chicago's Laboratory School (Morrison, 1926).

J. Franklin Bobbitt was one of the strongest and most powerful proponents of the planned curriculum based on objectives during the first quarter of the twentieth century. The year before he died, Bobbitt published his final book, *The Curriculum of Modern Education* (1941). In his last major work, Bobbitt spoke out strongly against the very curriculum making he had advocated in his book, *How to Make a Curriculum* (1924). Bobbitt stated: "Curriculum 'making' belongs with the dodo and the great auk [1941, p. 298]."

What caused Bobbitt to change his position so radically that he now considered someone to be an "auk" if he followed the very recommendations that Bobbitt had made in print 25 years before? Bobbitt's last major work contains some clues.

> It has long been assumed that a general curriculum can be laid out in the form of printed courses of study for a uniform guidance of pupils in mass. The assumption was a natural outgrowth of the conception that education is a mass implementation of prepared subject matter that can be managed more or less mechanically by a system of regimentation . . . but as text books and work books were made more and more elaborate, and as highly searching standardized tests were made an organic portion of the plan, the flexibility was reduced to the least possible. The educational profession now realizes that this type of curriculum . . . is no more justified for education than would be a uniform mass treatment of the patients in a hospital. For this reason, we turn now in education toward the discovery of individual natures and needs and toward the guidance of individual lives [1941, pp. 297–298].

Bobbitt was reacting against the widespread implementation of his earlier recommendations in the highly structured, regimented curriculum in which all the students performed the same activities at the same time. If the planned curriculum produced instruction that omitted individual discovery and prevented the curriculum from being adapted to individual students' needs, Bobbitt wanted none of it. Though Bobbitt rejected curricula that could not be adapted to individual students' needs, in other sections of his last major work he emphasized the importance to students of mastering basic skills, such as spelling and handwriting. He stressed that the instruction designed to promote such mastery should be adapted to the individual student's developmental level and should continue into high school and junior college if necessary.

Bobbitt's recantation focuses on one of the great mysteries of the educational process: How can the educational curriculum promote mastery of basic skills as well as individual inquiry and discovery? How can instruction focus on mastery without precluding discovery or focus on discovery without precluding mastery?

The educational curriculum needs to balance instruction aimed at promoting discovery with instruction aimed at promoting mastery. All of the instruction must be adapted to the needs and interests of the individual students involved. The mastery structure is most appropriate for those segments of the curriculum designed to teach the core of basic skills, concepts, facts, and attitudes. The amount of instructional time and resources which the mastery aspects of the curriculum need will vary according to the proportion of the curriculum devoted to the basics and to the amount of time the students require to master the basics. But in every curriculum, there should be portions devoted to inquiry and discovery in which students pursue their most salient problems and interests. Striking this balance between mastery and discovery is one of the great arts of curriculum design and implementation.

In 1950, Tyler reemphasized the position that a curriculum should be organized around educational objectives. Tyler stated:

> If an educational program is to be planned and if efforts for continued improvement are to be made, it is very necessary to have some conception of the goals that are being aimed at. These educational objectives become the criteria by which materials are selected, content is outlined, instructional procedures are developed and tests and examinations are prepared. All aspects of the educational program are really means to accomplish basic educational purposes. Hence, if we are to study an educational program systematically and intelligently we must first be sure as to the educational objectives aimed at.
>
> The most useful form for stating objectives is to express them in terms which identify both the kind of behavior to be developed in the student and the content or area of life in which this behavior is to operate [1950, pp. 3, 46–47].

This statement continues to receive frequent reference in current professional literature.

Much of the current interest in the mastery structure was rekindled by the theoretical model for school learning presented by John Carroll (1963). Carroll's model for school learning outlined major factors influencing the student's success in academic learning. A major contribution of this model is the proposition that most students can learn much of what is taught in the regular school curriculum if sufficient time is allotted. Carroll defined the student's aptitude for learning as the amount of instructional time he needed in order to attain mastery. Carroll stated:

> When the task is very difficult, or when it depends upon very special aptitudes, there may be quite a number of students who will never "make it." ... But for most of the tasks in the school curriculum, it can be expected that every student will reach criterion if given enough time—time with reason. This is one of the optimistic aspects of the model of school learning.
>
> The amount of time that a student needs to learn a given task under optimal learning conditions is, in the author's opinion, a reflection of some basic characteristic' or characteristics of the student that may be called "aptitude." Why students vary in the amount of time they need for a given learning task is not known; variations in aptitude are, in the author's opinion, simply a given for the educator to deal with in the best possible way [Carroll, 1971, pp. 31–32].

The original statement of the Carroll model (1963) proposed the following:

$$\text{Degree of learning} = f \left(\frac{\text{Time spent to learn}}{\text{Time needed to learn}} \right).$$

Assume that a student needs 10 hours to learn an arithmetic unit so that he can perform acceptably on an arithmetic test. According to this model, the student will perform adequately if 10 hours of instruction are allotted in the program, when the arithmetic instruction is of good quality and appropriate for him and the student spends the time allotted actively engaged in learning. More instructional time may be needed if the instruction is not of good quality or if the instruction is inappropriate for the student. Additional instructional time will be needed if the student does not spend all of the allotted time actively engaged in learning. The student is not likely to perform acceptably on the arithmetic test unless the instructional time he needs is allotted to him. Since different students are likely to need different amounts of time, the amount of instructional time allotted should be varied according to the individual student's needs.

This model had important implications for the design of competency-based instructional programs in which each student was expected to reach a fixed achievement level. The model suggested that each student would reach that achievement level when sufficient instructional time was allocated, given that he had the innate capacity to reach the achievement level, he spent the time allotted actively engaged in learning, and the instruction was appropriate for him. The allocation of additional instructional time would even compensate, at least to some extent, for inappropriate instruction and student procrastination. Thus, instructional programs should be designed to permit variations in amounts of instructional time available to students.

In 1971, Bloom presented an additional model for school learning (Bloom, 1971; 1976) which proposed that the amount a student learns is a direct result of the amount of time he actually spends in learning (time on task). The amount of time the student spends in learning is influenced by the quality of a given learning environment, which, in turn, is influenced by the student's cognitive entry behaviors (such as his aptitude and preparation for this particular task) and his affective entry characteristics (such as his attitude toward and interest in the task).

Bloom accepted Carroll's proposition that most students can attain mastery of basic skills if they are given sufficient learning time and if the instruction is of sufficiently high quality that they can understand and profit from it. Using this proposition as a basic assumption, Bloom developed the following argument. The intelligence tests usually used to measure aptitude indicate that students tend to be normally distributed with respect to the trait. If all students are given the same instruction (the same amount and quality of instruction and the same amount of time allowed for learning) then students' performance measured at the end of the instruction would be normally distributed as well. A strong relationship would exist between the students' aptitude prior to entering the instructional situation and his performance at the completion of the instructional program.

Research subsequently conducted by Carroll (1973) indicated that measures of students' aptitudes for a particular subject were reliable predictors of their performance at the end of an instructional program in that subject when all students in a group were allowed the same amount of time to learn. However, if the instruction and the time allowed for learning were varied to meet the individual student's needs, most students attained mastery.

The mastery model is designed to structure the curriculum and instructional program to maximize the likelihood that each student will have sufficient opportunity to learn from high quality instruction and adequate instructional time to enable him to attain mastery. The mastery model also incorporated principles and programs derived from Goodlad and Anderson's work with the nongraded elementary school and the open classroom (1959), Glaser's work in Individually Prescribed Instruction at the Pittsburgh Learning Research Development Center (1968), and the work in computer-assisted instruction by Suppes and Atkinson (Suppes, 1966; Atkinson, 1968a). The distinction between formative evaluation, which yields information to be used in the course of learning, and summative evaluation, which measures final achievement in the course, made by Michael Scriven (1967) was also incorporated.

The mastery process was influenced by the work of Gagné and Paradise (1961), which suggested that some learning can be organized into a sequence in which mastery of each unit or task is a necessary prerequisite for mastery of the later, more difficult or more complex tasks. The work of Bloom *et al.* (1956) and others in developing taxonomies of educational objectives provided a strong influence on the mastery process, as did B. F. Skinner's work with programmed instruction and reinforcement (1954). Skinner's emphasis on the importance of reinforcing desirable behavior and of immediate feedback to correct the inaccurate information to prevent the student from retaining wrong responses was particularly influential.

School Performance Model

These concepts and the two models presented by Carroll (1963; 1971) and Bloom (1971) were incorporated by this author into the theoretical school performance model shown in Figure 5.2.

This school performance model proposes that a student will attain a specific level of performance when the following conditions are met. The student has adequate intellectual, affective, and physical aptitude. His prior learning and prior and concurrent experiences, both in and outside of school, have given him adequate preparation and continuing support for the tasks involved. The instructional methods and materials, the teachers, the learning environment, and other services are adequate to provide instruction of good quality that the student can benefit from and understand. The student can learn at a rate adequate to reach the prescribed level of performance

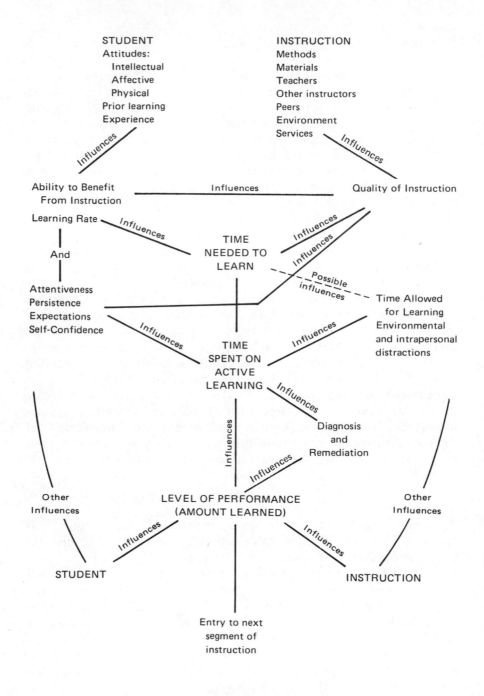

STUDENT
Attitudes:
  Intellectual
  Affective
  Physical
Prior learning
Experience

INSTRUCTION
Methods
Materials
Teachers
Other instructors
Peers
Environment
Services

Influences

Influences

Ability to Benefit
From Instruction

Influences

Quality of Instruction

Learning Rate

Influences

TIME
NEEDED TO
LEARN

Influences

Influences

And

Possible influences

Attentiveness
Persistence
Expectations
Self-Confidence

Time Allowed
for Learning
Environmental
and intrapersonal
distractions

Influences

TIME
SPENT ON
ACTIVE
LEARNING

Influences

Influences

Diagnosis
and
Remediation

Influences

Other
Influences

Influences

LEVEL OF PERFORMANCE
(AMOUNT LEARNED)

Influences

Other
Influences

Influences

Influences

STUDENT

INSTRUCTION

Entry to next
segment of
instruction

Figure 5.2. *School Performance Model.*

in the time allowed, using the available instruction. The time the student needs to learn is allocated in the instructional program. The instruction and the student's prior experience influence the student to feel confident that he will perform successfully, to expect to perform well, to remain attentive to the instruction, and to persist in completing the prescribed learning activities. As a result, the student spends the time he needs actively engaged in learning so that he reaches the level of performance defined as adequate for mastery.

The student's experiences in attaining one level of performance, as well as his newly acquired learning, influence his reactions to the next segment of instruction he encounters. His experiences and learning also determine whether the instruction will be of good quality for him. In addition, the student and the instruction in any instructional segment are subject to influence by forces not included in the prior segment of instruction. Research investigations of the hypotheses composing this model can increase knowledge of the processes involved in classroom instruction as well as the effectiveness with which this instruction can be implemented.

While mastery was receiving renewed attention in the 1960s through work in education, educational psychology, and curriculum development, a similar approach to instruction deriving from experimental psychology was developed by Fred S. Keller (1968). Keller's approach to instruction, often referred to as the "Keller plan" or the "Personalized System of Instruction," was strongly influenced by behaviorism and programmed instruction.

The Keller plan is one example of an implementation of the mastery structure. In this implementation, the student learns primarily from written materials. He usually works independently from other students. The instructional materials are divided into units. A unit is usually a text chapter. At the end of each unit, the student takes an exam that is graded by a proctor, a student who has previously passed the course. He must pass each exam at a high level, often 100%, before he can proceed to the next unit. Lectures and demonstrations are used as means of motivating students and rewarding them for good performance rather than as sources of critical information (Keller, 1972).

Keller used his method to teach introductory psychology at the New University of Brasilia, Brazil, in 1964. Beginning in 1965, the method was also used at Arizona State University (Wilson & Tosti, 1972). Keller listed the following features which, in his opinion, distinguished his method from conventional procedures within a mass education framework.

> 1. *The go-at-your-own-pace feature* which permits a student to move through the course at a speed commensurate with his ability and other demands upon his time.
> 2. *The unit-perfection requirement* for advance, which lets the student go ahead to new material only after demonstrating mastery of that which preceded.
> 3. *The use of lecture and demonstrations as vehicles of motivation* rather than sources of critical information.
> 4. *The related stress upon the written word* in teacher—student communication.
> 5. *The use of proctors*, which permits repeated testing, immediate scoring, almost unavoidable tutoring, and a marked enhancement of the personal—social aspect of the education process [1972, p. 176].

The Keller system is most effective for teaching students who can learn under self-paced instructional conditions. A recent survey (Clinton, 1976) found that the Keller plan is currently implemented in 1200 courses, of which 70% are at the postsecondary level, 65% are undergraduate, and 5% are graduate courses.

Other forms of the mastery model have also been used extensively in the United States and abroad. For example, over half a million students have used the basal mathematics program, *Mathematics Learning System* (SRA, 1974), which incorporates the mastery structure.

Obviously, the mastery model has gained considerable acceptance within a rather short time period. In addition to being used in programs involving hundreds of thousands of students, mastery has been investigated in numerous research studies. This research is the subject of Chapter 6.

6
Mastery Model Implementation: Cognitive Consequences

Thousands of students at various educational levels have participated and continue to participate in educational programs structured according to the mastery model. These curricula employ all six of the components of the mastery model described in the Chapter 5.

This chapter summarizes the results of research that investigated the impact of mastery model implementations upon students' cognitive performance. Indeed, most of the research incorporating implementations of the mastery model has focused upon this topic. The most common research format has been a comparison of an experimental group, which learned a particular topic using a mastery structured curriculum, with a control group of students, purportedly identical to the experimental group with the exception that their curriculum did not include all six components of the mastery model. The performance of the experimental and control groups on post-assessment measures, either criterion tests of the mastery curriculum objectives or norm-referenced standardized achievements tests, usually served as the data source. The data analysis typically consisted of simple comparisons of group mean scores. Separate comparisons are usually made for the experimental and control groups at each age or grade level, and analyses across age or grade levels are infrequent.

The present summary of research investigating the impact of mastery model implementation upon dimensions of student cognitive performance focuses upon the following cognitive outcome measures: student performance on objective-referenced measures administered following the completion of the entire instructional sequence; student performance on standardized norm-referenced achievement tests administered at the completion of the instruction; student retention of skills and knowledge learned in the mastery curriculum measured by objective-referenced tests administered no less than 2 weeks after the completion of the instruction; changes in students' learning rates and proportion of instructional time students spent in active learning.

In general, the research demonstrated that when the mastery model was implemented, students achieved higher levels of performance on objective-referenced posttests and increased the amount of instructional time spent in active learning. Results of research involving standardized norm-referenced achievement test scores were mixed, with some studies demonstrating higher scores for the mastery model curriculum and other studies demonstrating no significant differences between mastery model and control group test scores. The appropriateness of the standardized norm-referenced achievement tests employed as postassessment measures is considered.

In this review of research investigating the cognitive consequences of mastery model implementation, primary emphasis is given to research in which the mastery model implementations were not dependent upon continued, extensive, and frequent use of technical equipment, such as computers or audiovisual equipment, not readily available in the vast majority of the schools. Numerous instructional programs employing the six components of the mastery model depend upon extensive and continued use of technical equipment. Examples include Computer-Assisted Instruction at Stanford (Suppes & Morningstar, 1972), Individually Prescribed Instruction at the University of Pittsburgh (Glaser, 1965, 1968), Individually Guided Education at the University of Wisconsin at Madison (Klausmeier, 1971), and the Plato System at the University of Illinois.

The extensive published descriptive and evaluative literature on these instructional programs has generally tended to support the conclusions concerning the mastery model presented herein. However, this research does not receive extensive consideration in the present volume for two reasons. First, sufficient evidence is not yet available to enable the impact of the dependence upon technical equipment to be evaluated. Second, the present volume is concerned primarily with implementations of the mastery model that are potentially accessible to schools on a large-scale basis. Funds for extensive purchase and maintenance of technical equipment are not likely to be generally available in the near future.

Objective-Referenced Postassessment Performance

Research employing objective-referenced postassessment measures of cognitive consequences of mastery model implementation has included both large-scale investigations of at least one school year duration as well as smaller scale studies of shorter duration. Results of a representative sample of the large-scale investigations are presented first.

At the elementary school level, a large-scale study was undertaken by Science Research Associates (SRA, 1975) to investigate the effectiveness of the *Mathematics Learning System* (MLS) text series, which implemented the six mastery model components. Approximately 2300 students in grades one through eight learned mathematics using the mastery curriculum for 2 successive years. Alternate forms of the SRA Assessment Survey, a standardized objective-referenced mathematics achievement measure, were administered prior to the onset of instruction, again following 8 months of instruction, and a third time following 2 years of instruction. This assessment survey, part of the SRA achievement testing program, was developed and normed independently of the MLS. The racial and ethnic composition of the research sample was as follows: 1% American Indian, 12% Black, 1% Oriental, 11% Spanish surname, 74% White, and 1% Other.

The expected mean mathematics achievement level for each grade group was determined, using national normative data for the SRA Assessment Survey, in conjunction with the baseline data attained by each grade of students in the pretest (administration of the Assessment Survey prior to the onset of instruction). This expected mean represented the level of achievement that each group of students would be likely to attain in each of the 2 years of the study, assuming that the curriculum emphasis and teaching methods were not significantly different from those typically in use when the achievement test norms were established (Bode & Larsen, 1974). MLS students' SRA Assessment Survey scores over the 2 year period of the research were then compared with the expected mean group scores.

The results of these analyses were as follows:

Over the two year period the MLS students in grades two through eight:

1. Averaged from two to five months above the norm after two years of MLS, although they had averaged below the norm before using MLS (this achievement was significantly greater than expected).

2. Showed a growth rate exceeding the national norm; and

3. Grew from 15% to 49% higher than expected.

The *t*-tests used to determine the statistical significance of the differences showed that differences of this magnitude could occur by chance less than one time in one hundred for groups of the sizes studied here. Thus it can be concluded that these students in grades two through eight achieved greater than expected growth in mathematics during their first year in MLS and that over the two year period in MLS their growth exceeded expectations by a statistically significant amount. A similar pattern can be seen emerging for the first grade students [Suchaniak & Larsen, 1975, pp. 4–6].

In another investigation at the elementary school level, Anderson, Scott, and Hutlock (1976) assessed the differential cognitive consequences of mathematics curricula structured according to the mastery model versus comparable curricula which did not employ systematically all six mastery model components. This research was conducted in grades one through six in two schools of the Lorain, Ohio, public school system. Students in both schools represented a considerable range of socioeconomic status, with approximately 15% eligible for the free or reduced-cost lunch program and an additional 20% of the families classified in a professional occupational category.

As preparation for the mastery instruction, teachers in the mastery model implementation school attended a series of summer workshops in which the three researchers participated. The contents of these workshops included the philosophy and assumptions underlying the mastery model, as well as practical considerations involved in planning and implementing a mastery program. Teachers devoted a portion of the workshop time to developing objectives, original and supplementary instructional activities and materials, diagnostic tests, and a system for recording and reporting individual student progress. Curriculum and evaluation experts were available to assist the teachers, and easy access to varied instructional materials was provided. Most of the planning was completed prior to the beginning of the school year, but substitute teachers were available throughout the academic year for teachers who desired additional planning time.

In the mastery school, the curriculum incorporating the six mastery components was employed to teach mathematics in grades one through six throughout the 1974–1975 school year. Teachers in the "nonmastery" school employed the mathematics instructional procedures used in prior years. Observations of the nonmastery program indicated that the following components were omitted: explicitly stated objectives, objective-referenced diagnostic assessments, corrective activities and materials, and an entire class mastery performance standard (mastery or minimum pass levels).

The objective-referenced postassessment test, administered to both mastery and nonmastery students immediately following the completion of the entire instructional program, was constructed by the project director, the third author of the research report. This test assessed student mastery of the skills and knowledge defined in the instructional program structured according to the mastery model. Items assessing mastery of skills and knowledge that were not included in the nonmastery curriculum were omitted from the measure. In addition to the objective-referenced test, other measures were employed to assess the impact of the mastery model. These measures and the results produced are discussed in Chapter 7.

For purposes of analysis, each student in the mastery curriculum was matched with a student at the same grade level in the nonmastery curriculum on the basis of performance on the Metropolitan Readiness Test or the Otis–Lennon Intelligence Test. On the objective-referenced test, grade-level means for students in the mastery program were significantly higher than grade level means for students in the nonmastery curriculum. A separate comparison was reported for each of the six grade levels; the differences in mean grade level scores were statistically significant at every grade level with the exception of grade five, though the latter difference was in the predicted direction.

In another study at the elementary school level, Smith and Wick (1976) employed a curriculum structured according to the mastery model to teach reading comprehension and word attack skills to 150 inner-city students of lower socioeconomic status who were achieving at approximately the third grade level in reading. Though data collection is still in progress, preliminary results are available. Prior to the implementation of the diagnostic assessment and remediation components of the mastery curriculum, approximately 65% of the students performed at or beyond the minimum passing levels. After completion of the diagnostic assessment and correction cycle, approximately 95% of the students attained or exceeded the minimum pass levels on each of the objective-referenced postassessment measures in each of the mastery units.

One of the larger implementations of mastery has been conducted in Korea under the direction of Hogwon Kim, Yung Dug Lee, and their colleagues. Kim (1971) used group-based mastery procedures for teaching students in elementary and secondary schools. Typically, one teacher was responsible for about 70 students. Kim began with a pilot study in which an eight session unit on geometric figures was taught to 272 seventh grade students. The students were randomly assigned to two groups. Half of the students learned under mastery conditions and the other half learned using the lecture–recitation approach. The groups of students were comparable in terms of measured aptitude and past achievement in mathematics. To attain mastery, the students had to perform correctly at least 80% of the items on the objective-referenced postassessment test. The results showed that 75% of the students who learned with mastery procedures attained the acceptable performance level; 40% of the nonmastery students attained this level.

Based on these results, Kim expanded his mastery program. In the next stage, 5800 seventh grade students from nine middle schools in Seoul were taught mathematics and English for 8 weeks. Grouping procedures similar to those in the pilot study were used. As in the pilot study, the criterion of 80% correct on the objective-referenced postassessment was used to define mastery. In English, 72% of the mastery students attained this criterion, whereas 28% of the non-mastery students performed at the minimum pass level. In mathematics, 61% of the mastery program students performed at criterion, and 39% of the nonmastery students performed at criterion.

Kim's next project involved teaching mathematics, English, physics, and biology to 25,887 seventh grade students from rural and urban schools over an entire school year. Again, similar procedures were used. In English, 50% of the mastery students performed at criterion, while 44% of the nonmastery students performed at criterion. In mathematics 48% of the mastery students performed at criterion, and 26% of the nonmastery students performed at criterion. In physics, 30% of the mastery students performed at criterion, and 8% of the nonmastery students performed at criterion. In biology, 22% of the mastery students performed at criterion, and 3% of the nonmastery students performed at criterion (Kim, 1971, 1974).

Lee *et al.* (1971) replicated Kim's procedures. This project involved 12,000 fifth and sixth grade students enrolled in courses in arithmetic and science during one school year. Mastery procedures were used for 7409 students in 99 classrooms. An additional 5095 students from 80 classrooms who learned under normal, nonmastery conditions served as comparisons. The following results were obtained: In fifth grade arithmetic, 42% of the mastery students reached the criterion, and 12% of the nonmastery reached the criterion. In fifth grade science, 39% of the mastery students reached the criterion, and 7% of the nonmastery students reached the criterion. In sixth grade arithmetic, 45% of the mastery students reached the criterion, and 18% of the nonmastery students reached the criterion. In sixth grade science, 46% of the mastery students reached the criterion, and 12% of the nonmastery students reached the criterion (Lee, 1971; Block, 1974).

The Korean research shows that mastery procedures have brought thousands to the attainment of acceptable criteria of performance. For example, in Kim's project involving over 25,000 students, a difference of 10 percentage points (between the number of students who attained the criterion of performance under mastery and nonmastery conditions) represents 2500 students. When mastery procedures increase by 10% the number of students who attain the minimum criterion of performance, mastery procedures produce adequate performance levels for 2500 students who might have performed less than adequately under nonmastery conditions.

A medical college curriculum structured according to the mastery model provides an example of large-scale implementation at the professional level. The College of Medicine at the University of Illinois in Chicago designed the entire medical school curriculum incorporating the six mastery components.

Using the mastery model, objectives were developed; diagnostic and postassessment tests measuring attainment of minimum pass levels were used in place of norm-based measures throughout the school year. Diagnostic assessment tests were administered at the end of each unit.

Tests were given frequently, at least once a week. All students were required to take these tests, but the grades on them did not "count." Students who did not attain the minimum level of acceptable performance on these tests were referred for additional instruction and retested. If a student did not pass a test, he was given immediate help from a faculty member or student volunteer. (A more extensive description of this curriculum is presented in Chapter 9.)

One major modification that occurred as a result of the implementation of mastery procedures affected the amount of time taken to complete the medical program. Prior to implementation of mastery, the medical program required 4 years of study. Using mastery procedures, approximately 10% of the students were able to complete the program in 3 years. Some students were allowed long as six years to complete the same program. The mastery procedures have proven effective for helping almost all students attain the minimum pass levels. At the present time, the faculty has taken the position that students will not be allowed longer than 6 years to complete the program. A major evaluation of this curriculum is in progress.

In addition to large scale research represented by the examples reported above, numerous smaller scale studies, employing smaller samples and having a duration of less than one academic year, have employed objective-referenced tests to assess cognitive outcomes associated with mastery model curriculum implementation. Following is a representative sample of this research.

Block (1970) used mastery procedures to teach elementary matrix algebra to 91 eighth grade students. Programmed instruction textbooks, which presented the instruction in a series of sequential learning units, were employed. The students in the control group, Group I, progressed through the self-instructional textbook at their own rate without further assistance. The text was designed so that the average eighth grader would learn only about 50% of the material contained in each unit. Four other groups of students were required to learn a specific percentage of the material of each unit before they could progress to the next unit. Students in Group II were required to master 65% of the material in every unit; in Group III, students were required to master 75%; in Group IV, students mastered 85%; and in Group V, the students mastered 95% of the material of every unit. Students in the four specific mastery groups were given diagnostic tests when they completed each unit. If the student's performance on the diagnostic test showed that he had not mastered the percentage of the material required for his group, he was given his corrected test, a review sheet, and an additional programmed textbook. The second text contained a more complete explanation of the material he had answered incorrectly on the diagnostic test. When the student completed his study of the additional materials, he was given a second form of the diagnostic test. If his achievement on the second test was less than the mastery level prescribed for his group, he was tutored on the material he had missed. When the tutoring was completed, he took a third form of the diagnostic test.

All of the students were given an objective-referenced postassessment test when they finished the algebra textbook. A few students were dropped from the study because they either exceeded the performance level required for their group or were consistently unable to attain the required performance level.

The results showed that students who were required to master at least 85% of each unit demonstrated significantly greater postassessment achievement and retention than did the other students. Students who had mastered 95% of each unit were better able to transfer their knowledge to other contexts. Students who mastered at least 85% of the material showed a more positive attitude toward algebra and greater interest in the subject than did the other students immediately after completing the algebra text. Further, when the students' interest and attitudes were retested 2 weeks later, students who had mastered 85% of each unit showed greater interest and a most positive attitude toward algebra. This study indicates that requiring students to master a high percentage of each subject matter unit before they progress to the next unit can increase their achievement, retention, ability to transfer their learning to other contexts, and interest in and attitude toward the subject matter.

Block's study also illustrates the complexities involved in determining the criterion level students should be required to master. In this study, the students who mastered 85% of the material showed a greater interest and a more positive attitude toward algebra 2 weeks after completing the unit than did students who mastered 95% of the material. Yet, the students who mastered 95% of the material earned the highest scores on tests of postassessment achievement, retention, and ability to transfer learning to other contexts. Block concluded: "No single performance level (that is, standard) could be chosen which would simultaneously maximize both student cognitive and affective learning [1970, p. 150]." This conclusion is based on the results of a short-term instructional program, administered under highly controlled experimental conditions, that involved fewer than 100 students. More extensive research investigating the effects of various criterion levels is needed.

In another study, Lierley (1973) taught an arithmetic unit on fractions to about 25 sixth grade students using mastery procedures. When the instruction was completed, relatively few of the students had attained the minimum level of acceptable performance. A diagnostic analysis of the posttest items was performed. Lierley determined that the students did not know how to reduce their answers to the lowest terms, and the textbook did not contain the necessary instruction. Students were given supplemental instruction on reduction of fractions. When the students were retested, 77% of the students gave accurate answers to 90% of the items on the test.

Walbesser and Carter (1968) reported their evaluation of a science curriculum called *Science—A Process Approach Curriculum*

Project. This project was designed to teach science to students in grades K through 3. The results indicated that 90% of the students who had begun the mastery curriculum in kindergarten attained minimum pass levels on 88% of the objective-referenced performance measures in grade one. Students who had learned under nonmastery conditions in kindergarten attained the minimum pass levels on only 54% of the performance measures in grade one. In grade three, students who had participated in the mastery program attained criterion on 64% of the performance measures. Students who had learned with the mastery approach in either grades one or two attained criterion on 42% of the measures. Students who had not participated in the mastery program attained criterion on only 22% of the measures.

At the high school level, mastery procedures were used to teach introductory algebra to 169 students (Hymel, 1974). Mastery students were compared with students learning algebra under nonmastery conditions. The results indicated that mastery students learned significantly more algebra than did nonmastery students. Feedback—correction procedures were used to adapt the instructional procedures to the needs of individual students in the mastery program. These procedures accounted for at least part of the increased achievement of the mastery students.

Mastery procedures have been used in numerous college courses. In many reported studies, students who learned using mastery procedures attain higher levels of objective-referenced postassessment achievement than did students who learned under nonmastery conditions. For example, Collins (1969) used the mastery model to teach modern algebra to liberal arts majors and calculus to engineering and science majors. The courses were broken into units. The mastery students received lists of objectives for each unit, each class session, and each assignment. In each class session, the mastery students spent 5 to 10 minutes solving a problem based on the objectives of the preceding session. The problem was discussed and questions were answered. Nonmastery students were not given the objectives or the daily problems. The results indicated that 75% of the mastery students achieved the minimum pass level criterion (a grade of A or B in the course), whereas only 30% of the nonmastery students attained the criterion. In the calculus classes, 65% of the mastery students attained the criterion, whereas 40% of the nonmastery students attained the criterion. In both mastery classes, almost none of the students received grades of D or F.

When mastery procedures were used to teach educational psychology (Gentile, 1971), the content was divided into small instructional units and students learned at their own pace. Study questions identifying major points to be mastered were given to the students. When a student completed a unit, he scheduled an interview session with a classmate. He used the session to explain, in his own words, what he had just learned. His classmate listened, questioned confusing points, and commented favorably when the explanation was clear. Both students decided when the student who initiated the session was ready to take a test on the unit. When the student was ready to take the test, he obtained the test from his proctor (a student who had previously completed the course). Then he completed the test and discussed the results with his proctor. If the student had attained the minimum pass level, the proctor advised him to continue to the next unit. If the student had performed below this level, the proctor recommended appropriate review material. Upon completion of the review, the student was retested. This cycle was repeated until the student attained mastery. The results indicated that the mastery students had better understanding of the material than did students who took the course under nonmastery conditions. In addition, the mastery students reported more favorable attitudes toward the course. In evaluating the course, 74% of the mastery students indicated they had enjoyed the course, whereas only 21% of the other students reported that they had enjoyed the course.

In another study, mastery procedures were used to teach introductory statistics at the university level (Mayo *et al.*, 1968). Weekly diagnostic assessment tests were administered to each student. Individual and small group help was available as needed. Students were told that their final grade would be determined by their actual performance, regardless of their standing among their peers. The students were given a final examination that had been used in the previous session of the course. A grade of A was attained by 65% of the mastery students. Only 5% of the students who had taken the course under nonmastery conditions received the grade of A.

Mastery procedures were used to teach a test theory course at the graduate level (Airasian, 1969). Achievement in the course was evaluated using a test comparable to the test that had been used in previous courses. Results showed that 80% of the students who learned with mastery procedures achieved at the level required to earn the grade of A. Only 30% of the students had earned A grades in a prior session of the course.

An additional summary of small scale, short duration research is contained in the forthcoming edition of *Review of Education in*

Research (Block & Burns, in press). Research investigations of the effectiveness of the mastery model, ranging in duration from 1 week to one semester, include the following: Anderson, 1973; Block, 1972, 1973, 1974; Fiel and Okey, 1974; Glasnapp, Poggio, & Ory, 1975; Hymel, 1974; Jones *et al.*, 1974, 1975; Kim *et al.*, 1974; Okey, 1974, 1975; and Wentling, 1973. Mathematics curricula were employed in the majority of these investigations; the content of other investigations included European historiography, moral education, auto mechanics, English, business, economics, biology, and social studies. Student grade level ranged from first grade through university.

An additional set of studies investigated the effectiveness of the PSI implementation of the mastery model: Born *et al.*, 1972; Born *et al.*, 1972; Breland and Smith, 1974; Coldeway *et al.*, 1974; Cole *et al.*, 1975; Cooper and Greiner, 1971; Johnston and Pennypacker, 1971; Karlin, 1972; McMichael and Corey, 1969; Nazzaro *et al.*, 1972; Rosati, 1975; Roth, 1973; and Sheppard and MacDermot, 1970. The majority of the curricula involved in the PSI investigations were employed to teach psychology courses at the university level, though two courses taught engineering and one taught history. In each of these investigations, posttest performance of students in the mastery curricula was compared with posttest performance of students in the nonmastery curricula. Most studies reported results for one comparison group, though some studies reported results for as many as fourteen comparison groups.

Summarizing the results of these comparisons, mastery students' posttest performance was significantly higher than posttest performance of nonmastery students (exceeding .05 confidence level) in comparisons of 45 groups. In an additional 16 groups, the mastery students performed higher than nonmastery students, though the differences were not statistically significant. In 2 additional groups, the nonmastery students performed better than the mastery students, though these differences were not statistically significant. There were no reported results indicating that non-mastery students performed significantly (at the 5% level of confidence) better than mastery students.

In sum, the results of research employing objective-referenced measures and investigating the impact of implementation of the mastery model upon students' cognitive performance strongly support the conclusion that mastery model implementation contributed to higher levels of students' cognitive performance. In addition, greater percentages of students in mastery classes attained or exceeded the minimum pass levels than did students in nonmastery classes. In the next section of this chapter, a different cognitive outcome measure, norm-referenced standardized achievement test performance, is employed in the research investigating the mastery model.

Norm-Referenced Standardized Achievement Tests

Some of the research investigations of the mastery model that employed norm-referenced standardized achievement tests as post-assessment measures to assess the impact of the model have found that students in curricula structured with the six mastery model components demonstrated significantly higher achievement test scores than did students in nonmastery curricula. Other such investigations have found no significant differences in standardized achievement test scores for students in mastery model and nonmastery model curricula. Following are some representative samples of the larger scale, longer duration research.

One of the largest studies investigated was the impact of the MLS (SRA, 1974) curriculum upon the standardized achievement test performance of approximately 2300 students, discussed previously in this chapter. This is the only research located that obtained both norm-referenced and objective-referenced standardized achievement test data. As reported, the mathematics norm-referenced standardized achievement test scores of students in grades two through eight of the MLS curriculum were significantly higher than the expected group scores derived from the normative test data. The differences for students in grade one of the MLS curriculum were in the predicted direction, though not statistically significant. The SRA Assessment Survey used to obtain the data was part of the SRA standardized achievement testing program, which was developed and administered independently of the MLS program. These results support the conclusion that the MLS mastery model curriculum implementation produced significantly higher scores on the norm-referenced standardized tests of mathematics achievement (Suchaniak & Larsen, 1975).

Prior to the production of the MLS, SRA developed and produced the Distar reading, arithmetic, and language packaged instructional programs which implemented the mastery components at the preschool and early elementary levels. Distar has been used primarily with students who are expected to have difficulty in mastering the basic skills of the normal school curriculum. Research conducted by SRA using norm-referenced standardized achievement test scores supported the following conclusion:

> Students in Distar programs have tended to come closer to grade level than similar students have done or have been expected to do in traditional curriculums. Students whom educators have often predicted to be academic failures have performed almost at grade level—or beyond—or have achieved academic growth that essentially equals that of more educationally advantaged groups. Students who have not started out with an educational disadvantage have attained achievement scores far beyond grade level [SRA, 1971].

This conclusion is substantiated by numerous research studies. Studies have included inner-city students, functionally retarded students, black and Spanish-American students, students on an Indian reservation, and students in both rural and urban areas.

Research conducted by Anderson, Scott, and Hutlock (1976) investigating the implementation of the mastery model in the mathematics curriculum of elementary grades one through six was referred to previously in this chapter. The concepts, computation, and problem solving subscales of the California Achievement Test were administered to all students in mastery and nonmastery classes at the completion of the mathematics instruction. Compared with nonmastery students, first grade mastery students demonstrated significantly higher performance on the computation subscale, and third grade mastery students demonstrated significantly higher performance on the concepts and computations subscales. Eight subgroups of mastery students demonstrated (statistically nonsignificant) higher performance levels than nonmastery students. Four subgroups of mastery students demonstrated (statistically nonsignificant) lower performance than nonmastery students. Finally, sixth grade mastery students demonstrated significantly lower performance than nonmastery students in each of the three subscales of the test.

Implementation of the PSI form of the mastery model in the teaching of economics at the university level (Abraham and Newton, 1974; Billings, 1974) demonstrated similar results. Summarizing the results, one group of mastery students demonstrated significantly higher norm-referenced achievement test performance than nonmastery students, one group demonstrated performance that was higher than nonmastery performance but not significantly so, and two groups of nonmastery students demonstrated performance higher than that of mastery students, though these differences, too, were not statistically significant.

These results do not support any clear conclusion concerning the impact of mastery model implementation upon standardized achievement test performance. In general, the frequency of research results indicating significantly greater scores in mastery curricula is approximately equivalent to the research results indicating either no significant differences or higher scores for nonmastery students.

Several issues complicate the interpretation of the results of mastery model implementation upon standardized achievement test performance. One issue is the appropriateness of the specific normative measures to the population of students to which they are applied. The second issue is the appropriateness of the standardized achievement test measures to the measurement of the outcomes of the specific instructional programs to which they are applied.

Research currently in progress at the City of Chicago Board of Education (Smith, Katims, and Steele, unpublished paper) is investigating the effectiveness of the Iowa Tests of Basic Skills (Reading) as a postassessment measure in an evaluation of implementation of the mastery model in a reading curriculum. In conjunction with the Smith and Wick (1976) mastery model implementation in the reading curriculum at the third grade level, discussed previously in this chapter, the researchers wanted to use standardized achievement measures to assess the impact of the mastery curriculum. Students participating in the research were performing at more than one of the levels designated in the standardized achievement test format. To investigate the comparability of two levels of the tests and to determine the appropriate level for various subgroups of the students, levels eight and nine were administered to approximately 20 students, with a time lapse of two weeks or less between administrations. Results of both administrations are presented in Table 6.1.

As these results demonstrate, level nine achievement (grade equivalent) test performance was an average of 1 year lower than level eight achievement test performance, when both tests were administered no more than 2 weeks apart and both test levels were equally appropriate according to the test administration instructions. Some students showed grade equivalent test score decreases of up to 2 years. The researchers suggested that one cause of the decrease in level nine scores was the introduction of machine-scored answer sheets in the level nine tests. The students had difficulty in using the machine-scored answer sheets. In the level eight tests, students recorded their answers directly into the test booklet.

TABLE 6.1

Grade Equivalent Scores on Two Levels
of the Iowa Test of Basic Skills (Reading),
Administrations Separated by 1 to 2 Week Intervals[a]

Student number	Level 8 score	Level 9 score
1	3.0	2.7
2	3.1	2.6
3	3.2	3.9
4	3.4	2.5
5	3.4	2.7
6	3.4	3.9
7	3.5	2.4
8	3.7	2.4
9	3.8	2.5
10	3.9	2.8
11	3.9	3.2
12	3.9	3.4
13	3.9	4.1
14	4.2	3.0
15	4.4	3.8
16	4.5	3.2
17	4.9	3.5
18	5.5	3.7
19	5.5	4.3
20	6.2	4.1
$\overline{X}$	4.1	3.1

[a]*Source:* Smith, Jeffery K., Katims, Michael
and Steele, Carolyn. *Mastery Learning and Read-*
ing Instruction. City of Chicago Board of Education (unpublished paper).

In this investigation, the level of the standardized achievement
tests administered was associated with greater variation in postassessment standardized achievement test performance than was any other
measured instructional variable, including implementation of the
mastery model. Rarely in educational research does any treatment
factor account for an average difference of 1 year in standardized
achievement test performance.

Factors such as the initiation of machine-scored answer sheets,
item variation and difficulty, and other factors accounting for variations across simultaneous administrations of various levels of achieve-

ment tests must be investigated if these tests are to continue in use as postassessment measures in instructional programs. Interpretation of the results of standardized achievement test performance relative to mastery model implementations should be reserved until these research results are in.

The second issue concerning the use of standardized achievement tests as postassessment measures concerns the appropriateness of the test items and test format to the objectives, content, methods of instruction, and outcome measures of the particular curriculum for which the standardized achievement measures serve as postassessments. If the standardized achievement tests do not measure outcomes attributable to this specific curriculum, then these data should not be used to evaluate the effectiveness of those curricula.

Retention

Student retention of skills and knowledge learned in the mastery curriculum was measured in research investigations by readministration of the postassessment objective-referenced measure after the entire program of instruction and the initial postassessment administration had been completed. Readministrations of the same postassessment measure employed in the instructional program have been separated from the completion of the instruction by varying time periods, usually ranging from 2 weeks to $1\frac{1}{2}$ years. As the Block (1970) research previously discussed in this chapter reported, students who attained high mastery levels (approximately 90%) during the instruction demonstrated greater retention than did students who attained lower mastery levels and students in nonmastery curricula. Similar results have been reported in the following studies: Anderson *et al.*, 1976; Anderson and Artman, 1973; Block, 1972, 1973; Breland and Smith, 1974; Burrows and Okey, 1975; Corey and McMichael, 1974; Corey *et al.*, 1970; Jones, 1974; Nazzaro *et al.*, 1972; Poggio, 1976; Wentling, 1973. In these studies, retention of learning in psychology, physics, mathematics, social studies, statistics, and auto mechanics was assessed. Grade level ranged from first through university level. Although most studies reported comparisons for one group, two studies reported comparisons for five groups.

Summarizing these results, students in mastery curricula demonstrated statistically significant greater retention in 17 comparisons, greater (but not statistically significant) retention in nine comparisons, and less (statistically nonsignificant) retention in only one comparison. These results support the conclusion that curriculum designs that implement the six mastery components produce greater student retention than do curriculum designs that omit one or more of the components.

Reduction in Extent to Which Cognitive Entry Characteristics Determine Postassessment Performance

One of the basic tenets of the Carroll model (1963a) postulated that providing each student with adequate opportunity to learn (high quality instruction and ample instructional time) would permit him to attain mastery of the skills and knowledge identified in the curriculum objectives. Thus, implementation of the mastery model was expected to reduce the relationship between measures of student subject-matter-specific (Bloom, 1976) and instructional-method-specific (Block & Anderson, 1975) entry characteristics to the student's postassessment performance.

An extensive consideration of subject-matter-specific cognitive and affective entry behaviors expected to affect student ability to benefit from instruction as well as student postassessment performance was presented in Chapter 5 and in other volumes (Bloom, 1976; Block & Anderson, 1975; Block & Burns, in press). Research results available to date suggest that these cognitive and affective entry characteristics do significantly affect the student's reactions to instruction and his postassessment performance. However, the results (see, for example, Carroll, 1962) indicate that the mastery model components tend to reduce the relationship of student cognitive entry characteristics to student postassessment performance on cognitive measures.

Results of other investigations of the effect of the mastery model upon the relationship of preassessment to postassessment cognitive performance have tended to support the conclusions of the Carroll (1963b,c) research (see, for example, Anderson, 1976; Born *et al.*, 1972; Burrows & Okey, 1975; Hymel, 1974; Nazzaro *et al.*, 1972). These studies have suggested that the following three conditions associated with mastery model implementation serve to help students compensate, in varying degrees, for deficient cognitive entry characteristics: provision of ample instructional time, diagnostic assessment and prescription, and high minimum pass levels required on each unit. The contributions of specific components and conditions associated with the mastery model are considered in greater detail in Chapter 8.

Conclusion

In sum, the research evidence available to date supports the conclusion that implementation of the six components of the mastery model contributes to higher student performance on objective-referenced measures of cognitive mastery and to increased retention, when compared with instructional programs that omit one or more of the mastery components. Preliminary evidence indicates that the mastery component may serve to reduce the extent to which student cognitive preassessment performance (student characteristics measured prior to the onset of instruction) predict postassessment performance. Results of evaluations incorporating norm-referenced standardized achievement tests are inconclusive. Further investigations of issues concerning the validity of the widely available existing standardized achievement tests as measures of the outcomes of curricula implementing the mastery model should be conducted before conclusions using these measures to assess mastery model impact can be drawn.

Most of the research investigating mastery model implementation has employed univariate rather than multivariate approaches to the evaluation process. Data from each group of subjects, grade level group or administration occasion group, were analyzed separately. Results obtained with each outcome measure were also analyzed separately. Information about effectiveness of component implementation, variations in implementation formats, and other classroom process variables have rarely been included.

Furthermore, the unit of analysis in most of the research investigations reported herein has been the class or group mean. As is the case with other instructional treatments, the mastery model components are likely to be more effective for some students within the group than they are for others. Likewise, specific implementation of the mastery model components may be more effective for specific subsections of the content as well as for specific subgroups of students. These important issues remain uninvestigated when results are reported and analyzed using group means on postassessment measures.

A multivariate model derived from Carroll's model for school learning and appropriate for evaluating mastery model implementations has recently been developed by William Cooley and Paul Lohnes (in press). This model specifies that information be obtained on the following components of instruction: (1) student initial ability upon entrance to the instructional program, (2) opportunity to learn, (3) student motivation, (4) curriculum structure, (5) instructional events, and (6) criterion ability (student postassessment performance). When information on each of these components of instruction has been obtained, a multivariate analysis procedure is used to determine the regression of criterion ability upon the other five components of the model. This permits analysis of the extent to which the total variance of postassessment performance can be attributed to: (1) initial student ability independent of classroom variables, (2) variance due to classroom variables independent of initial ability factors, (3) interactions of initial ability and instructional processes.

A more extensive multivariate model for analyzing the impact of mastery model implementation, developed by this author, is presented in Chapter 9. Multivariate investigations of mastery model implementations, employing the Cooley and Lohnes model (in press), the Torshen model, or other procedures, will increase knowledge of the specific components and implementation conditions that contribute to the increased postassessment performance levels found in mastery model curricula.

The present chapter has focused exclusively upon cognitive consequences. In the next chapter, the research investigating the impact of mastery model implementation upon student affective consequences is considered.

7

Mastery Model Implementation: Affective Consequences

Numerous practitioners have proposed that the most significant outcomes associated with mastery model implementation lie in the affective domain. Practitioners have reported that students in mastery model curricula demonstrate increased interest in the subject matter and in learning, greater satisfaction with the academic curriculum, increased academic confidence, more positive perceptions of the self in school-related areas, and increased optimism concerning future performance.

In contrast with the practitioners, researchers evaluating mastery model implementation have tended to focus on cognitive rather than affective outcomes. Relative to the number of investigations evaluating cognitive factors, few studies have included assessments of affective factors.

In those investigations of mastery model implementation in which affective outcomes have been measured, the results have tended to support the conclusions observed by practitioners. The present chapter reviews this research. In addition, research investigating affective factors associated with the conditions created by mastery model implementation is considered herein.

In Chapter 6 the research designs of the mastery model implementation studies were criticized for overdependence on univariate pretest–posttest or posttest-only designs employed to investigate complex multidimensional phenomena. The same criticisms apply to most of the research reviewed here. In addition, most of the studies have used relatively short self-report questionnaires to measure highly complex affective variables. Furthermore, either the underlying dimensionality of the inventories has not been considered and the underlying structure has not been investigated, or the results of such consideration and investigation have not been reported. Notable exceptions include Lynch, 1975, 1976; Torshen, 1969, 1973, 1974, 1976, 1976, which investigated the underlying dimensionality of the affective measures. In spite of these deficits, the research in this area is interesting in that the results are reasonably consistent and indicative of positive affective outcomes associated with mastery model implementation.

Teachers' Perceptions

It has been proposed that one of the primary advantages associated with mastery model implementation is a change in teachers' expectations concerning student performance (Bloom, 1968). The mastery philosophy asserts that most students in a classroom can master the basic skills and knowledge (attain the minimum pass levels) in instructional settings in which the six mastery model components are implemented (Bloom, 1971; Carroll, 1971).

Such a change in teacher's expectations for students' performance is needed because of the strong and dominant influence which average-based education and the normal curve have had upon these expectations. Bloom (1968) asserted that teachers begin a new term or course with the expectation that one-third of the students will learn the material adequately, one-third will learn some of what is taught but not enough to be regarded as good students, and one-third will fail or just get by. However, these expectations are incorrect because "most students (perhaps over 90 percent) can master what we have to teach them [Bloom, 1968, p. 1]."

The proposition that teachers typically do not expect most of their students to master the curriculum objectives was supported in the investigation by Good and Dembo (1973), in which 163 in-service teachers were asked to estimate the percentage of their students whom they expected to "really master the material" that they intended to teach. Over one-half of the teachers expected fewer than 50% of their students to master the material. Expectations that

95% or more of the students would demonstrate mastery were reported by a mere 6% of the teachers.

Results of one series of investigations, conducted by Okey, 1974, 1975, 1976; Okey and Ciesla, 1975, and a second series conducted by Anderson *et al.*, 1976, indicated that mastery model implementation was associated with highly positive teacher expectations concerning student performance. Okey and Ciesla developed an in-service teacher-training module to teach the basic mastery philosophy and procedures to preservice and in-service elementary and middle school teachers. This module, which requires from 7 to 10 hours of instructional time, employs a slide–tape or filmstrip–tape format with an accompanying manual containing objectives and practice exercises. The manual includes self-tests with answers for each of the seven sections, as well as a pretest on prerequisites in a project section.

In investigating the effectiveness of *Mastery Teaching*, Okey and Ciesla (1975) used this instruction to train 20 preservice and 20 in-service teachers. Pretest data indicated that, prior to the instruction, the teachers were unfamiliar with the mastery philosophy and procedures, although some of the teachers were familiar with or had implemented portions of the mastery components. Upon completion of the module, all of the teachers demonstrated that they had mastered the philosophy and procedures. Furthermore, 75% of the teachers reported that they intended to incorporate the philosophy and procedures into their own teaching. A subsequent replication with an additional 40 teachers (Okey, 1976) demonstrated comparable results.

In the preceding chapter, the investigations of Anderson *et al.*, (1976), which employed a summer workshop to teach mastery philosophy and practice to in-service teachers, received considerable attention. When the teacher-training program had employed the mastery curriculum for several months, a 15-item questionnaire was administered to all teachers in the experimental and control groups. Of the mastery teachers, 100% gave affirmative answers to questions concerning the following: (*1*) By writing and using objectives, I have more knowledge about the math I should teach. (*2*) I believe I am doing a better job teaching math this year than in the past. Most teachers gave affirmative answers to the following question: In comparison with last year, I find it takes me less time to complete math units. Significantly fewer teachers in the nonmastery curriculum format gave affirmative answers to these questions. Almost all teachers in the experimental and control groups gave affirmative answers to the following question: Most of my students are meeting the objectives that I have set in mathematics. Although the difference was not statistically significant, more mastery than nonmastery teachers disagreed with this statement: I believe that it is very difficult for many of my students to actually master the objectives that have been designed for my grade level.

Teachers' Attitudes toward the Curricula

In accord with the results of the Anderson studies, other investigations have demonstrated that implementation of the mastery model is associated with positive attitudes on the part of the teachers toward the curricula. Okey (1976) found significant improvements in teachers' attitudes toward the mastery model components. In the evaluations of the *Mathematics Learning System* (SRA, 1974) instructional materials, implementing the mastery components in mathematics instruction in grades one through eight, 80% of the teachers surveyed reported favorable attitudes toward the curriculum and the instructional materials (Suchaniak & Larsen, 1975). In both investigations, teachers reported positive attitudes toward the objectives, the diagnostic assessment and correction process, and the objective-referenced assessments.

An investigation employing mastery components to teach fifth-grade arithmetic to 12 classrooms of students (Kersh, 1971; personal communication) indicated that the teacher's encouragement and persistence were crucial factors significantly related to student performance. When teachers encouraged students to complete the instruction and when they supervised carefully those students who were reluctant to finish needed remedial instruction, most of the students in the class attained mastery in the mathematics units. However, implementation of the mastery curriculum had no significant measured impact upon student posttest performance when teachers did not provide this encouragement and supervision.

In the research conducted by Smith and Wick (1976), discussed in the preceding chapter, considerable effort on the part of the researchers was needed to guide the classroom teachers to employ the information derived from the diagnostic testing in the prescriptive component of the curriculum. Teachers tended to supply students with answers to the questions they had missed rather than to investigate the causes of individual student problems. If half of the students in the class performed below the minimum pass level on one diagnostic measure, the teacher tended to present review instruction for all of the students in the class. When the experimenters were successful in teaching the teachers to implement the diagnostic and prescriptive components of the model appropriately, teachers developed more positive attitudes toward the mastery model.

In sum, these results indicate that implementation of the mastery model is associated with higher teacher expectations for student performance and more favorable teacher attitudes toward the curricula. However, teachers who do not implement the components correctly or do not provide sufficient encouragement and supervision of students did not demonstrate these positive perceptions.

Parents' Perceptions of Curricula
Structured according to the Mastery Model

Parents' opinions and attitudes have rarely been measured in mastery research. However, those studies that measured parents' attitudes have reported favorable opinions of the mastery curricula. In the series of studies by Anderson *et al.*, 1976, questionnaires were distributed to parents of students in the mastery and nonmastery curricula. Parents of students in the mastery curriculum gave significantly more positive responses than did parents of students in the nonmastery curriculum to the following items:

1. I received adequate information concerning the skills my child has in arithmetic.

2. I believe that the school is doing a satisfactory job of educating my child in arithmetic.

3. My child seems to enjoy arithmetic.

4. I believe that my child is learning the necessary math skills.

5. I believe my child is confident about his/her work in school.

6. I think my child is expected to learn an appropriate amount of arithmetic in an appropriate time [Anderson *et al.*, 1976].

Comparable results were obtained in assessment of parents' evaluations of the MLS curriculum (SRA, 1976). Parents responded anonymously to questionnaires and mailed the completed questionnaires directly to the researchers. Approximately 70 to 80% of the parents of students in grades one through six reported favorable evaluations of the MLS curriculum. In grades seven and eight, the percentage of positive evaluations dropped to approximately

60%. Parents of fifth grade students reported that their child enjoys math: Usually (73%); sometimes (23%); seldom (5%). Of the parents surveyed, 88% reported that they judged mathematics to be very important to their child's education.

Students' Perceptions

Among research investigating student affective consequences associated with mastery model implementation, the most frequent measurement was the student report of his interest in or attitude toward the subject matter or the teaching method. Students' reports of their attitudes toward the instruction and subject matter were often obtained in courses taught using the PSI procedures. Two studies (McMichael & Corey, 1969; Sheppard & MacDermot, 1970) found that students who took PSI courses in introductory psychology reported greater satisfaction and more favorable attitudes toward psychology than did students who took non-PSI versions of the introductory psychology course. Similar results were reported for other PSI courses in psychology (Born, 1972; Breland & Smith, 1975; Morris & Kimbrill, 1972; Witters & Kent, 1972).

Other studies, which investigated students' attitudes toward PSI instruction but did not compare those attitudes with the opinions of students in non-PSI courses, also reported that students viewed the PSI instruction favorably. For example, 98% of the students in a PSI course in introductory psychology made favorable comments about the course (Gallup, 1969). In a course in fluid mechanics, 93% of the students reported that they preferred the PSI method to other teaching methods (Flammer, 1971). Similar results were reported for courses in introductory psychology (Born & Herbert, 1971), physics (Green, 1971), nuclear, mechanical, electrical and operations research engineering (Hoebrock, 1972), library science (Knightly & Sayre, 1972), abnormal psychology (Walen, 1971), general physics (Philippas & Sommerfeldt, 1972), and digital systems engineering (Roth, 1973).

Similar conclusions were reached in studies that investigated student attitudes associated with other implementations of the mastery model in elementary classrooms. When 40 teachers completed *Mastery Teaching* (Okey, 1975), the teachers taught various subjects to elementary and middle-school students using curricula structured according to the mastery model. A 10-item pupil attitude questionnaire was administered to students twice, once prior to the onset of mastery instruction (nonmastery condition) and a second time at the completion of the mastery units (mastery condition). Total group mean scores indicated that, under the mastery condition, students reported favorable attitudes toward the instruction on all 10 items of the pupil attitude scale. Statistical significance of relationships of attitude scores under mastery and nonmastery conditions were not reported (Okey, 1976).

Anderson (1973, 1976) included items on student questionnaires to investigate students' perception of instructional quality (two items) and students' predictions of how interesting the next instructional unit would be (one item) prior to the onset of a unit of mastery instruction. One portion of the research investigation employed the three-unit mastery and nonmastery sequences of programmed material in matrix arithmetic developed by Block (1970), described in Chapter 6. Students in the mastery sequence gave significantly more positive responses to the single question, administered following the first and second units, requiring them to predict how interesting they expected the next unit to be. In the portion of the research in which arithmetic and algebra were taught using the mastery model, mastery students gave more positive responses to the two items measuring their perceptions of instructional quality, but the differences between the mean responses of mastery and nonmastery students did not reach statistical significance.

In the evaluation of the MLS instructional program (SRA, 1975), 72% of students surveyed reported that they liked the mastery curriculum better than the nonmastery curricula that they had used during the preceding academic year. Only 6% of the students reported that the mastery curriculum was not as good as the preceding curriculum.

In two studies conducted by Block (1972, 1973) which employed the mastery matrix algebra instructional sequence (Block, 1970) to teach 1 week sequences to eighth grade students, two groups of students in the mastery curriculum reported significantly more positive attitudes toward the subject matter, three groups reported more positive attitudes that were not statistically significant, and one group reported (statistically nonsignificant) less positive attitudes than did students learning matrix algebra in the nonmastery curriculum. In a third study (Block & Tierney, 1974), mastery components were employed to teach European historiography to college students. Students in the mastery curriculum reported (statistically nonsignificant) less positive attitudes toward the subject matter than did students in the nonmastery curriculum. As reported in Chapter 6, Block's research indicated that less positive student attitudes toward the subject matter are associated with the enforcement of high (90%+) mastery levels. Further research is needed to determine whether these relationships are representative of other subject matter instruction and of instruction of longer duration. Research should also investigate whether these negative attitudes toward the subject matter associated with 90% mastery levels were caused by factors specific to the high mastery level conditions of the instruction in the Block research.

Satisfaction of Student Performance Expectations

Okey (1976) employed student questionnaires to measure student perceptions of instruction and performance in the nonmastery and mastery conditions described above. Though statistical significance levels are not reported, students gave more positive responses following the mastery instruction to the following questions:

1. I learned what the teacher expected in this unit.
2. I am satisfied with my achievement on this unit.

Students' Concepts of Self

In the research of Anderson *et al.* (1975, 1976), the National Longitudinal Study of Mathematics Self-Concept Inventory was administered to students in fourth through sixth grades following completion of each of 2 academic years of mastery instruction (experimental group). This inventory measured students' self-reported self-concepts in areas specific to mathematics. Following the first year of mastery instruction, students in the mastery curriculum reported higher self-concepts in math-related areas (differences were statistically significant for one group only) than did students in nonmastery curricula. Following the second year of instruction, mastery students continued to report higher academic self-concepts in mathematics (differences were statistically significant for grades five and six).

In an earlier study, Anderson (1973, 1976) administered the same self-concept inventory prior to the onset of mastery instruction to approximately 55 students. The results indicated that student reported academic self-concept specific to mathematics was positively (statistically significant in one group only) related to the amount of time the students spent actively engaged in learning during the mastery instruction.

If students who have more positive feelings about their academic competence in mathematics areas devote more of their allotted instructional time to active learning, this relationship provides one explanation for the demonstrated relationships of student-reported academic self-concept and academic achievement. Further investigations of these relationships could provide extremely useful information about interactions of affective and cognitive factors in learning.

Other studies have added additional support to the above findings. In the mastery research conducted in Korea, Lee (1971) found that students who learned with the mastery methods reported significantly greater academic self-confidence than did students in curricula that did not employ all six mastery components. Jones *et al.* (1975) found that college students' self-reported academic self-concepts were significantly greater in the mastery sections of the following courses: business, economics, English, humanities, and social studies. Ely and Minars (1973) reported that college students' self-reported general self-concepts were higher in mastery than in nonmastery curricula, though the differences were not statistically significant. Finally, Okey (1976) found that students in the mastery curriculum reported more positive feelings about themselves than did students in the nonmastery curricula.

Lee (1971) also found that mastery students who had participated in small group cooperative learning activities reported significantly more positive cooperative feelings than did other students. Similar results were found by Okey (1976). In this investigation, mastery students reported that they were encouraged more frequently to help one another during the instruction.

Student Motivation and Persistence

The most frequent measure of student motivation and persistence employed in the mastery model research conducted to date consists of student withdrawal from or completion of the sequence of instruction. The research on this topic that could be located was conducted with college students exclusively. In investigations employing the PSI form of mastery instruction, significantly greater numbers of student course withdrawals under the PSI conditions were reported by Born *et al.* (1972), Born and Whelan (1973), McMichael and Corey (1969), Philippas and Sommerfeldt (1972) and Sheppard and MacDermot (1970). Kulik *et al.* (1974) found significantly fewer student course withdrawals under PSI conditions, and Jones *et al.* (1975) also found fewer student course withdrawals with another form of mastery model implementation. These latter investigations employed techniques that encouraged students to reduce procrastination during the early portion of the instructional sequence.

Student Anxiety Associated with Testing

This anxiety factor was investigated in only one of the studies (Poggio *et al.*, 1975) of the affective factors associated with mastery model implementation. In this particular implementation of the mastery model, students' course grades were determined by their performance on a single administration of the posttest. Students in the mastery instruction demonstrated higher anxiety associated with this type of posttest administration and grading than did students in the nonmastery instruction. It is possible that this test anxiety could be reduced by providing multiple opportunities to demonstrate competent performance and earn final course grades.

In sum, implementation of mastery model curricula was found to be associated with increased teacher expectations relevant to student mastery, favorable teacher, parent, and student attitudes, increased student interest, and more positive student self-concepts. Increased student course withdrawals in PSI courses and higher test anxiety in one experiment were also reported. In general, the research indicated that favorable affective consequences resulted from mastery model implementation.

Affective Consequences of Instructional
Conditions Created by Mastery Model Implementation

Since the research investigating affective consequences associated with the mastery model is rather sparse to date, additional research relevant to one or more of the conditions associated with the mastery model is considered herein. This research provides valuable insights even though the studies were not designed specifically to investigate the mastery model.

The research considered here supports the following conclusions.

1. Teachers form expectations concerning how their students will perform. Even when inaccurate, these expectations affect teachers' evaluations of students' performance, as well as students' opportunities to attempt difficult instruction and to demonstrate competent performance. Increasing teachers' access to objective assessments of students' performance can increase the accuracy of the teachers'

expectations. Since implementation of the mastery model provides ample access to performance information, this model may increase the accuracy of teachers' expectations.

2. Evaluations of students' academic performance determined by their teachers and communicated directly and frequently to the students, usually in the form of grades, were significantly related to students' self-concepts in academic areas, expectations concerning future performance, motivation and perceptions of their power of influence over what happens to them in school. Students who received frequent positive evaluations demonstrated positive self-concepts, realistic expectations concerning future performance, persistent and active participation in learning and acceptance of responsibility for their own performance. These positive affective conditions were not characteristic of students who received consistent and frequent negative feedback from their teachers.

Experimental investigations in classroom settings demonstrated that employing well-defined goals to evaluate students' performance, teaching students to accept responsibility for their performance, providing encouragement and a supportive environment in which negative evaluations were minimized, and providing positive evaluations to each student who demonstrated competent performance contributed to positive changes in students' self-concepts, expectations concerning future performance, motivation, and acceptance of responsibility. Since these instructional conditions are characteristic of the mastery model implementation curriculum, they may be significant factors contributing to the positive affective consequences reported by practitioners who employed the mastery model.

Teachers' Expectations about Students' Performance

Teachers' expectations concerning how students will perform are normal components of the daily classroom functioning. Accurate expectations are extremely useful in helping teachers organize and prepare for instruction.

Willis (1972) investigated the judgments about students' achievement potential made by first-grade teachers after only a few days of experience with the students. The teachers made many accurate judgments about the students' achievement potential. They correctly distinguished between students' actual ability and their readiness. Students who had lower ability but high readiness because they had been coached at home were identified as such. Students who had high ability but low readiness because they had received little or no preparation at home were also accurately identified. However, the accuracy of the teachers' judgments was increased when they had access to readiness test information. The records of prior performance and the diagnostic evaluations included in the mastery procedures are designed to provide teachers with extensive relevant information to help them develop accurate expectations about each student's achievement potential.

Some of the studies gave teachers inaccurate information about students, which caused them to develop inaccurate expectations concerning students' performance. The results of this research indicated that teachers' expectations affected their behavior toward students even when those expectations were inaccurate (see Braun, 1976, for a current review of this literature). Teachers tended to interact more often with high-expectation students, to attempt to teach them more information, and to praise their successes more frequently than they did for low-expectation students. The teachers' behavior toward the high-expectation students could encourage these students to perform at high levels. The teachers' behavior toward lower-expectation students might discourage them from attempting to perform well (Rubovits & Maehr, 1971; Kester & Letchworth, 1972).

Brophy and Good (1970) found similar teaching behavior patterns when teachers developed their expectations concerning students' performance in the normal course of their teaching. Students for whom teachers had higher expectations received significantly more praise following correct answers and significantly less criticism following wrong answers than did students for whom teachers had low expectations. When high-expectation students gave wrong answers, teachers repeated or rephrased the questions or supplied a clue more frequently than they did for low-expectation students. The same results were found when the students demonstrated reading problems. When low-expectation students gave answers to the teacher's questions, they received significantly less information about their answers than did high-expectation students.

Follow-up studies (Brophy & Good, 1974) indicated that some teachers consistently demonstrated these behavior patterns while other teachers did not. Teachers who were least likely to demonstrate harmful behavior patterns associated with expectations were labeled "pro-active." These teachers established and maintained the initiative in their actions with their students. They used their expectations concerning students' performance as a basis for individualizing instruction and designing instructional methods and materials appropriate for the needs of each student. Though these teachers generally made accurate predictions concerning students' achievement potential, they were flexible concerning their expectations. They frequently observed the changes in their students and modified their expectations accordingly.

The mastery model is designed to employ the characteristics associated with the pro-active teacher. The needs of each student are considered when the instructional program is prepared. Alternative learning procedures are available when needed. The frequent diagnostic evaluations provide information that students and teachers can use to modify and correct inaccurate predictions about the students' needs, interests, and potential as well as the effectiveness of the instruction.

When one teacher must supervise 30 or more students simultaneously, it is extremely difficult to give equal attention and help to each student. The research identifying differences in teacher behavior associated with different teacher expectations about students' performance indicates that inequities can occur in the classroom even when teachers have no intention of slighting any student. Perhaps the mastery procedures may reduce some of these inequities.

Teachers' expectations concerning students' performance may affect both the evaluations that they make of the students' performance and the students' performance itself. Several studies found that teachers' expectations significantly influenced the grades that they gave to students' work (Cahen, 1966; Finn, 1972; Simon, 1969).

In two additional studies, first grade reading teachers who did not believe that boys could learn as well as girls were identified (Doyle, Hancock, & Kifer, 1972; Palardy, 1969). In the Doyle study, the teachers systematically overestimated the IQs of girls and systematically underestimated the IQs of the boys. The results of both studies indicated that the boys showed significantly lower reading achievement than did the girls in the courses in which the teachers expected boys to achieve lower than girls. In both studies, students' aptitude for reading was controlled. The performance of students in classes where teachers had equal expectations for boys and girls was compared with the performance of students in classes in which teachers expected lower achievement from the boys. When the teachers' expectations for boys and girls were equivalent, equivalent levels of reading achievement were found for boys and girls.

In another study, Brookover (1973) investigated social environment factors associated with students' achievement. Students in 24 schools participated in the study. The results indicated that teachers' expectations concerning their students' performance were significantly related to the students' actual performance. These results suggest that the expectations that teachers hold concerning their students' performance may actually affect how the students perform.

One of the most obvious ways in which expectations concerning students' performance are formalized is through tracking. When tracking procedures are used, students are placed in homogeneous groups on the basis of an estimate of their ability. The students in each group or track receive only the instruction judged to be appropriate for their level. If the student is placed in the track inappropriate for him or if the instruction presented to him is inappropriate for him, then his performance is likely to suffer. In addition, his expectations and those of his teachers, parents, and peers, which are influenced by the level of the track to which he has been assigned, may strongly influence him to judge himself and his own ability according to the track label.

Mackler (1969) studied the tracking procedures in the Harlem area of New York. Students were tracked informally in kindergarten. Track assignments were based on teachers' judgments concerning students' maturity, politeness, passivity, and willingness to listen to and follow directions. The tracking assignments made in kindergarten were used when the students progressed to first grade. Students who had not attended kindergarten were placed in the lowest track in the first grade. Though the initial tracking was based largely on teachers' initial impressions and on students' preschool experience rather than on a diagnosis of the students' actual level of performance, very few changes in the tracking assignments were made. By the end of the first grade, the students in the lowest track were achieving at a level approximately one-half year below the students in the highest track. By the time the students reached third grade, the students in the lowest track were approximately 1 year behind the students in the highest track. Mackler concluded that the tracking procedure influenced the expectations and attitudes of the teachers, their parents, and the students which, in turn, affected the students' performances.

Tuchman and Bierman (1971) investigated the effect of track assignment on the performance of 805 black junior and senior high school students and their teachers. The students who participated in the study attended high schools in which they were tracked into three ability groups. In this experiment, half of the students assigned to the middle ability group were moved to the highest group, and half of the students assigned to the lowest ability group were moved to the middle group. Students who were moved to the higher tracks showed statistically significant increases in standardized achievement test performance compared with those students who remained in their original track placement. In most cases, the grades, levels of satisfaction with school, and attendance records of the students who had been moved to higher tracks did not differ from the students in the original track placements. Students placed in higher tracks maintained approximately the same grade-point-averages and levels of satisfaction even though they were required to perform more difficult academic work. Many of the students placed into higher groups were subsequently recommended by their teachers for continued placement in those higher groups. Over half of the senior high school students moved to higher tracks were subsequently recommended for higher group placement, as compared to only 1% of the students who remained in their original tracks. Tuchman and Bierman concluded that the ability group placement affected the performance expectations held by the students and their teachers, which, in turn, significantly affected the students' academic performance. The students placed in higher tracks were given the opportunity to do more difficult work. The resulting increases in their academic performance showed that they had the ability to perform at a higher level than was indicated by their original track placement. The increased academic performance shown by the students placed in higher tracks may have resulted from increased expectations concerning their performance as well as the opportunity to do more difficult academic work.

Teachers' expectations concerning students' performance and labels such as those included in the tracking process may significantly influence the students' expectations about their own performance. These expectations may, in turn, affect how the students perform.

Teachers' Evaluations Have
Powerful Effects upon Students

An investigation at the elementary school level showed that students used the grades they received from their teachers as the measure of how well they did in school. Students from grade one through grade six were asked: "How do you know when you have done well or badly in school?" Almost every student answered that he evaluated how well or how poorly he did in school by the marks he received on his report cards. Interviews with the students showed that they often lacked an understanding of the origin and the meaning of the marks they received. Nevertheless, the students were extremely concerned about their marks, and they devoted considerable energy to determining where their marks ranked them in the "pecking order" of the classroom (Boehm & White, 1967).

In a survey of over 9000 high school students to study the impact of standardized ability tests in American secondary schools (Brim *et al.*, 1965a), the students were asked what source of information had been most important to them in deciding how much intelligence they really had. The most frequently chosen response was: "The marks I have received in school." The students were also asked to identify the criteria that had been most important to them in assessing the intelligence of other people their own age. Here again, the most frequently chosen response was: "The marks they have received in school."

In another study, 1500 adults were interviewed about their experiences and attitudes concerning standardized intelligence tests (Brim *et al.*, 1965b). The adults were asked to name the most important source of their own intelligence estimate. "Success in my work" was the most frequently chosen response, and "school grades" was the second most popular response. The response "intelligence, IQ or aptitude test scores" was selected by only 3% of the people surveyed.

This research indicated that the grades students received from their teachers had a very strong impact on their own judgments about their academic competence. If the students' grades and other evaluations received from teachers significantly affect the students' views of themselves, then students need to earn positive academic evaluations in order to develop healthy self-perceptions.

Student Self-Concepts

There is abundant evidence indicating that evaluations of students' academic performance are positively related to their self-concepts. Students who received positive evaluations tended to report positive views of themselves; students who received less than positive evaluations tended to report less than positive views of themselves.

Numerous studies have reported significant, positive correlations between measures of students' self-concepts and their academic achievement test scores (correlations range from .22 to .72). These significant positive relationships were found for students at all grade levels from kindergarten through college (Alberti, 1971; Bledsoe,

1967; Bledsoe & Garrison, 1962; Bodwin, 1957; Brookover *et al.*, 1962, 1965; Campbell, 1967; Caplin, 1968, 1969; Coopersmith, 1959, 1967; Hughes, 1968; Ozehosky & Clark, 1970; Piers & Harris, 1964; Sears, 1963; Torshen, 1969, 1973, 1974; Wattenberg & Clifford, 1964; Williams & Cole, 1968).

Significant positive relationships between students' self-concept assessments and their grades were also found by many researchers. Most studies that included a measure of self-concept of academic ability reported correlations in the range from .45 to .60 and some researchers found correlations as high as .70. As was the case with achievement test scores, significant relationships between students' self-concepts and their grades were found for students at the full range of age and grade levels (Binder *et al.*, 1970; Brookover, 1962, 1964; Coopersmith, 1967; Dyson, 1967; Hughes, 1968; Jones & Grieneeks, 1970; Kifer, 1973; Modu, 1969; Paschal, 1968; Torshen, 1969, 1973). See Alvord (1972), Badwal (1969), Beebe (1972), Green (1971), Marx & Winne (1974), and Hatcher *et al.* (1974) for examples of investigations finding no significant relationships among these variables. Refer to Combs (1963) for a discussion of the problems inherent in self-report measurement, and to Landry (1974) for an example of research identifying curvilinear relationships among these variables. The issue of self-report measurement is discussed more extensively elsewhere (Torshen *et al.*, in press).

Although both students' grades and their achievement test scores demonstrated significant relationships to their self-concepts, students' grades may have a greater impact on students' concepts of themselves when grades play a larger role in the classroom than do achievement test scores. A study conducted by the author (Torshen, 1969, 1974) sought to isolate that particular evaluation of a student's classroom performance which most strongly influences his self-concept. Achievement test scores and teachers' grades were selected for examination because they are the most widely used measures of formal evaluation. The aspects of students' self-concepts that are most likely to be affected by the classroom were considered.

The study was based on the proposition that the evaluation a person receives for his performance affects his self-concept when that evaluation occurs within his immediate environmental context. The importance of the immediate environmental context was assessed by investigating differences between the effect of grades, which may have direct impact on the classroom, and standardized achievement test scores, which may affect the student indirectly. The investigation included 400 fifth grade students selected from six school districts. The students represented lower, middle, and upper socio-economic classes.

This investigation tested the general hypothesis that the evaluation that is most important to the student's immediate social environment will have the strongest effect on his self-concept. Grades and achievement test scores differ in the impact they have on the classroom. In most classrooms, the grade is the formal evaluation used most frequently to assess students' cognitive performance. When teachers, classmates, and parents consider a student's academic status among his peers, they are likely to place substantial weight on his grades. Standardized achievement test scores do not play an equally important role in the daily routine of the American classroom. Typically, the achievement tests are given once a year. The results are usually filed in the student's permanent record folder, which is accessible only to the teacher and other school personnel. The scores may be meaningful to the student largely through the influence they can have on his teacher's evaluations of him. While grades have a strong direct impact on the student in the classroom, most of the influence of achievement test scores appears to be indirect.

Many educators consider grades and achievement test scores to be equivalent measures of students' cognitive performance in classrooms. If this were true, it would not matter if grades influenced students directly and achievement test scores influenced them indirectly. But these two evaluation measures do not always yield the same assessments of students' academic work. Teachers' grades can be influenced by factors such as the student's conformity to institutional norms, his rank in his own classroom, or the expectations his teacher had for his performance. It is not likely that standardized achievement test scores will be affected to an equivalent degree by these factors. If the influence of teachers' grades on students' perceptions of themselves is stronger than the effects of standardized academic achievement tests, factors that influence teachers' grades can have important consequences for students' self-concepts even if those factors are irrelevant to the students' actual achievement.

The following model summarizes the findings of the study.

Achievement Test Scores ⟶ Grades ⟶ Self-Concept

_____ indicates direct impact
- - - - - - - indicates indirect impact

As the model illustrates, students' grades remained significantly related to their self-concept reports when the effects of their standardized achievement test performance were removed using statistical procedures. When the effects of grades were removed, the remaining relationship of achievement test scores to students' self-concepts was not statistically significant. These results support the conclusion that grades are the evaluations of students' cognitive performance that directly influence their self-concepts. Achievement test scores appear to affect students' self-concepts indirectly; their primary impact can be accounted for by the influence they have on grades. The impact that a form of evaluation has upon a person's immediate social environmental context may be the significant factor that determines the effect of that evaluation on the person's self-concept. Because students' grades have a tremendous impact on daily classroom life, they may play an important role in determining students' self-concepts.

Several research students have found that students' concepts of themselves became more positive when the students learned in educational settings in which negative evaluations for their school work were kept at a minimum. When the students' work merited positive evaluations, students were given evidence that they had performed well.

Purkey, Graves, and Zellner (1970) created an ungraded elementary school program that differed from the normal program in the following ways. Students were grouped according to the number of years they had attended school. There was no grouping on the basis of ability and no student was failed. Individualized instructional methods were used when needed within the normal peer group. Children were regrouped frequently. Compared with students who did not participate in this experimental program, the students in the special program showed higher self-esteem in grades four through six. In the special program, students' self-esteem increased in each subsequent grade level. Self-esteem of students who did not participate in the program decreased in grades three through five and then stabilized.

In another study, White and Allen (1971) designed a special summer school art program for preadolescent boys who had histories of underachievement. The boys participated in an art class where they were given success-oriented tasks, encouragement for creative expression, and encouragement for self-awareness. Their work was evaluated in relation to clearly defined goals, and no grades were given. Although the class was designed to increase the positiveness of the students' self-concepts, the students were unaware of this purpose. A similar group of students were given traditional nondirective counseling; these students served as the control group. Students in the special art class showed significant increases in their self-concept scores. Three tests given 14 months later showed the increases had remained. The students in the control group did not change their self-concepts. These results suggest that a supportive classroom environment in which clearly defined goals are used to evaluate student performance can produce positive changes in students' self-concepts, even for students who have already established patterns of low self-concepts and underachievement.

Felker, Stanwyck, and Kay (1973) conducted a teacher-training program designed to help participants understand and apply classroom methods that increased self-rewarding behavior of students. The program encouraged teachers to praise themselves and to help their students evaluate themselves realistically. Students were guided to set reasonable goals for themselves, to praise themselves, and to praise others. Two programs were suggested to the teachers. In one program, student tutors were trained by the teachers to provide social reinforcement to the students they were tutoring. In the second program, students participated in a classroom game in which their attention was focused on positive characteristics of their classmates. The results indicated that the program was responsible for producing moderate positive changes in the students' concepts of themselves.

Results of several studies indicated that students' concepts of themselves tend to become more negative as the students progress through school. Educational programs that produce positive changes in students' concepts of themselves are even more important in the light of this conclusion. Stanwyck and Felker (1974) measured the self-concepts of 55 students as they progressed from fourth through seventh grades. The results indicated that self-conceptions concerning feelings and the self in social situations became increasingly positive. Self-conceptions concerning the student's behavior and the student's perceptions of himself in school became increasingly negative over the period of the study. Research conducted by Morse (1964) and by Cyrier and Carpenter (1973) also found that students' concepts of themselves became increasingly negative as the student progressed through school.

When Felker, Stanwyck, and Kay (1973) investigated the effects of their teacher-training program upon students' self-concepts, they measured the self-concepts of a group of students comparable to those whose teachers had received training. The students whose teachers did not participate in the training program served as a comparison group in the investigation of the effects of the teacher-training program. Felker *et al.* found that students' self-concepts were more negative as the grade level increased. Positive changes in students' self-concepts were found in classes in which the teachers had participated in the training program.

In sum, the research suggests that students' concepts of themselves tend to become somewhat more negative as the students progress through school. Part of this change in self-conceptions may be a natural result of the maturation process. As the student develops and becomes less self-centered and egocentric, he may come to realize that others are at least as talented, attractive, and popular as he. If he entered school with an extremely positive view of himself, this view may become somewhat less positive and more realistic as a result of his interactions with his peers.

While some negative changes in students' self-concepts may be a normal consequence of maturation, students' concepts of themselves in areas related to school showed greater negative changes than did self-concepts in other areas (Stanwyck & Felker, 1974). These results suggest that school experiences may have excessive negative effects on students' self-concepts. Average-based educational programs may give some students so much evidence that their performance is less than successful that they become convinced they cannot do well in school. Some students may realize that success in school is not available to them because they lack the skills needed to benefit from the instruction. The frequent less-than-positive feedback they receive in school may serve to reinforce these negative self-impressions.

Instructional programs designed to help students set reasonable goals and to provide praise and other positive reinforcement for each student were shown to be successful in producing positive changes in students' concepts of themselves. The mastery structure is designed to set reasonable goals for each student himself and to give positive evaluations for good performance. The research reported here suggests that these procedures can encourage the students to develop more positive concepts of themselves.

*Student Motivation and
Perceptions of Personal Power*

Kifer (1973) found that students who were successful in school tended to believe that their actions produced the positive evaluations they received. Students who were unsuccessful in school believed that rewards and punishments they received were given at the discretion of powerful others or were controlled by luck or fate.

Students who have high expectations for success may spend more time actively engaged in learning and be more persistent than students who have low expectations. Battle (1965) found significant positive relationships between students' expectations for success and the persistence they showed in solving difficult problems.

Brookover (1973) found that students' academic achievement was significantly related to the students' reports about their own sense of futility, which included feelings of hopelessness or lack of caring about their academic achievements. The students' reported sense of futility accounted for 45% of the variance in their achievement test scores. Students who reported that they did not care about doing well in school or that they lacked hope that they would do well earned substantially lower scores on achievement tests than did students who reported that they could do well in school if they worked hard. Students who reported a high sense of futility indicated that they believed they had to be lucky in order to get good grades in school. They also indicated that people like them almost never do well in school even though they try hard.

Meichenbaum and Smart's (1971) experiment included 24 freshmen engineering students who had barely passed the first semester of a three semester sequence in mathematics, physics, and chemistry. Half of the students were told that test data indicated they would perform considerably better in the next semester; these predictions were used for purposes of the experiment, but they were not based on actual data. At the end of the semester, the students who had received positive predictions about their performance achieved significantly better in two courses than did students who had been given no information. In addition, the students who had been induced to develop high expectations about their performance reported that the testing programs helped them to realize that they could do better and to become more interested in their course work. High-expectation students also viewed the course as more relevant to their future careers. The false test information suggesting that their achievement would improve may have altered the students' self-confidence and expectations for success which, in turn, influenced their increased achievement. These results suggest that students' expectations concerning their performance may affect their actual performance through the effects that these expectations may have on the students' willingness to persist and on their self-confidence.

The student who believes that he can succeed if he works hard may be encouraged to put forth the effort needed to successfully complete the learning activities in the mastery program. The student who believes that he can succeed only when he gets lucky or that success in school is meaningless to him may be unwilling or unable to put forth the effort needed to attain mastery.

Lewis (1974) found that students' reports of whether they had a chance to do well in school and whether school achievement mattered to them differentiated students who achieved well in a remedial reading program from those students who did not improve their reading skills in the program. The administrators of a remedial reading program in a large urban public school system requested research to investigate why some students substantially improved their reading skills in the program while others did not. Previous investigations indicated that the students who improved and the students who did not improve were roughly comparable in socioeconomic status, past performance, and measured IQ. The remedial program served eighth- and ninth-grade students, drawn from several school districts, who were below their age group in grade placement and/or not achieving at grade level in reading. About 50 students participated in the study. The students' self-concepts of their academic ability, their perceptions of significant others' academic evaluations of them, their reports of whether they cared about doing well in school and whether they thought they had a chance to do well in school, and their reading achievement were measured when they entered the program and again five months later. Within the 5 month period, the students received two report cards containing reading grades.

At the beginning of the program, some students reported that they cared about doing well in school and they believed that they did have a chance to do well. For these students, self-concept of academic ability and perceptions of significant others' evaluations of them were significantly related to improvements in reading achievement at the end of the 5 month period. The students who saw school as important to them and believed that they had a chance to succeed showed significant improvements in reading achievement.

Other students reported that school was not important to them and they did not believe they had a chance to succeed there. These students did not show significant improvements in reading achievement. In addition, the reading achievement of these students was unrelated to their self-concepts of academic ability and their perceptions of significant others' evaluations of them.

In explaining these results, Lewis proposed that the high self-concepts reported by students who were achieving at low levels were defensive rather than realistic. According to Horney (1950), Rosenberg (1971), and others, a person attempts to see himself in as favorable a light as possible in order to protect his feelings of self-worth. If a student's feelings of self-worth are threatened by his school experiences, he may attempt to protect himself by adopting the position that school is unimportant to him and he has no chance of doing well there. Through this position, the student can maintain his self-esteem. He can continue to see himself as a good student, though he receives no evidence of this in school, rationalizing that he has sufficient intellectual ability but does not achieve well because he is not trying. His academic failure is not a humiliation because he has not seriously attempted to succeed. While this defensive reationalization protects the student's self-esteem, it does not contribute to development of basic academic skills.

Repeated failures may cause the student to believe that he lacks the power to exercise control over what happens to him in his own environment. The individual who has learned that he is helpless may not try as hard as he can because he believes his actions make little or no difference. (Seligman, 1973; Seligman & Haier, 1967).

Dweck (1975) asked school psychologists, principals, and classroom teachers to identify the children who were most helpless (characterized by expectation of failure and giving up easily in the face of failure) out of a group of 750 students. The students who frequently showed helpless behavior were given specialized treatment. Some of the subjects were given frequent experiences of success. Other subjects were taught to take responsibility for their failures and to attribute their failure to lack of effort on their part. All of the subjects were then asked to do problem solving tasks. The tasks were designed so that each subject failed a few of the tasks and could succeed on most of them. The students who had received only experiences of success showed a severe deterioration in performance after they failed one of the tasks. The students who had learned to take responsibility for failure and to attribute failure to lack of properly directed effort were able to maintain or to improve their performance following failure. In addition, the students who had learned to attribute failure to factors that they could control associated their failures with insufficient or improperly directed motivation rather than lack of ability.

In another study, Tessler and Schwartz (1972) asked college students to perform a social adjustment task. The experimenters designed the task so that each student performed poorly and needed to seek help from a written source available to him. Some students were told that 90% of the people who worked on the task could complete it successfully without help and that the procedure involved in the task had been well refined. Other students were told that the majority of people who worked on the task needed to consult the readily available written materials for assistance and that the procedures involved in the task might need refinement. These latter instructions were designed to encourage the students to see their failures in performing the task as the result of defects in the task itself. The first set of instructions were designed to encourage the students to see their failures as the result of their own deficiencies since they were told that most people could complete the task successfully without help. The results of the study showed that students who could reasonably attribute responsibility for failure to sources external to themselves sought help significantly more than did those students who saw their failure as resulting from their own deficiencies.

These results suggest that instructional procedures should encourage students to see their failures as the result of deficiencies in the instructional program or lack of effort, and not as the result of a lack of ability on the part of themselves or their teachers. Students who perceived their failures as caused by their own deficiencies were less likely to seek help when needed. Students can be taught to recognize that their failures are caused by lack of properly directed effort and/or needed modifications in the curriculum.

DeCharms (1972) developed an education process designed to increase students' intrinsic motivation for achieving in school by increasing the extent to which they took personal responsibility for their classroom activities and perceived their world realistically. In this experiment, teachers were given training designed to help each student (1) determine realistic goals for himself, (2) know his own strengths and weaknesses, (3) determine concrete action to help him reach his goals, and (4) decide whether he is approaching his goal and whether his action is having the desired effect. The results indicated that the teachers who had received the special training showed increased motivation, and their students showed increased motivation and higher academic achievement.

In another study, Luginbuhl (1972) compared students' reactions to their performance on a randomly assigned task with their reaction to their task performance when they had selected the task for themselves. The results indicated that students who selected the tasks themselves felt less successful and less competent after their performance on these tasks, irrespective of whether they succeeded or failed, than did students who did not choose the tasks they performed. Perhaps the students who chose their own tasks consciously selected the tasks that would be easiest for them. Knowing that they had selected the easiest tasks might have decreased the extent to which they felt successful and competent when they completed the tasks successfully.

The results of these studies pointed out the extreme complexity of the problems involved in designing instructional programs to maximize positive affective outcomes. The mastery procedures can be used to structure an instructional program that helps students see themselves as "origins"—individuals who initiate intentional goal-directed behavior intended to produce changes in their environments and who accept responsibility for their actions (DeCharms, 1972). Students can participate in selecting the goals and objectives of the program. They can examine the results of the diagnostic evaluations so that they know their own strengths and weaknesses. They can select instructional activities that will help them reach the objectives they have identified for themselves. They can examine the diagnostic assessment results to determine whether the activities are guiding them toward their goal. However, the results of the Luginbuhl (1972) research suggest that students' successes in activities they have chosen for themselves might not contribute to the development of their self-esteem and feelings of competence as much as their successes on tasks that have been assigned to them. This conclusion suggests that students should not select entirely by themselves all of the instructional activities that they perform. Although students need the opportunity to select tasks that are interesting and pleasant for them, they also need the opportunity to work on tasks that are moderately difficult and challenging.

The mastery procedures begin with the expectation that each student can reach the level of performance defined as acceptable for competence. In contrast, average-based procedures may encourage teachers and students to begin an instructional program with the expectation that some students will achieve very well, but others will be only moderately successful and still others will be minimally successful at best (Bloom, 1968). These expectations are important when they influence teachers' behavior toward students, students' willingness to persist and self-confidence, and students' ultimate performance. Students also need to see that they can succeed in school as a result of their own efforts in completing academic activities. To this end, the mastery procedures clearly define the activities the student is to perform as he works toward mastery. In addition, the evaluation procedures modify the activities or provide alternative activities when necessary. These procedures give students additional opportunity and encouragement as they work toward mastery.

The mastery procedures are advocated here because they are expected to lead to positive affective as well as cognitive consequences. As the research reported in this chapter suggests, relationships between students' affective development and their achievement in school are extremely complex. Our research efforts have just begun to scratch the surface. Many of the studies reported here have included only small numbers of students in limited, short-term educational settings. Available research enables us to draw only the most tentative conclusions. Much more research is needed to facilitate the design of instructional programs to produce positive affective and cognitive consequences.

8

Research Relevant to
Specific Mastery Model
Components

The curriculum, instruction, and evaluation literature contains numerous research studies that investigated one or more, but less than all six, components of the mastery model. In this chapter, research that was not designed to investigate the entire mastery model but that contributes important information concerning specific components of the model will be considered.

Objectives

The mastery model places considerable emphasis upon the selection of the objectives of the curriculum. The objectives determine the content to be included in the curriculum as well as the amount of instructional time and emphasis that will be allocated to specific subsections of the content.

The issues of objective formats and the role of objectives in the curriculum are points of current and continuing controversy, receiving considerable attention in the professional literature. The format issue concerns whether objectives must be stated in behavioral terms (Mager, 1962; Gagné & Briggs, 1974) or in more general terms, as recommended by Tyler (1950). The restriction of the objective format to the use of behavioral indicators has received considerable criticism. For example, Cronbach (1971) asserted that "operational-izing" objectives by substituting observable and measurable phe-nomena for less tangible forms of learning denies the usefulness of theoretical terms or constructs by substituting behavioral indicators for them. Overdependence upon behavioral indicators in objective formats has the added disadvantage of obscuring the issues con-cerning the origin of the objectives (MacDonald-Ross, 1973).

Most of the research investigating the role of objectives in the curriculum focused on the impact of presenting behavioral objectives to students upon students' posttest performance. (See Duchastel & Merrill, 1973, for a review of research in this area.) Rothkopf and Kaplan (1972) and Morse and Tillman (1972) found that relevant learning was greater than incidental learning when students were presented with behavioral objectives prior to the beginning of the instruction. Objectives salient to the instructional tasks were found to be most effective (Dalis, 1970; Huck & Long, 1973; Lawson, 1973). Behavioral objectives presented to students had a greater impact upon student performance in traditional types of teaching than in programmed instruction and computer-assisted instructions (Sink, 1974).

The presentation of behavioral objectives to students prior to the onset of instruction was associated with increased posttest scores for students of middle ability but not for students of higher or lower ability (Cook, 1969). The presentation of objectives had the least impact upon students who were submissive, self-controlled, consid-erate, and conscientious (Kueter, 1971). These results suggest that presentation of behavioral objectives was most effective for students of moderate ability and for students who tended to be independent and less conscientious than their peers.

For students, the most helpful objectives communicated un-ambiguously the expectations of the instructional program. Exces-sively complicated and confusing objective statements further com-plicated the instructional process. In addition, objectives directed students' learning only when the students were convinced that the objective related directly to the achievement measured on the tests assessing the students' performance in the course (Tiemann, 1968). Once students determined that an objective was unrelated to what was measured on the final course examination, students paid less attention to the objective statements and used them less often to direct their learning.

In research investigating the differential impact of behavioral objectives versus more general objectives, Oswald and Fletcher (1970) found the general objectives to be at least as effective as the more specific behavioristic objective statements. Other studies (see, for example, Jenkins & Deno, 1971; Janeczko, 1972) found no significant differences between the effects of specific and the more general objectives, and Rothkopf and Kaplan (1972) found the more specific behavioristic objectives to be the most effective.

Training teachers in the use of objectives as teaching guides was associated with increased student achievement (McNeil, 1969; Piatt, 1970; Bryant, 1971). However, training students in the use of behavioral objectives showed no significant association with changes in student postinstructional performance (Brown, 1971; Morse & Tillman, 1972; Sink, 1974).

The results of the above research indicate that developing objective statements, teaching instructors the use of these statements in guiding teaching, and communicating these objectives to students can facilitate student learning, at least as demonstrated by the associations of these factors with increased student achievement. No clear conclusions concerning the advantage of one objective format over another can be reached given the results available to date.

An additional advantage of developing objective statements, which has received relatively little attention from researchers, is the fact that these statements permit more objective evaluations of the value-laden nature and the oversimplification represented by the selection by educational professionals of specific outcomes which serve as the goals of instructional programs (Stake, 1970). Educational goals are strongly influenced by the values and subjective judgments of the people who select them. Furthermore, any statement of educational goals is an oversimplification or an incomplete statement of desired instructional outcomes. The priority attached to specific objectives and the minimum pass levels and other standards incorporated in the objectives also represent value-laden subjective judgments.

Statements of objectives (high-value targets) enable values analysis to be conducted. Stake (1970) suggested two types of analyses: (1) a check on the logic of the objective selection from a given value position (see Jensen, 1950); and (2) an empirical assessment of the desirability of specific objectives and the extent to which specific value positions are accepted among faculty groups, community groups, professional groups, and so forth (see Larkins & Shaver, 1969).

Research available to date suggests that measures of student mastery of specific method and content prerequisites and affective entry characteristics are more effective preassessment measures than are measures of student general intellectual ability, including IQ test performance. Yeager and Kissel (1969) measured the IQs of students who were about to begin a self-paced instructional program in mathematics. The students were also given a pretest measuring skills relevant to the mathematics instruction. The students then completed the instructional program. Results of subsequent analyses indicated that students' IQs were not related to the amount of time needed to complete the instruction. However, students' scores on the pretests were significantly related to the time required to complete the program. In this study, the students' general intellectual ability was not related to their learning rates, but their mastery of prerequisites needed in the instruction was significantly related to their learning rates.

Research conducted in individually paced programs indicated that measures of students' preparation for the particular instruction involved were efficient predictors of the amount of time the students needed in order to attain mastery. Carroll (1963) found that students' performance on the Carroll–Sapon Modern Language Aptitude Test significantly predicted the amount of time the students needed to complete a programmed instruction course in Mandarin Chinese. Students who showed lower aptitude for language learning required significantly more time to complete the course than did students who showed higher aptitude for language learning. In a second study, all of the students were allowed the same amount of instructional time. Under these conditions, those students who had lower aptitude for language learning were not allowed sufficient instructional time, and they performed at lower levels on the final achievement tests. These results suggest that students can achieve at high levels when they are allowed sufficient instructional time, though some students will require more time than others.

Students' learning rate on the first unit in an instructional program was found to predict efficiently the amount of time they needed to complete a computer-assisted instructional program (Suppes, 1972). Students who completed the first unit faster than their peers also completed the entire program in less time. The amount of time the student needed to complete the first unit could be used to obtain an accurate estimate of the amount of time the student needed to complete the program. This instruction was administered under controlled conditions, and the units were homogeneous in form of presentation and form of response required from students. Predictions based on performance on the first unit may not be quite so accurate when the other units in the program employ different instruction or evaluation methods.

These results indicate that there are substantial variations in students' learning rates. If all students in a group are expected to attain a specific level of performance, then the curriculum may need to be structured to provide sufficient learning time for each student. Flexible time scheduling can be used to accommodate variations in students' learning rates. Preassessments, including pretests of relevant skills and measures of initial learning rates on typical units, can be used to estimate how much time each student will need in order to complete the instructional program. The study conducted by Yeager suggests that IQ tests and other measures of general ability may not be efficient predictors of the amount of learning time students will need. Pretests of skills specific to the instruction in the program are likely to be more efficient preassessment measures.

Sequencing of Objectives and Instructional Activities

The preassessment component incorporates the theoretical proposition that people process information in hierarchical sequence such that basic skills and knowledge serve as the foundation upon which more complex processes are built (Suppes, 1974). This postulate of a hierarchical organization involved in the learning process is in agreement with a conception of intelligence as problem-solving capacity based on a hierarchical organization of symbolic representations and information processing strategies (Hunt, 1961).

If intellectual skills develop in a hierarchical order, then the student must learn A before he learns B, and he must learn B before he can learn C. If he fails to learn B, he lacks the necessary skills and knowledge that enable him to learn C. If this is true, then a crucial question for education is: What skills and knowledge must be learned in step A before the student can progress to B, and so forth? What is the most efficient sequence in which these skills and knowledge can be taught?

One approach to investigating propositions concerning the hierarchical organization of learning has been to identify prerequisite skills that function as necessary but not sufficient conditions for particular types of learning. Various research efforts have been directed toward identifying processes that facilitate particular kinds of learning. For example, Rohwer (1970, 1971) has investigated the process called "mental elaboration," in which a person recodes or transforms information presented to him by elaborating upon the content. As an example, a person presented with the words "girl" and "cookie" can picture a girl eating a cookie or can make up a sentence using these words. His research indicated that skills in mental elaboration facilitated learning in general. Young learners could be taught to develop these skills.

As another example, Rosner (1972) studied individual differences in visual and auditory preceptual processes. He related these differences to students' competence in organizing and extracting patterns of information presented in geometric patterns and in solid combinations. He concluded that students' skills in visual perception processes were significantly related to their arithmetic achievement, and their skills in auditory processing were significantly related to their reading achievement. His work also indicated that students could be taught to develop these processing skills.

Research results available to date indicate that, when students have adequate intellectual skills to deal with the instruction, practitioners have considerable flexibility in determining the sequence in which units of instruction are to be presented. The *Taxonomy of Educational Objectives: Cognitive Domain* (Bloom *et al.*, 1956) presented a sequence of objectives in which lower order objectives, those dealing with factual material, were taught early in the instructional sequence, and higher-order objectives, those dealing with problem solving and evaluative strategies, were taught later in the instructional sequence. This work significantly influenced many curriculum designers so that numerous curricula were organized according to this hierarchy.

Madaus, Woods, and Nuttall (1973) tested the proposition that the six major taxonomic levels in the *Taxonomy: Cognitive Objectives* (Bloom *et al.*, 1956) had to be learned in the prescribed hierarchical sequence. The results indicated that there were numerous direct and indirect links among the various levels and that learning of material at the various levels could be influenced significantly by the student's general ability. These results raise important questions about the proposition that the hierarchy of cognitive objectives presented in this *Taxonomy* is the most efficient organization for these objectives.

Another line of research investigating learning hierarchies stems from the work of Gagné (1962). In a preliminary study, Gagné established a hierarchy of prerequisite skills to be used in teaching seven students how to find formulas for sums of terms in a number series. Gagné proposed that a student could not master this higher order skill if he had not mastered one or more of the subordinate prerequisite skills in the hierarchy. To identify the skills in the hierarchy, Gagné began with the highest skill to be taught and posed the question: What must the learner be able to do in order to perform this task successfully, if given only instruction? This inquiry identified the prerequisite skills immediately subordinate to the highest level of the hierarchy. The same question was applied to these skills, and the process continued until the basic skills that the students had already mastered were reached. Gagné called this network of skills a "hierarchy of knowledge."

Richard White (1973) summarized the results of this research and its impact upon subsequent investigations:

> He (Gagné) taught the skills to the seven children, and observed that none of them acquired a skill without also acquiring all of the skills that were shown as subordinate to it in the hierarchy. This result suggested that, if hierarchies were generally valid representations of the sequences in which skills or elements of knowledge must be learned, then they would be valuable too for shaping more effective instruction for the acquisition of problem solving skills and knowledge in general. Despite this important implication, few investigations of the validity of hierarchies were performed in the subsequent decade, and these were almost totally restricted to subject matter in mathematics and science, and generally ended in inconclusive results [1973, p. 361].

White proceeded to study the validation of a learning hierarchy, proposing nine stages in the validation process. This process began by defining in behavioral terms the element that was the pinnacle of the hierarchy. This stage was comparable to the defining of the objectives in the mastery process. In the second stage, the following question was asked: What must the learner be able to do in order to learn this new element, given only instruction? This question was applied to the standard of performance defined as the desired outcome of the instruction program. The question was then applied to the answer to each preceding question until the instructor arrived at the skills and knowledge that students had acquired in previous instruction. The reasonableness of the postulated hierarchy was checked with experienced teachers and subject matter experts. Very precise definitions of each element of the hierarchy were obtained.

An investigation was carried out to determine whether the divisions represented different skills. An instructional program was written for each of the elements, and a sample of students worked through the program. The results were analyzed to determine whether any of the proposed connections between the elements could be rejected. Finally, the rejected connections were removed from the hierarchy. This hierarchy served as the basis for constructing instructional programs.

Constructing an instructional program around a validated hierarchy has numerous advantages. First, instruction can be designed so that students attain mastery of each of the steps in the hierarchy. Second, the subordinate skills in the hierarchy, derived and validated in the manner recommended by White (1974), may compose a complete set of the prerequisites needed to attain mastery of the objective. Instruction based on this hierarchy could teach all of the enabling skills students need to attain mastery of the objective.

White's work with this hierarchy suggested that general intellectual skills may be learned hierarchically, but specific individual facts are not hierarchically learned. While the learning of intellectual skills was predicated on mastery of lower order skills, the learning of facts appeared to be independent of prior factual learning.

These results raise further questions concerning the order of cognitive objectives prescribed in the *Taxonomy of Educational Objectives* (Bloom, *et al.*, 1956). This taxonomy suggests that factual objectives should be taught first, but White's research suggests that factual learning may be less dependent upon hierarchical organization than had been assumed. Thus, if students have the necessary intellectual skills, factual information may be presented in any reasonable order. But the students' intellectual skill development should be considered in the curriculum organization.

Another extremely interesting line of research in this area investigated relationships of text content structure to learned cognitive structure. (See, for example, Shavelson, 1971, 1974; Shavelson & Stanton, 1975; Geeslin & Shavelson, 1975; Rudnitsky & Posner, 1976.)

Many curricula organizations are based upon assumptions about sequencing that need to be tested by research. For example, medical school curricula are often organized on the proposition that medical students need to learn about children (pediatrics) before they can learn about adults. At the University of Illinois College of Medicine, the organization of the curriculum in which pediatrics was taught early in the curriculum proved to be inconvenient. The medical students had to work in ten different hospitals, and it was extremely difficult to coordinate all of these programs so that each student studied pediatrics before he progressed to adult medicine. Research was conducted to investigate the proposition that teaching pediatrics early in the sequence was the most efficient organization. The results indicated that once the student had completed a year of basic medical instruction, the sequence in which he was introduced to the various specialties did not affect the efficiency with which he learned. Based on this conclusion, the sequence in which students learned the various specialties was modified according to the needs of the ten hospitals in which the students were taught.

In sum, this research provides some recommendations for the practitioner involved in establishing a sequence of learning activities. The research suggests that there are intellectual skills that are learned hierarchically and that serve as necessary but not sufficient prerequisites for successful achievement in academic subjects. These results suggest that it is important to identify the intellectual skills that are to be taught in a particular instructional program. Instruction pertaining to these skills should be sequenced so that the students master the basic skills before they attempt to learn more advanced skills. Structured maps provided to aid teachers in placing students into the curriculum and directing attention to needed prerequisite skills or the appropriateness of advanced skills can be most beneficial here (see Resnick *et al.*, 1973). Placement tests and other pretests should be used to determine whether the students entering the program have the skills they need to understand the instruction to be used to teach the first skill included in the program. If the students lack the necessary prerequisite skills, then instruction for these skills should be included in the curriculum or the curriculum should be revised so that it is not dependent upon mastery of the prerequisite skills the students lack. The research indicates that there is considerably more freedom possible in determining the sequence of instruction that does not pertain to intellectual skills.

Once a sequence for teaching factual material is established, the sequence itself establishes a hierarchy. For example, students need to know some facts about the Civil War in the United States before they study political and geographic factors pertaining to this war. However, a study of the Civil War can begin with a study of the political factors so long as the instruction takes into account the possibility that the students may be totally unfamiliar with relevant factual information.

When the prerequisites needed to progress through a curriculum are an artifact of the particular curriculum sequence used, teachers have the option of reorganizing the curriculum when the sequence proves to be inefficient. For example, a social studies instructional program can begin with factual information about a particular event in history. If the students do not appear interested in this approach, the sequence can be modified so that it begins with a problem solving activity. Students can be given historical documents that figure prominently in the history of the times. Even though the students have minimal knowledge about that period in history, they can use these documents to draw general conclusions. Then they can proceed to learn additional factual information about the period.

Instruction

The content selected to be taught and the emphasis given to specific aspects of the content are two significant variables affecting student learning and the educative process (Walker & Schaffarzick, 1974). These factors appear to be more significant than the instructional method employed. Few consistent significant differences have been found to be directly related to instructional methods, including traditional lecture and discussion, audiovisual aids, programmed instruction, and computer-assisted instruction (Stephens, 1967; Jamison, Suppes, & Wells, 1974).

The IEA evaluation of student achievement in seven subject matter areas in 22 countries represents the most comprehensive evaluation of educational achievement conducted to date. A major goal of this research was the identification of the aspects of the curriculum and instruction that significantly affected student performance. The results of this evaluation demonstrated that students' performance was significantly influenced by the extent to which students were exposed to specific subject matter content and by the amount of instructional time devoted to teaching specific subjects in school (Bloom, 1974). Considerable weight is given to both student exposure to content and instructional time allocations in the implementation of the mastery model.

Exposure to Content

The IEA results indicated that what was included in the curriculum significantly affected what students learned. The National Longitudinal Study of Mathematical Abilities (Wilson, Cahen, & Begle, 1968–1972), which compared the achievement of 112,000 students in 1500 schools in 40 states in the Unites States across grades 4 through 12 over a 5 year period, added further support to this conclusion. This research found that student achievement in mathematics mirrored, to a substantial extent, the content treated in the textbooks that the students used in their mathematics courses. Students were more likely to learn what had been taught in their classrooms than they were to learn what had not been taught.

Several experiments conducted on a much smaller scale have related instructional content to student learning of higher order skills. The following are a few examples of these studies. Feldman and Klausmeier (1974), of the Wisconsin Research and Development Center for Cognitive Learning, studied concept learning among 4th grade students. Some of the students received instruction consisting of a definition of the concept. Other students received instruction containing only a rationally chosen set of examples and nonexamples for each critical aspect of the concept. A third group of students received a definition and a rationally chosen set of instances. The fourth group of students received the definition and three rationally chosen sets of examples. The results indicated that students learned an equal amount from either a definition or a rationally chosen set of instances. Students learned slightly more from the combination of the two. And the students learned substantially more from the definition and the three rationally chosen sets. The students learned more when the instruction they received included more information.

In another study, McGuire and Page (1972–1973) investigated clinical problem solving behavior and diagnostic processes used by experienced physicians. This research found a high level of intraindividual variation in problem solving performance, suggesting that problem-solving skills may be far more content specific than has previously been assumed. Physicians who were efficient in solving some types of problems were often inefficient in solving other types of problems. Efficiency and proficiency in the diagnostic work-up were found to be independent of the accuracy of the diagnosis reached. These results suggest important implications for medical education. If problem solving performance is, indeed, highly content specific, then medical education should include specific instruction aimed at producing proficiency in each of the essential problem solving skills.

These results strongly support the conclusion that students tend to learn what is taught in school. If a topic is not covered in school, the students are less likely to learn it. Since the content included in the curriculum may affect what the students learn, selecting this content is extremely important.

In some curricula, students are taught facts with the expectation that they can use these facts to solve problems. Students are taught definitions of concepts with the expectation that these definitions, by themselves, will teach the concepts.

But this approach is extremely risky. While some students might be able to take a definition of a concept and come up with their own sets of examples and nonexamples, other students might not be able to go much beyond the definition of the concepts without specific instruction. A much safer approach is to design the curriculum to include sufficient instruction in each area defined as important to guide the student toward the proficiency levels needed for competence.

Time Devoted to Learning

The IEA research and other studies indicated that students' achievement may be influenced by the time devoted to instruction as well as by the students' exposure to the content. There are considerable variations in the number of hours that students spend in school every year.

Wiley and Harnischfeger (1974) reanalyzed the data from the Study of Equality of Educational Opportunity (Coleman *et al.*, 1966) collected in Detroit. They found that the total number of hours that students spent in school in 1 year ranged from 710 to 1,150 hours. The amount of time spent in school was significantly related to students' achievement:

> In terms of typical gains in achievement over a year's period, we concluded that in schools where students received 24% more schooling, they will increase their average gain in reading comprehension by 2/3 and their gains in mathematics and verbal skills by more than one-third. These tremendous effects indicate that the amount of schooling a child receives is a highly relevant factor for his achievement [1974, p. 9].

Students who spent more time in school achieved at higher levels than did students who spent less time in school. Low-achieving students enrolled in instructional programs containing fewer hours might be able to raise their achievement levels significantly if they have the opportunity to receive more hours of instruction.

Increasing the amount of time students spend in school may increase their achievement only when the students spend that additional time actively engaged in learning. Time, in the Carroll model for school learning (1963), referred to the time that the student actually spent being attentive and trying to learn. If the instruction is inappropriate or if the student spends the time available on activities unrelated to the objectives of the instructional program, then increasing the time allotted for schooling may not increase the student's achievement level substantially.

Research conducted by Anderson (1973, 1976) demonstrated that use of the mastery structure increased the amount of time that students devoted to active learning. The students' attentiveness to learning activities was measured in two ways. First, an observer watched each student to determine what percentage of his time he appeared to be spending in active learning. Second, students were stopped at periodic intervals during a "seat work" activity. At each interval, each student was asked to write a sentence indicating what he had been thinking just prior to being told to stop (this technique was developed by Bloom (1953)). The students' responses were coded to indicate whether they had been paying attention to the task.

The results of this experiment indicated that the amount of time the students spent in active learning was significantly related to their achievement in the instructional program. Students who entered the instructional program with adequate prerequisite skills and knowledge, with positive concepts of their own ability and interest in the activities tended to spend more time engaged in active learning than did students who were less well prepared, less confident of their own ability, and less interested in the activities.

In Anderson's (1973) study, one randomly selected group of the students had received instruction based on mastery procedures. These students made more efficient use of the time allotted so that they spent more time actively engaged in learning than students in nonmastery groups did, even though equivalent amounts of time were allowed for both groups.

Students who are successful achievers may make the more efficient use of the time they devote to learning. Combs (1964) investigated how high-ability students (IQs of 115 and higher) used the time allotted for learning. Students whose achievement test scores placed them in the lower 25% of their grade showed inefficient and less effective approaches to problems than did students who achieved at or above the grade average. In another study, Lahaderne (1967) found that students who achieved at high levels spent more of their classroom time paying attention to what went on in class than did students who were low achievers. Several studies (Lloyd, 1971; Sheppard & MacDermot, 1970; Zeaman & House, 1963, 1967) have found that "slower" learners take much more time to get started on learning activities than do "faster" learners.

These results emphasize the importance of using instructional methods and materials that encourage students to participate actively in the learning process. (See, for example, Davies & Semb, 1976; Glick *et al.*, 1976.) The instructional program should be structured so that students are encouraged to start working on the learning activities when the instruction begins in order to decrease procrastination. Students can be given extra points or other rewards when they perform the first learning activity as soon as possible after the instruction begins. Frequent formative evaluations can discourage procrastination. Frequent feedback can be given throughout the instructional process so that students can correct their errors quickly without wasting valuable time. If possible, distractions in the educational environment should be minimized so that students are able to concentrate on the learning activities.

Implementation of the diagnostic assessment and prescription components may reduce the amount of time students need to learn more complex material because the students will have mastered the prerequisite skills and knowledge before they attempt to learn more advanced material. Merrill, Barton, and Wood (1970) required college students to learn a five lesson teaching machine course in science. Some of the students were given a specific review procedure to be used when the student encountered learning difficulties. This procedure consisted of a thorough explanation of the material the student had misunderstood. The comparison group of students did not receive this review material. The results indicated that students who received review and explanation when they had made mistakes systematically decreased the amount of learning time they needed as they progressed through the five lessons. The students who received review spent less total time in the instructional program and were exposed to more instructional material than the comparison group. The review and explanation procedures used in this experiment are one example of an implementation of the diagnostic evaluation procedures in the mastery program. This experiment suggests that the diagnostic evaluation procedures can reduce the total amount of learning time students need.

Block (1971) used a series of sequential learning tasks to teach elementary matrix algebra to eighth grade students. Some of the students were required to master 95% of the material in each task before they could proceed to the next task. No mastery requirement was made for a comparison group of students. By the third unit, the students who were required to master 95% of the material had learned more of the material than the comparison group did even though both groups spent the same amount of time in learning. Diagnostic assessment and prescriptive procedures were available to the students who were required to master 95% of the material, but these students had very little need for these correction–review procedures after the third unit because they made very few mistakes.

In another study, Arlin (1974) also provided instruction consisting of learning activities organized in sequence. Some of the students who received this instruction were required to master each activity at the 85% level before they could proceed to the next activity. Other students, the comparison group, were not required to maintain any fixed mastery levels. By the time the students reached the eighth unit, the students who were required to maintain 85% mastery had learned more of the material in that unit even though they had spent no more time than the comparison students.

The student whose errors were diagnosed and who were given corrective instruction and the students who were required to achieve high levels of mastery may have acquired a solid foundation of basic skills upon which they could build. When they approached more complex instruction, they had the basic skills needed to learn the more complex material. The results of the above studies suggest that students may require less learning time and make fewer errors when they approach more advanced material with a solid foundation of basic skills.

Students' learning rates vary, even when the curriculum is designed to encourage attentiveness and persistence. Atkinson (1968) reported finding great variability in the rate at which first graders learned in a self-paced computer-based instructional program in initial reading. In the 7 month period, the slowest students completed 1000 problems whereas the fastest students completed 5000 problems. In addition, the slowest students learned at approximately the same rate throughout the program. The rate at which the faster students learned increased steadily as they progressed through the program. Glaser (1968) also reported finding a learning rate difference of 5:1 between the fastest and the slowest students as they progressed through the Individually Prescribed Instruction project at

Pittsburgh. These students were also in a self-paced individual instruction program. If all of the students in the group were to attain mastery of a particular performance level, then some students might require five times more instructional time than other students needed. In both of these individually paced programs, sufficient time was allocated so that students could attain the mastery levels in each of the basic instructional units. However, some students mastered considerably more units than did other students.

Matching Instructional Variables
to the Individual Student's Learning Characteristics

In a recent summary of the research on achievement treatment interactions, Tobias (1976) concluded:

> Despite this persistent interest in individualized instruction, there are few systematic attempts to adapt the *method* of instruction to student characteristics. Existing adaptations generally consist of varying instructional *rate* to student needs rather than instructional *method* [1976, p. 61].

Research in this area conducted to date (see Cronbach & Snow, in press, for a current review of this literature) provides relatively little guidance to assist the practitioner in selecting instructional methods matched to individual student needs on a daily basis. However, the concepts involved remain of considerable interest to researchers and practitioners, and recent research is yielding some conclusions applicable to the classroom.

One of the most productive lines of research in this area investigated relationships between teaching methods employed to teach addition and subtraction to young children and students' eventual performance (Suppes & Groen, 1967; Woods *et al.*, 1975; Resnick, 1977). First, the children were taught to solve a single-digit addition problem (e.g., 6 + 8) by counting first six blocks, then eight blocks, and then the combined set of blocks. When the blocks were taken away, the children shifted first to counting their fingers and then to internal processing. Analyses of their internal processing indicated that they appeared to set up a mental counter that identified the larger of the two numbers and then added the smaller number in increments. However, children who learned most efficiently were able, without direct instruction, to convert the routine taught in the experiment to a more efficient procedure involving commutativity and requiring fewer steps. The most efficient performers found the methods taught in the experiment to be awkward and slow.

The criticism that Tobias (1976) applied to individualized instruction is applicable to many of the instructional programs employing the mastery model. These programs have, generally, varied the instructional rate but not the instructional method, except during the prescriptive (remedial or enrichment) phase of the instruction. The subject matter, instructional method sequences, mastery criteria, and other factors have been aimed at the typical or average student. The slower learner may not suffer substantially if ample instructional time and remediation are provided and if he has mastered enough of the prerequisites to enable him to benefit from the instruction. Research in this area has supported the conclusion that mastery procedures have been particularly effective with slower learners, handicapped learners, and culturally different students (Suppes, 1974; Block & Burns, in press).

However, the rapid learners and highly creative students have often resisted when they are forced to complete each of the steps in an extended instructional sequence. In the early elementary grades, the faster learners were often satisfied with any form of instruction that permitted them to proceed at their own rate and gain access to enrichment instruction. Students in the later elementary and upper grades were less tolerant. Often, the faster learners and more creative older students refused to complete instruction that forced them to proceed through a fixed series of steps that were too small for them. They preferred to learn in larger "chunks." When this option was not available, some students refused to complete the instruction. Those gifted students who consistently did not complete instruction often fell far behind their less talented classmates. Eventually, the gifted students no longer had attained mastery of the prerequisites for the classroom instruction and they posed a significant instructional and classroom management problem.

Instruction that presents larger chunks of content, requires more complex information-processing strategies, or employs other techniques appropriate for the most efficient learners should be incorporated as instructional method options in the mastery curricula. (See Spencer *et al.*, 1976, for an example.) The availability of such options enables talented students to derive benefits from the instruction that are comparable to those derived by the average and slower learners.

Though considerable research has investigated relationships of instructional methods and materials to students' achievement, considerably more research is needed if practitioners are to receive adequate guidance. For example, the current state of research relating teaching skills to student achievement was summarized by Barak Rosenshine (1974):

> Most papers on teacher education contain the embarrassing recognition that the present scientific base for teaching and teacher education is primitive. . . . The results of these studies are *not* sufficiently strong or clear to direct teacher training practices or certification or evaluation of teachers [1974, p. 1].

Rosenshine reviewed the literature relating teaching skills to student achievement (Rosenshine, 1971; Rosenshine & Furst, 1973). Nine teaching skill variables were selected as "most promising" for future research.

1. Clarity of teacher's presentation.
2. Variety of teacher-initiated activity.
3. Enthusiasm of teacher.
4. Teacher emphasis on learning and achievement.
5. Avoidance of extreme criticism.
6. Positive responses to students.
7. Student opportunity to learn criterion material.
8. Use of structuring comments by teacher.
9. Use of multiple levels of questions in cognitive discourse [1974, p. 2].

Brophy and Good (1970, 1974) and Brophy and his colleagues at the University of Texas at Austin investigated instructional factors associated with student learning. Results indicated that teacher warmth and enthusiasm did not significantly affect students' adjustment to school or achievement in the early grades, though other investigations have indicated that these teacher factors are crucial for older students. Conclusions of this research concerning the impact of teacher expectations were discussed in the preceding chapter. (Refer to *Teachers Make a Difference*, Good, Biddle, & Brophy, 1975, for an initial summary of results concerning crucial teacher variables. Most of the analysis of the volumes of data collected at the Austin Research and Development Center has been completed, and publications of the results, currently in preparation, will be available during the next few years.)

The mastery procedures incorporate most of these teaching skills, and the remaining skills can easily be used in a mastery program. A mastery program would provide an excellent opportunity for conducting research to investigate the effectiveness of these skills in relation to student learning.

Future research in this area should focus on the effects that particular instructional programs have for individual students. In addition, assessment procedures used to evaluate the outcomes of a program should not be restricted to paper-and-pencil achievement tests. A most serious shortcoming of most of the comparative curricular studies performed to date is the restricted range of outcomes measured in these studies (Walker & Schaffarzick, 1974). Future research should include an assessment of each of the outcomes the program was designed to produce.

One example of curriculum evaluation research that measured varied outcomes is the evaluation of the Project Physics conducted at Harvard University (Welsh & Walberg, 1972). The outcomes of the project were assessed using 11 measures: a physics achievement test, a test of the students' understanding of the scientific enterprise, a test measuring knowledge of activities, assumptions, products, and ethics of science, the measure of interest in physical science, a questionnaire assessing course satisfaction, an inventory of science-related activities, final course grade, a questionnaire measuring reactions to the course, an inventory characterizing classroom climate, a semantic differential test of perceptions of physics, and a semantic differential test of attitudes toward physics.

Research studies that have related aspects of instruction to various aspects of students' performance have produced promising results. One example is the language arts study in which programmed instruction in language arts was given to 42 high IQ (136 and higher) fourth- and fifth-grade students for about 3 minutes per day for a period of 2 months. The subject matter involved vocabulary building and word attack skills. All of the students made significant gains in achievement. But the less creative students made greater achievement gains than did the more creative students. Many of the highly creative students expressed a strong dislike for the programmed instruction. The less creative students reported that they liked the programmed instruction very much (Strom & Ray, 1971). While the programmed instruction appeared appropriate for the less creative students participating in this study, the more creative students might have benefited more from another type of instruction.

Results of a study conducted by Yando and Kagan (1968) indicated that the degree to which a teacher pauses to evaluate the quality of cognitive products in the course of problem solving (referred to as differences in reflection and impulsivity) can influence the extent to which first-grade students pause to evaluate the quality of cognitive products. First-grade students who learned from experienced teachers who had a reflective style became more reflective themselves during the course of the school year. When first-grade teachers had impulsive problem-solving styles, their students tended to become more impulsive during the course of the year. Should this finding be substantiated by further research, the results can be used to match the teacher model with the students' cognitive problem-solving style. For example, the student who is overly impulsive can be placed in the class of the teacher who uses a reflective style.

No matter what type of instruction is used, the instruction is not likely to be efficient in guiding students toward mastery unless the instruction is of good quality. Carroll and Spearitt (1967) studied the effects of high and low quality instruction on learning about verbs in an artificial language. Self-instructional booklets were used. One booklet contained high quality information. In this booklet, each rule was presented and tested before the next rule was presented. When a student made a mistake, he was referred to pages on which his mistakes were fully explained. The second booklet, containing the low quality instruction, presented too much information at one time in a disorganized manner. In addition, the explanations of the students' mistakes were inadequate. Results indicated that students required significantly more time to achieve mastery when they used the low quality instruction. Students who had high IQs and students who had relatively low IQs tended to lose interest soon after they were presented with the low quality instructional materials. These results indicate that instructional materials of poor quality can contribute to decreased persistence and increased learning time needed to reach minimum pass levels.

The results of these studies suggest that the learning process is more efficient when the instruction is of good quality and instructional methods and materials are matched to the needs and learning styles of the students involved. The mastery procedures are likely to be most efficient when these conditions are met. Future research may provide more information that will help improve the general quality of instruction and facilitate appropriate matching between instruction and learner characteristics.

Diagnostic Assessment

As indicated in Chapter 5, the diagnostic assessment component of the mastery model employs evaluation procedures which Scriven

(1967) classified as formative, and the postassessment component employs summative evaluation procedures. Extensive consideration of the theoretical issues involved in formative and summative evaluation, as well as numerous examples of both measurement procedures, are available from other sources (see, for example, Bloom, Hastings, & Madaus, 1971; Grobman, 1968).

The diagnostic and postassessment components employ measures that assess whether each student has demonstrated adequate performance in each of the cognitive, affective, and psychomotor categories specified in the objectives. The terms "objective-referenced," "domain-referenced" and "criterion-referenced" have been used in the literature to refer to this type of evaluation. Though this type of evaluation has been used in the educational process for centuries, both the philosophy and the measurement issues involved have received considerable attention in the literature since the early 1960s (see, for example, Glaser, 1963; Glaser & Nitko, 1971; Livingston, 1972; Millman, 1973; and Tyler, 1970). In spite of the increased professional interest in objective and criterion-referenced testing, a substantial portion of educational measurement continues to focus almost exclusively upon norm-referenced measurement. Robert Glaser's recent consideration of the components of a psychology of instruction emphasized the need to shift from norm-referenced towards criterion-referenced measures:

> For effective instructional design, tests will have to be criterion referenced in addition to being norm referenced. They will have to assess performance attainments and capabilities that can be matched to available educational options in more detailed ways than can be carried out with currently used testing and assessment procedures [1976, p. 21].

For additional consideration of problems associated with criterion-referenced testing, refer to Davis (1975), Harris, Alkin, and Popham (1974) and Meskauskas (1976). The latter reference includes an interesting assessment of various mathematical models employed in setting standards for criterion-referenced testing.

Of the evaluation issues associated with the assessment components of the mastery model, one of the most important concerns the establishment of mastery or minimum pass levels. The standards did not originate with the recent interest in criterion-referenced testing. For example, minimum pass levels were employed in the departmental physics course taught at the University of Chicago more than 20 years ago (Nedelsky, 1954). At least six physics instructors participated in establishing the standards for this program. Other examples of the successful use of minimum pass levels include University of Illinois, College of Medicine, 1967, and Taylor *et al.*, 1971.

In conformity with the Nedelsky (1954) process for establishing minimum pass levels, Meskauskas and Webster (1975) employed six professionals to serve as judges in establishing the minimum pass levels for recertifying examinations for physicians. They found a wide range of differences among professional judgments. Based on these results, they recommended that multiple judgments be employed in establishing minimum pass levels.

Levine and Forman (1973) investigated the impact of minimum pass levels that were developed based upon the judgment of one professional. They found that an excessively high percentage of students failed to perform successfully when these standards were employed. These results support the conclusion that numerous judges should participate in establishing performance standards. A method for classifying judgmental information in determining minimum pass levels was developed by Ebel (1972).

In spite of the research recommending that multiple judgments be employed to establish appropriate minimum pass levels for specific measures, most of the implementations of the curricula employing the mastery components employed either a single standard for an entire instructional program (e.g., 80% to 85% mastery in IPI programs; 90% mastery in learning for mastery programs, as recommended by Block & Burns, in press) or the minimum pass level decision was left up to the individual teacher (Hambleton, 1973). In reviewing research relevant to the setting of mastery levels, Block and Burns concluded:

> It has been the *unit mastery requirement* that has consistently produced the strongest effects. The failure to impose a unit mastery requirement or to ensure that the requirement has been met has tended to produce less achievement and retention and less-consistent study behavior. . . . A unit mastery requirement of a 90% correct score on at least one of the unit diagnostic-progress tests has proved optimal [in press].

Two studies by Block (1972, 1973) were referenced by Block and Burns (in press) in support of the conclusion that the mastery level is optimal. Both studies investigated mastery levels in the context of 1 week instructional programs teaching matrix algebra to students having no prior experience with the subject matter. One of these investigations (1972) was described in greater detail in Chapter 6. The only other study (Johnson & O'Neill, 1973) referenced by

Block and Burns in support of this conclusion considered performance standards for students exclusively at the college level. Additional research investigating the impact of various performance standards in mastery programs of greater duration and for students at various age levels is needed before any recommendation of optimal program-wide mastery levels can be made.

On each diagnostic assessment measure, the minimum pass level should define the level of mastery of skills, knowledge, attitudes, and so forth, that the student needs in order to perform successfully in subsequent more advanced instruction and to meet long-range learning goals. Research available to date strongly supports the conclusion that enforcement of student attainment of these minimum pass levels is extremely important. Students who attained the minimum pass levels on the diagnostic assessment measures demonstrated significantly higher posttest performance on subsequent units than did students who performed below the minimum pass levels (Arlin, 1974; Anderson, 1973; Block, 1972, 1973; Calhoun, 1973; Carlson & Minke, 1975; Davis, 1975; Johnston & O'Neill, 1973; Semb, 1974).

In the implementation of the mastery curriculum at the Abraham Lincoln College of Medicine, diagnostic assessments were provided to students initially as optional instructional aids. When students were not required to take these tests, those who needed them most did not do so. While the diagnostic assessments were optional learning aids, they had no measured impact upon student learning or performance. Based on these conclusions, the faculty required every student to complete each diagnostic assessment. Attainment of the minimum pass levels was strictly enforced, using the procedures described previously in Chapter 6. The achievement levels of students performing below the minimum acceptable standards increased significantly when the diagnostic assessments were required and the minimum pass levels were enforced.

While enforcement of the most important minimum pass levels appears crucial, one of the most serious mistakes made in mastery model implementation has been excessive enforcement of insignificant or irrelevant passing levels. In too many cases, all of the students in a group have been forced to answer correctly most or all of the items on all the diagnostic and postassessments in each unit before they could proceed to the next. Some of the items they were expected to answer correctly were actually irrelevant or insignificant to the course objectives. When unnecessarily high minimum pass levels on every diagnostic and postassessment were strictly enforced, some of the slower students spent the entire academic year on the first unit. Consequently, they were never exposed to the instruction of most of the course. This is a misuse of the mastery components.

When students fail to master subcategories of minimum pass levels after a reasonable amount of instructional time has elapsed, the portion of the instruction that the student has failed to master should be evaluated. If the student has failed to master high priority segments of the objectives, then he should continue receiving appropriate instruction on these segments. Another alternative is to place the student in an alternate instructional sequence in which successful performance is not dependent upon the skills he has failed to master. A third alternative is to place him in portions of the instructional sequence that do not depend upon mastery of skills and knowledge he lacks while he is receiving continued instruction relevant to the high priority objectives. However, the student should proceed directly to subsequent portions of the instruction if the segments of the minimum pass level he has failed to attain represent low priority objectives.

The diagnostic assessment component of the mastery model must be implemented in conjunction with the prescriptive component if the information obtained through the diagnostic assessment procedure is to have a significant impact upon student learning. Simply providing feedback to students concerning their performance is not sufficient to produce optimum student learning (McKeachie, 1974). The information obtained in the diagnostic assessments must be used to select appropriate instruction for each student if this information is to have a significant impact upon the instructional process.

Prescription

When students fail to attain the minimum pass level on the diagnostic assessment measure, they are frequently required to review the same content that they have covered immediately prior to the administration of the diagnostic test. Repeated study of the same text chapter is a frequently prescribed method of remedial instruction (Smith & Wick, 1976). However, this form of remedial correction has been demonstrated to be the least effective.

More effective remedial prescriptions have provided students with alternative methods and materials for different approaches to the subject matter (Block, 1971; Block & Anderson, 1975; Kersh, 1969; SRA, 1974). Another effective form of corrective instruction provided the student with learning activities that helped him increase his mastery of cognitive and/or affective entry characteristics (Bloom, 1976) relevant to the specific subject matter and instructional methods of the instructional program (Fiel & Okey, 1974).

The instructional program itself can cause students' learning problems. The program objectives may not accurately represent the domain of competence they were designed to implement. The objectives may concern insignificant aspects of the domain of competence, and the important aspects of the domain may have been omitted. The students and/or the teacher may have negative attitudes toward the program. The instruction may be of poor quality, and the methods may be inappropriate for the context and students. The program may pose scheduling problems or other administrative and resource problems that cannot be resolved. The preassessments may not accurately measure students' preparation for the program, and the students may lack prerequisite skills and knowledge essential for success in the program. Either substantial remediation procedures or a change of program may be needed.

Analyzing Information
Produced in Formative Evaluations

When a student does not demonstrate mastery on a diagnostic assessment measure, the student's problems need careful analysis in order to determine the appropriate decision. A flowchart summarizing the steps in a process of employing diagnostic information to select appropriate prescriptions in educational settings appears in Figure 8.1.

The first step is to define the problem and the objective deficits as clearly as possible. A complete description of performance discrepancies should be made. The common threads running through the performance discrepancies should be identified. It may help to discuss the problems with the student to gain a better understanding of his perspective.

When the performance problem has been described, the significance should be considered. If the deficits are minor or insignificant, they can be ignored. The student can be advised to continue progressing through the program.

If the problem is considered important and the student is not likely to be successful unless he corrects his deficits. the following analysis can be made: Could the student have performed adequately if his life depended on it? Did he have the cognitive and psycho-

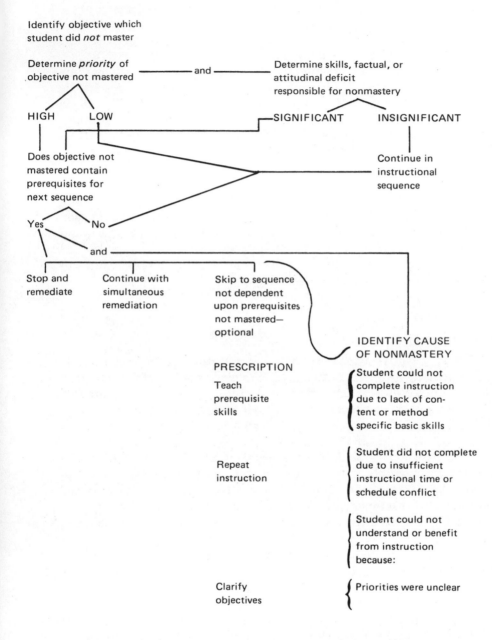

Identify objective which student did *not* master

Determine *priority* of objective not mastered ——— and ——— Determine skills, factual, or attitudinal deficit responsible for nonmastery

HIGH   LOW   SIGNIFICANT   INSIGNIFICANT

Does objective not mastered contain prerequisites for next sequence

Continue in instructional sequence

Yes   No

and

Stop and remediate   Continue with simultaneous remediation   Skip to sequence not dependent upon prerequisites not mastered— optional

IDENTIFY CAUSE OF NONMASTERY

PRESCRIPTION

Teach prerequisite skills

Student could not complete instruction due to lack of content or method specific basic skills

Repeat instruction

Student did not complete due to insufficient instructional time or schedule conflict

Student could not understand or benefit from instruction because:

Clarify objectives

Priorities were unclear

Figure 8.1. *Using diagnostic assessment information to select approximate prescriptions.*

Select alternate method	{ Instructional method was inappropriate
Select alternate instructional methods/materials	{ Instruction was of poor quality
Refer to medical or psychological specialist and modify instruction in accord with professional advice	{ Student had physical or psychosocial problem which prevented competent performance
Repeat or continue instruction when appropriate	{ Crisis occurred in student's personal life which prevented competent performance
Use this information to select/create a higher quality program	{ Entire instructional program is inappropriate or of poor quality
	Student would not complete instruction due to:
Change attitude, select alternate content or method, or omit instruction	{ Lack of interest or negative attitude toward content or method
Identify problem and remediate	{ Excessively low expectations or fear of accepting responsibility
Identify problem and remediate	{ Other psychosocial problems—e.g., conflict among students in study group
Remove punishment	{ Student would have been punished for performing well
Remove that reward	{ Performing poorly produced a reward
Provide reward or change instruction	{ Good performance was not rewarding

motor subject matter and instructional method specific entry characteristics needed for adequate performance? If so, then changes in the
psychosocial and reward systems of the educational program may be
required. If the answer is no, repairs in the content and instructional
method aspects of the program may be necessary.

As one example, for the student who has the skills and knowledge necessary to perform adequately, reward-system problems may
cause his inadequate performance. First, the student might be pun-
ished if he performs well. For example, a group of Joe's classmates
makes a game of beating up any boy who gives the right answers to
the questions the teacher asks in class. Joe knows the right answers.
But if he gives the right answer when called upon, he knows he will
be beaten after school. So he gives the wrong answers. If the teacher
discovers this situation, he can attempt to remove the conditions that
punish good performance. He can stop calling on Joe to give answers
in class. And he can try to provide instructional programs that will
capture the interest of the other students. If these students can become interested in the instruction and perform successfully, they may
be less concerned with punishing other students who perform well. If
the punishment can be removed, then the instruction can continue.

Second, a student may not be performing adequately because not
performing adequately is rewarded. Sally may be afraid to go out at
recess time because the other students do not include her in their
games. If Sally completes her work on time, then she goes out to
recess with the rest of the class. If she does not complete her work
on time, then she stays in during recess to finish her work and
correct her errors. For Sally, inadequate performance produces the
reward of being able to avoid recess. To correct this situation, the
consequences of doing well should be changed. The student can
receive a good grade or a special privilege when he performs adequately. In addition, in the case such as that of Sally, an attempt
should be made to deal with the problems the student is having in
getting along with the other children.

Third, it may not matter to the student whether he performs well
or not. Perhaps the student does not believe that it is important for
him to learn what is taught in school. He may view the instruction as
irrelevant or meaningless. Or the student whose work is evaluated
using average-based methods may have become convinced that he
cannot earn high grades no matter how hard he tries.

For example, Sam generally achieves at a level somewhat below
average compared to his classmates. He usually earns grades of C and
D, with an occasional failure. When his weekly grades are averaged to

determine his final grade, he generally receives Cs. Occasionally, if he tries very hard to perform well, he may earn a B. But the averaging process washes out the Bs as well as the Ds and Fs. Sam knows that he can earn Cs without too much effort. And the effort needed to earn Bs doesn't make much difference in his final grades. So he doesn't work to increase his performance level.

Students must see adequate performance as valuable and worthwhile if they are to put forth the effort needed to perform adequately. The student who perceived the instruction as irrelevant or meaningless can be made aware of the long-term benefits associated with that learning. In addition, activities that the student sees as relevant to him can be incorporated into the curriculum. Instruction that is truly irrelevant and meaningless can be omitted from the program.

Rewards such as high grades or special privileges should be available to each student who performs well. Each student should have the opportunity to earn the reward no matter how much time and effort are required to earn it. There should be no restriction on the number of students who can earn rewards for good performance.

Fourth, a student may perform inadequately because there is an obstacle to prevent him from performing well. Perhaps he has to work in a small group with three other students, and the group members spend most of the time fighting. Perhaps the student knows that he does not understand something but is afraid to ask because he does not want to look stupid. Perhaps the student must complete his homework if he is to perform adequately. But he cannot work at home because there is no proper space and he has too many other responsibilities there. Deemphasizing homework, encouraging and not punishing students who ask questions, and helping students to deal constructively with group process problems can remove the obstacles to performing well. Once the obstacle has been removed, students can continue with the instruction or with the repair procedure.

When the problems in the reward system have been identified and dealt with, a student can be retested. If he performs adequately, he can continue in the program. If his performance is inadequate, possible problems in the knowledge, skill, content, and method areas should be considered.

The student may not be performing adequately because he lacks the necessary skills and knowledge or because he has not learned enough from the instructional program. When this is the case, the following alternatives can be considered.

First, the student may not have completed the instruction. If so, he can be given more learning time and then retested.

Second, the student may not have learned a portion of the material covered in the instruction. The instruction may have been adequate for some students but inadequate for others. If so, small group or individual supplemental instruction can be given to the students who need it. The instruction may have been insufficient. If more instruction is needed, additional materials can be prescribed. A portion of the instruction may have been of poor quality. When this portion is identified, different methods and materials can be used and the topic can be retaught to all the students.

Third, the student may have forgotten or never have learned a portion of a previous unit or course that is essential to success in this course. The student's problems should be located and appropriate supplemental instruction prescribed. The student can perform the remedial procedures as he continues in the regular instructional sequence, or he can stop the regular sequence until he has completed the remediation. Whether he stops or continues in the regular sequence depends on the dependence of subsequent instruction upon skills in which he is deficient and the amount of effort and time required to complete the remediation procedures.

Fourth, the student may never have learned or he may have forgotten skills and knowledge that are prerequisites for this type of instruction. Deficits here often include problems in reading comprehension, understanding of number concepts, or other basic skills that are prerequisites for the program. When there is a deficit of this type, the student may need to stop until he has completed the remediation procedures. Extensive remediation may be required to deal with these basic skill deficits.

Fifth, this type of instruction may be inappropriate for the student's optimum learning style. The program may begin by presenting large amounts of facts and rules. The student may not be able to integrate all of the diverse pieces of information. Perhaps an overview of the concepts and problems involved would be a more beneficial initial method. Or an inquiry-based problem solving format may be more appropriate.

Sixth, this type of instruction may be inappropriate for the student because he has a psychomotor problem that prevents him from benefiting from it. The student may have a hearing problem so that he can't hear the lecture. This problem can be dealt with by preparing a written transcript of the lecture material. The student may have a visual problem, making it extremely difficult for him to read large amounts of textual material. This problem can be dealt with by preparing audiotapes of the text material. In addition, services of developmental disabilities specialists may be needed.

Seventh, the student may have an emotional problem that is interfering with his performance. Special services may be needed to diagnose and deal with this problem.

Eighth, a crisis may have occurred in the student's personal life that interfered with his academic performance. If the interference is temporary, the program can be modified slightly to give him a chance to compensate. If the interference is lasting, special services may be needed to deal with the problem.

Last, experience in implementing a portion of the program may have indicated that the program is inappropriate or ineffective. When this is the case, an alternative program can be substituted.

When the performance problem has been analyzed and the appropriate psychosocial or reward system modification or the remedia-

Student's Name _____

Date _____

Class _____

☐ Read pages (page numbers) of test, workbook, alternate test, supplemental reading, programed instruction material.
Book name _____

☐ View_____(name of film)_____film or filmstrip.

☐ Listen to_____(name of recording)_____recording.

☐ Consult teacher_____(name)_____or student tutor
_____(name)_____at_____(time)_____am/pm in
Room_____(number)_____.

☐ Meet with study group consisting of_____(student's_____
name)_____,_____(student's name)_____,_____(student's
name)_____,_____(student's name)_____at__(time)__am/pm in
Room__(number)__.

After completing above, take alternative form (test form number) of formative evaluation test.

Figure 8.2. *Sample prescription form.*

tion procedures have been identified, the student can be recycled, changed to another program, or permitted to continue in the existing program and to conduct the remediation procedures simultaneously. If the student's performance on the readministration of the diagnostic assessment indicates that additional instruction is needed, the record of his errors should be accompanied by an explicit prescription to correct his errors and learn the material he missed. Figure 8.2 contains an example of a learning prescription form.

Postassessment

The issues surrounding objective-referenced and criterion-referenced testing and the setting of minimum pass levels applicable to the postassessment component have been discussed above in conjunction with the diagnostic assessment component.

Advocates of mastery have proposed that almost all students can acquire adequate levels of the basic skills and knowledge taught in the normal school curriculum when mastery procedures are used (Bloom, 1971; Carroll, 1971). Research results available to date indicate that student cognitive and affective subject-matter-relevant (Bloom, 1976) and instructional-method-relevant (Block & Anderson, 1975) characteristics, which have been established prior to student entry into the instructional program, significantly influence student postassessment performance (Block, & Burns, in press). Significant subject-matter-relevant cognitive entry characteristics include the information processing and other intellectual skills assessed by subject matter aptitude tests, postassessment measures from prior units in the sequence, and other diagnostic and readiness pretests. Subject-matter-relevant affective characteristics include student interest in and attitude toward the subject matter and student self-confidence (Anderson, 1973, 1976; Block, 1970, 1972; Born et al., 1972; Bowen & Faissler, 1975; Burrows & Okey, 1975; Fiel & Okey, 1974; and Oczelik, 1973).

Method-relevant cognitive entry characteristics include information processing and problem solving skills, short-term memory capacity, learning speed and efficiency, and resistance to distraction (see, for example, Estes, 1974; Hunt, Frost & Lunneborg, 1973; Resnick, 1977; Caponigri, 1972; Contreras, 1975; and Reviere & Haladyna, 1974). Method-relevant affective characteristics include self-confidence in areas relevant to the instructional method and openness or positive attitude toward the instructional methods (Anderson, 1973; Billings, 1974; Born *et al.* 1972; Falstrom & Abbot, 1973; Newman *et al.*, 1974; Oczelick, 1973; Poggio *et al.*, 1975; Reynolds, & Gentile, 1975).

The results of these research investigations generally support the conclusion that students' cognitive and affective entry characteristics significantly affect their ability to benefit from the mastery program and their postassessment performance. However, those students who are moderately deficient in subject-matter- or method-relevant cognitive entry characteristics and who persist in using the diagnostic assessment and remedial prescriptive components of the mastery model to reach prescribed minimum pass levels on the diagnostic assessment do, in general, attain the minimum pass levels on the postassessment measures. Research relevant to this conclusion was summarized in Chapter 6.

Consequently, the mastery components cannot and should not be used to produce identical patterns of postassessment performance among large groups of students. Rather, these components are appropriate for helping those students who are willing to persist in completing the diagnostic and prescriptive phases to attain adequate competence in the basic skills, knowledge and attitudes which comprise the core of the curriculum.

Reinforcement and Grading

The mastery components are designed to maximize the likelihood that each student will attain the minimum pass levels defined as adequate for mastery. Every student who attains the minimum pass levels has demonstrated the performance that earns him positive evaluations. The student who performs at or beyond the minimum pass level on the final or summative evaluation in a unit or course is evaluated as one who has performed successfully in the course. The grades can be administered by the teacher, a proctor (see, for example, Conrad *et al.*, 1976), a classmate (see, for example, Phillips *et al.*, 1976), or the student himself.

If the course is graded on a pass–fail basis, the student receives a pass. If letter or number grades are assigned to students, the student who performed successfully receives a high grade. The mastery procedures place no limits on the number of high grades or passing grades that can be earned by the students in the group. Average-based procedures limit the number of high grades that students in any group can earn. The mastery procedures include no such limitations.

The students in a classroom group may work at different rates, and they may enter the instruction with different levels of prerequisite skills and different goals, needs, interests, and other motivations. In addition, the instructional methods and materials may not be equally effective for all of the students in the class. As a result, some students may master more objectives than others master. Some students may require more time to reach the same level of mastery that other students attain in shorter time periods. Students in the same class may work towards several different sets of objectives. Lower mastery levels may be prescribed for some students whereas higher levels are prescribed for others. Nevertheless, when a student arrives at a mastery level prescribed as adequate for him, he receives the passing grade, the high grade, or whatever response is given to indicate that a student has performed successfully. This positive response is intended to reinforce the student behaviors that produced the successful performance.

The mastery procedures propose to structure the curriculum so that each student can perform successfully. In effect, they promise the student that if he will persist in completing the learning activities and whatever alternative corrective activities are also prescribed, he will arrive at the level of achievement defined as acceptable for competence. If the student believes this promise, puts forth the effort required, and arrives at the level defined as adequate for competence, then he has earned the evaluation of successful performance. If he arrives at the mastery level only to be told, "Sorry, we gave out all the good grades already," then he may be very suspicious the next time someone tells him that he can perform successfully if only he will put forth the necessary effort and complete the prescribed activities.

Though students who attain mastery should receive both evidence that their performance has been successful and some recognition or reward at the end of the instructional unit or program, this recognition and reward does not have to take the form of a grade. Any consequence is appropriate when it serves to reinforce the productive behaviors that the students demonstrated in the program. Grades may not serve as positive reinforcers for some students; for these students, other consequences that they see as desirable should follow the classroom behaviors that are to be reinforced.

Grades and other consequences received for acceptable behavior in the classroom and adequate academic performance may become incentives for some students because they can be exchanged for other reinforcers, such as access to responsible positions or other special privileges. In addition, social reinforcements in the form of teacher, parent, and peer approval that accompany acceptable behavior and performance can also serve as reinforcers.

For some students, grades, smiling faces, and stars on papers, and positive social reinforcement in the form of smiles and favorable comments are not effective reinforcers (Cohen *et al.*, 1965; Meichenbaum, Bowers & Ross, 1969). Token reinforcement systems, in which students receive points or chips or other objects that they exchange for other things or privileges, have been effective for these students.

Token reinforcement has been defined as the use of "tangible objects . . . which attain reinforcing power by being exchanged for a variety of other objects such as candy and trinkets which are back-up reinforcers [O'Leary & Becker, 1967]." A number of research studies found token reinforcers to be effective for shaping the behavior of delinquent students, retarded students, and students who posed considerable discipline problems.

For example, Sloggett (1974) developed a token reinforcement system for increasing the academic achievement and reducing the disruptive classroom behavior of 24 adolescent boys. The boys were placed in four groups of six persons each. Each group worked together as a team. Each student contributed to a team score; each team achieved rewards as a unit. The boys were encouraged to work together and to help each other. Points were used as token reinforcers. The students earned points and approval for various achievement-related activities during the school day. The points were totaled at the end of each week, when they were translated into letter grades. Each boy contributed his points to the team total and he received the grade his team earned as a unit. Each boy earned points for being present in class or having an excused absence, for appropriate classroom behavior (which was clearly defined), for having needed materials and participating in learning activities and for producing accurate work. Team points were earned for contacting remiss students about school attendance, tardiness, or misbehavior and for contacting students about school or personal problems, including notifying absent members concerning classroom activities and helping classmates outside of school. Each team that earned an average of at least 1000 points per member at the end of the week could earn a grade of A and an award. Thus, each team was competing against the standard of known value. In addition, grading was not on a curve basis so that there was no limit on the number of students who could earn the highest reward.

In addition to the high grades, the students could use their points to earn "backup reinforcers." Within limits, the students were allowed to choose these rewards. Adults often assume that they know what students like, but this assumption is not always valid. Allowing students to select some of their own rewards may ensure that they will select consequences that are truly rewarding to them.

In this experiment the boys' initial requests were for cokes, candy, and doughnuts. Other choices included playing basketball during class time, a picnic in the park adjoining the schoolgrounds, and permission to play radios in class.

When the experiment was completed, the students showed substantial increases in academic achievement, increased productivity, reduced amounts of disorderly behavior, increased self-imposed peer pressure for good conduct, and improved attendance. The reinforcement system proved to be a rather inexpensive procedure for producing numerous positive results.

In most school settings, many reinforcers are available for use in a systematic reinforcement program such as the one employed in the previously mentioned experiment. Games, recess, toys, snacks, rest periods, free and play periods during regular class time, television and movies, social approval and other special privileges are usually included in the regular school programs. However, students normally receive these privileges whether or not they produce desirable behavior; these events are normally not contingent upon the production of specified behaviors. But reinforcement programs can easily be designed that incorporate these available events into a reinforcement system designed to elicit desirable behaviors from students. These events can be used to reinforce the behaviors that are beneficial for students to repeat, such as good study habits, attentiveness, persistence, cooperation, creativity, initiation of ideas and projects, promptness, and so forth.

For example, Hughes (1973) found that students who received consistent and frequent praise from their teachers when they answered correctly and who received supporting statements from their teachers when they answered incorrectly achieved at higher levels on science achievement tests than did students who received no verbal praise or other indication of support. The comparison students, who received no praise, did receive acknowledgment when their answers were correct, but this acknowledgment did not appear to be of sufficient force to encourage them to achieve at the high levels that were attained by the students who received consistent praise and support from their teachers.

In another study, Tyler (1958) required four groups of students to perform problem solving tasks. First, each group performed an initial task in which the students achieved an average amount of success. On succeeding tasks, each group received a different pattern of verbal reinforcement. The first group received consistent encouragement. The second group received consistent discouragement. The third group received inconsistent feedback, including both encouraging and discouraging statements. The fourth group served as a comparison group and did not receive verbal reinforcement at all. The results indicated that the encouragement group performed significantly better on the problem-solving tasks than did the discouragement group. However, the comparison performed almost as well as the encouragement group. The performance of the discouragement group was almost comparable to the performance of the group that had received inconsistent feedback. These results suggest that verbal reinforcements containing discouragement or inconsistent feedback may significantly hamper students' performance.

Though positive evaluations and encouragement are important parts of the learning process, mistakes and criticism are also part of this process. An instructional program in which students make no errors may *not* be ideal for most students. Pask and Scott (1972) found that many students became bored or reported that they did not feel they were learning enough when the error rates in an instructional program were set too low for them. Students varied in the error rates they preferred.

In sum, the research on grading and reinforcement indicated that consistent negative feedback could be detrimental to students. However, consistent positive feedback with criticism and negative comments omitted did not prove universally beneficial. The results favored providing every student with positive evaluations for good performance and maintenance of an appropriate error rate in conjunction with constructive criticism, encouragement, and high-quality corrective instruction.

In Chapter 9 examples of the many instructional programs implementing the mastery model are presented.

Practical Concerns

9

Implementation Examples and Evaluation

This chapter begins with a brief review of some examples of widely used and continuing mastery model implementation programs. This review is not intended to provide the practitioner with a step-by-step procedure for developing and implementing a specific mastery model curriculum in a specific classroom. Numerous "how to do it" manuals are currently available. Examples include Block and Anderson's *Mastery Learning in Classroom Instruction* (1975), Davies' *Competency Based Learning: Technology, Management, and Design* (1973), Keller and Sherman's *The Keller Plan Handbook* (1974), and Okey and Ciesla's *Mastery Teaching* (1975).

Following this brief summary of some of the high quality mastery model implementations, the issue of formative and summative evaluations of mastery model implementations conducted to date is considered. A model for conducting these evaluations developed by the author is presented.

Competencies

When the mastery model is used to structure a competency-based curriculum, the objectives serve as the working definitions of the competencies selected for the program. The performances that students are expected to demonstrate as evidence that they have attained competence are defined in the objectives.

In the process of identifying competencies, the needs, potentials, and preferences of the students who will participate in the program are considered, as are the needs and values of the society in which the program operates. What competencies will the students need when they complete the instructional program? Which aspects of their intellectual, emotional, social, and physical potential should be developed in the instructional program? What outcomes can the students reasonably be expected to attain, given their present level of development?

Selecting Competencies for a Preschool Program

An interesting approach to selecting competencies to be used as the basis for a preschool program was employed by Troutt and Jennings (1974). The expert judgments of 31 scholars in the area of child growth and development were obtained. These judgments were used as a basis for selecting the competencies for a curriculum for preschool education of children in the mountains of Appalachia. Troutt and Jennings sought to determine the degree to which agreement could be established among the scholars about the competencies of children, up to age 6 years, 0 months. They surveyed the theoretical and research literature to obtain a list of these competencies. The list was submitted to the national panel of scholars and to a panel of Appalachian scholars for systematic judging. Examples of the competencies that the experts judged to be appropriate for children up to age 6 included:

Category: Classification

    Competency: Ability to form concepts

        Example: To recognize repetition of patterns
                To establish and label categories
                To generalize from one situation to another

    Competency: Ability to discriminate by sound

        Example: To distinguish between sounds
                To distinguish rhythm
                To identify sources of sounds

Category: Habits and Attitudes

    Competency: Ability to initiate action

        Example: To realize when an action would improve existing conditions
                To know the range and probable results of actions

      Competency: Ability to plan action

         Example: To make choices based on the dynamics of a given
                situation
             To assess resources
             To anticipate end results [1974, pp. 13–14].

Objectives

The objectives in the mastery program define the performances the student is expected to demonstrate when he successfully completes the educational program. The objective statements may follow the strict behavorial format specified by Mager (1962, 1975) and Gagné and Briggs (1974). However, restriction of objective statements to the behavioral format is not mandatory.

In the more complex subject matter areas and at university and professional instructional levels, professionals serving as curriculum designers often have great difficulty in stating objectives when they are forced to restrict themselves to the strict behavioral format. This author has served as a consultant to programs in which the entire mastery model implementation would have been terminated if the behavioral format for stating objectives had been strictly enforced. Following are some examples of objectives from curriculum materials that have been discussed in preceding chapters.

Objectives for a Preschool and Primary Level Arithmetic Program

Two examples of behavioral objectives for the Distar arithmetic program (SRA, 1971) are:

Behavioral Objective 1: When the teacher counts from 1 to a particular number, the student should be able to tell her what number she counted to.

Behavioral Objective 2: When the teacher specifies a number, the student should be able to count from one to that number.
Subobjectives:

a. With the teacher first demonstrating the sequence.
b. Without the teacher first demonstrating the sequence [SRA, 1971, p. 6].

In the Distar arithmetic program, the objectives are presented in conjunction with complete instructional materials and with diagnostic and postassessment tests that measure each student's performance on these materials. Each test includes specification of the minimum pass level.

For example, one test includes the following instructions:

> If any child in the group fails more than one problem, return the group to Lesson 46. Do Lesson 46 today but omit the Counting Events in Time tasks. Do Lessons 46–59, one lesson a day including the Counting Events in Time tasks. Then test the children again.
>
> If the group passes the test, proceed with Lesson 60, and continue doing one lesson a day [SRA, 1970, p. 7].

The materials also contain alternative supplemental instruction appropriate for students who performed below the minimum pass levels after completing the initial instruction.

The next example is a portion of the mastery curriculum developed at the College of Medicine of the University of Illinois. In this mastery curriculum, the professional participants serving as curriculum designers developed their own format for stating objectives. The following administrative procedures were established to develop and monitor the curriculum:

A committee on instruction was established to develop and implement the curriculum. This committee consisted of representatives of the various disciplines in the medical school.

A committee on appraisal was formed to determine the effectiveness of the curriculum. This committee was responsible for measuring each student's achievement of the stated objective and determining the degree of mastery of the objective achieved by the student.

A committee on student progress (promotion) was formed to receive and evaluate the results of all appraisal instruments. This committee was empowered to direct the academic advisory system to prescribe remedial work for students who failed to meet the instructional objectives of the curriculum. Repeated failure to perform commensurate with the objectives could result in recommendation for dismissal to the College Committee on Promotions. The College Committee on Promotions reviewed the activities of this committee on a periodic basis and heard appeals from the action of this committee.

A student academic advisory system was established to review the test results of those students whose performance required the remediation of academic deficiencies. With the help of departmental liaison members, this committee constructed a plan for the repair of deficiencies and supervised the implementation of this plan.

These committees worked in conjunction with the Center for Educational Development. This center performed the service of constructing and administering assessment procedures. In addition, the center conducted research and development with the goal of continually improving the curriculum.

The medical curriculum that has been implemented has two component parts. One part, the core curriculum, contains the minimal competencies, the knowledge, skills, and attitudes expected of all students graduating from the medical school. The second part, the selective curriculum, gives students the opportunity to structure their own program, with the advice and counsel of the faculty. As an example, a set of habits, attitudes, and value objectives, intended to be emphasized and achieved throughout the entire curriculum, includes the following:

The student should be able to:

Demonstrate sensitivity to patients, colleagues, and society which will be manifested by:

1. Promptness in keeping appointments
2. Adaptability to the unscheduled events of illness
3. Patience with the demanding, the ill-informed, the frightened patient
4. Nonjudgmental acceptance of unfamiliar life patterns, values, language [University of Illinois College of Medicine, 1973b, p. 30].

Samples of Curricula Which Implement the Six Mastery Components

A wide variety of curriculum designs and instructional materials is currently available to aid the instructor in implementing a mastery model curriculum. Some of these materials have been developed on the local level by the faculty in a professional school or school district. Other materials have been developed and published by professional publishers. Following are two examples of mastery model units selected to illustrate both types of curriculum development. The first unit was selected from the medical curriculum described above, and these materials were developed by the medical school faculty. The second unit was selected from the Mathematics Learning Systems (SRA, 1974).

A Sample Unit in the University of Illinois College of Medicine Curriculum

Unit Plans

Following is an example of the plan for a unit in microbiology on the topic Gram-Positive, Pathogenic Bacilli.

GOAL

This topic is designed to consider *Corynebacterium diphtheriae* and the *disease it causes; to describe Bacillus anthracis* and discuss its role as the etiologic agent of anthrax; to characterize *Erysipelothrix* and *Listeria* and the diseases they cause.

OBJECTIVES

A. Describe the characteristics of *Corynebacterium diphtheriae* and explain the procedures used in a diagnostic laboratory to isolate and identify this organism.

B. Discuss the pathogenesis of *C. diphtheriae* and note the roles of bacteriophase and medium iron concentration on toxin production by the organism.

C. Identify the mechanisms which confer immunity to *C. diptheriae.*

D. Explain the rationale of the Schick test.

PERFORMANCE SKILLS

The student should be able to:

A. discuss the role of exotoxin in the pathogenesis of diphtheria.

B. explain how many strains of diphtheria-like organisms are unable to produce clinical diphtheria in the nonimmune, while the classical strains can be very virulent.

C. analyze the factors which lead to swift, high mortality when *B. anthracis* infection is initiated in the lungs or GI tract and contrast this outcome with that observed in cases of cutaneous infections by the same organism.

KEY WORDS

Corynebacterium

Listeria

Erysipelothrix

Bacillus

Diptheria

Granulomatosis
   infantiseptica

RECOMMENDED STUDY AND RESOURCES

A. Required reading: *Microbiology*, Davis *et al.*, 1973, chapters on
    corynebacteria, aerobic, spore-forming bacilli and pages on *Listeria*
    and *Erysipelothrix*, or
    Zinsser Microbiology, Joklik & Smith, 1972, chapters 32 and 49,
    and pages 610–612.

B. Recommended reference reading:
    Manual of Clinical Microbiology, 1970, Chapters 10 through 13.
    Pathology, Robbins, 1967, pages 313–315, 332–333.
    Textbook of Medicine, Cecil & Loeb, 1971, pages 219–224,
    267–272.

C. Resources: One lecture.
    Lecture outline and representative learning feedback questions
    (available from the Microbiology Department office or from the
    lecturer). Slide/tape lecture on this topic in the Pathology A/V
    library [University of Illinois College of Medicine, 1973a,
    pp. 638–640].

The "representative learning feedback questions" are the diagnostic assessments of this implementation of the mastery model. For
students who fail to attain the minimum pass levels on one or more
of these measures, alternative instruction is available from the course
instructors and from the learning center, containing alternate learning aids available under the direction of professional supervisors.
Students who fail to attain the minimum pass levels after receiving
considerable additional instruction are referred to the diagnostic
assessment committee. The summative evaluations given in the medical curriculum are confidential and cannot be reproduced here.

A Sample Multiplication Unit in
the Mathematics Learning System (SRA, 1974a, b, c)

A fourth grade level multiplication unit is described here to
illustrate the MLS implementation of the six mastery model components. Since the entire unit is too long to reproduce here, samples
of each component are provided. The MLS program is available for
students from ages 5 through 14 (grades kindergarten through 8).

The instruction in this unit is divided into two sections. The first
section, covering text pages 98 through 105, teaches multiplying a
1-digit factor by a 1-digit factor and extension of estimation skills.
The second section, covering text pages 106 through 117, teaches
multiplication facts, multiplying 2- or 3-digit numbers by 1-digit

numbers, multiplying 2-digit by 2-digit numbers, and solving problems by multiplying. Two survey tests are administered to all students, the first before the students begin the first section of the chapter and the second survey preceding the second section of the chapter. Two diagnostic assessments (referred to as "progress checks" in this textual material) are administered, one following each section of the chapter. Three sets of enrichment or remedial prescriptive instructional activities are provided. The summative measure (called the "check-out" in this textual material), covering all of the chapter objectives, is administered to students who perform successfully on both progress checks.

Students can proceed through this unit individually, in small groups, or as an entire class. The "Pathfinder," an instructional aid provided with the MLS, illustrates the student's route of progress through the unit. The Pathfinder for this multiplication unit is illustrated in Figures 9.1A and B. For example, if a student were to proceed through this instruction individually, he begins by taking the first survey test, illustrated on side two of the Pathfinder. He scores his own test using the correct answers provided on side one of the Pathfinder, and records his score in the place provided. If he fails to answer all items correctly, he proceeds with the instruction on page 98. If he answers both items correctly, he proceeds directly to the first progress check, which is provided in his text. If he gives incorrect answers to three or more items, he proceeds to page 98 of the text. If he misses no more than one item on the progress check, he proceeds to the second survey. The student continues this progress through the unit as indicated on the Pathfinder.

Samples of each of these components of this MLS unit are provided below. The first presents the unit objectives and the relationship of these objectives to the other objectives in the instructional sequence, as described in the teacher's guide accompanying the instructional materials.

Unit Objectives

In this unit, the learner is
1. Multiplying a 2- or 3-digit factor by a 1-digit factor
2. Multiplying two 2-digit factors
3. Estimating products to check the reasonableness of a computed product.

Summaries of objectives from preceding and subsequent units are presented to establish the unit sequence:

Before this unit the learner has—
1. Mastered the multiplication facts
2. Rounded numbers to the nearest ten or hundred
    In later units the learner will—
1. Master multiplying any 2- or 3-digit factor by any 1-digit factor
2. Master multiplying any two 2-digit factors to find their product [SRA, 1974a, p. 96].

Preassessment

The next sample contains one preassessment measure (called "survey" in this text) and the accompanying student instruction and recommendations for the teacher. A second survey is shown on Figure 9.1.

Specification of prerequisites In the teacher's guide, the skills emphasized in the unit and the skills and facts which the student should master prior to beginning the unit are described:

The development of the multiplication computational skills is based on the same knowledge that was used for addition and subtraction.

1. Mastery of the basic facts must come first. Every child must be able to confidently name the product of any multiplication combination.
2. The knowledge of place value is the key to making any pupil independent in computation. If the child knows the facts and place value, he can multiply any of these problems with no trouble:

27	285	3261	465,120
$\times$ 7	$\times$ 9	$\times$ 8	$\times$ 6

It will take only a minimal amount of instruction to have the pupil confidently operating with 2- or 3-digit multipliers if he knows the basic facts and understands place value.
3. Knowing how to estimate answers will help eliminate careless mistakes and serve as a guide to the computation itself. If a pupil can look at 28 × 529 and think "30 × 500 is 15,000, so the product will be close to that," he will have mastered the skill of multiplication in no time at all.

Rounding numbers is of course a prerequisite to the development of estimation skills. Since estimation is a mental operation, most numbers will be rounded in such a way that the pupil will be operating with a number fact while also keeping in mind the place value (the number of zeros).

In general, a 2-digit number is rounded to the nearest ten, a 3-digit number to the nearest hundred, a 4-digit number to the nearest thousand, and so on.

ANSWERS

PROGRESS CHECK
p. 117

1. 63
2. 48
3. 15
4. 28
5. 66
6. 68
7. 348
8. 2511
9. 4025
10. 546
11. 2730
12. 7719
13. $62.25
14. $23.45
15. $13.80
16. $8.50
17. $12.40
18. $24.75

* $145.15

SURVEY

1. 76
   × 9

Right?

2. a.   37
      × 86

b. 29 people.
Each sold 15 tickets.
How many tickets sold?

Both right?

SCORECARD

DATE	TEST	SCORE
	Progress Check p. 106	
	Progress Check p. 117	
	Checkout p. 120	

ACTIVITIES

Try some of the activities listed below.

1

AM	W 36, 37, 38, 39
PS (4)	28, 29 •
STP (4)	21-23, 28, 30
AFK	Multiplication cards
CT	MD 10, 11, 21, 22
CSDK	Whole Numbers Multiplication 1-4, 8
CNP (WN)	Multiplication 1-4, 8
SMM (I)	C 3, 6, 8, 13, 14, 18, 22

2

AM	W 53, 54, 55
PS (4)	30-32
STP (4)	24, 49, 50, 67
CT	MD 12, 23, 24
CSDK	Whole Numbers Multiplication 5, 9, 11
CNP (WN)	Multiplication 5, 9, 11, 14-16
SMM (I)	C 4, 5, 7, 11-17, 20-24
SMM (II)	C 26, 27

EXTENSIONS

3

AM	W 56
PS (4)	33
STP (4)	29, 40, 44, 46, 51-53, 59, 64, 68

What I did on my own:

Would you like to be a tutor for this chapter? _____

Figure 9.1A. *Multiplication Pathfinder (Side 1) (SRA, 1974c).*

5 MULTIPLICATION
PATHFINDER

Your goal is to learn even more about multiplication.

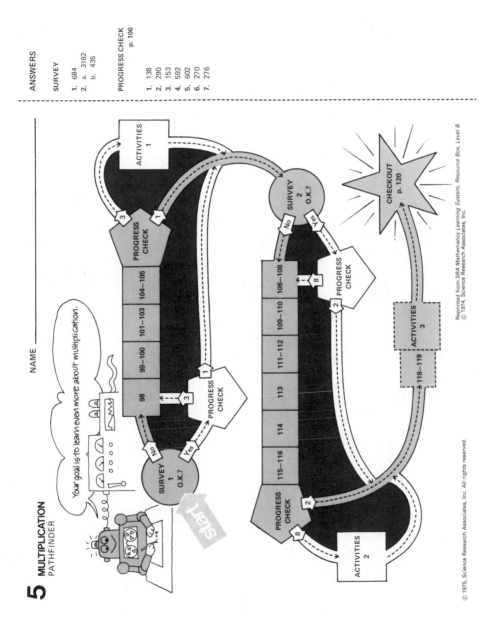

ANSWERS

SURVEY

1. 684
2. a. 3182
   b. 435

PROGRESS CHECK
p. 106

1. 138
2. 290
3. 153
4. 592
5. 602
6. 270
7. 276

You will find a heavy emphasis on rounding and estimation throughout the chapter. And you will see the computational form for multiplication build from the multiplication skills that the learner has already developed.

The major computational emphasis will be on 1-digit multipliers so that an understanding of the operation itself, the related place-value implications, and the computational form can be thoroughly developed. Multiplying two 2-digit factors is introduced at the end of the chapter, but minimal practice is provided at this point. Let's get knowledge of 1-digit multipliers mastered first. That's the goal [SRA, 1974, 96d].

Administration of the Preassessment Measure: Instructions Presented in the Teacher's Guide

Use questions 1 through 6 for discussion. You'll probably use a large map to locate the territory illustrated to make the discussion more meaningful. Emphasize the illustration is only a part of a larger map. The questions set the theme for the next several pages that focus on Virginia City. This small ghost town in Montana is located about 50 miles from Yellowstone National Park. Be alert for confusion—the famous Virginia City is located in Nevada.

Questions 7 and 8 will give you the most information about an individual pupil's previous knowledge of multiplication. (These questions serve as the unit preassessment.) Make sure you emphasize the learning goal.

Discussion Questions 1–6:
(Desired Student Response)

1. What part of North America is shown?
   (The Northwest)

2. What countries are partly shown?
   (United States, Canada)

3. What provinces are partly shown? What states are partly shown?
   (British Columbia, Alberta, Saskatchewan, Washington, Oregon, Idaho, Montana, Wyoming)

4. What's the difference between a province and a state?
   (Province—political division in Canada)
   (State—political division in U.S.)

5. Would this part of the country have been settled at about the same time? Find out when towns were started in this region.
   (Middle 1800s)

6. Can you find out what brought people to this region?
   (Mining, lumber, trapping, farming)

7. Way back then, a man was lucky to get paid $1 for 1 day's work. He worked 6 days a week, so he got paid $6 a week. How much money would he earn in 26 weeks? in 52 weeks? in 104 weeks (that's 2 years)? in 260 weeks (that's 5 years)? ($156, $312, $624, $1560)

8. If a man was lucky, he might find gold. The price of gold was as high as $12 an ounce. How much money could the man get if he sold 15 ounces? ($180) [SRA, 1974, p. 98]

Instruction: sample learning activities. Following are two examples of the teaching instructions and sample learning activities appropriate for students who answered incorrectly one or more items on the first survey or three or more items on the first progress check.

Sample Learning Activities
(Desired Student Response)

Teaching Instructions: Example

goal Introduction to the algorithm for multiplying a 2-digit factor by a 1-digit factor

Develop the page (shown on page 156) with the group. Stress the importance of place value in the partial products. Aligning ones and tens in straight columns is necessary in order to add the final product. (You might suggest that the pupils turn lined paper sideways to reinforce the ideas of columns.)

Don't require the youngsters to write the thinking step when writing the partial products. They need write only this:

$$\begin{array}{r} 12 \\ \times\ 6 \\ \hline \left(\begin{array}{r} 12 \\ 60 \\ \hline 72 \end{array}\right) \end{array}$$

Problems 1 through 7 should be completed independently. Watch for those pupils who are already in trouble. Check on mastery of multiplication facts. Addition errors are another possibility.

Ask your pupils to hunt for newspaper grocery ads and bring them to class tomorrow. And then plan on at least one day of computation practice outside the text. Use activity 2, part a described on page 120a of the Resource Section.

Student Activities: Example 1
(Desired Student Response)

If Dirty had known how to multiply, this is how his work would have looked.

Day 1		*Day 2*		*Day 3*	

$$\begin{array}{cc} 10 & 8 \\ \times\ 3 & \times\ 3 \\ \hline (30) & (24) \end{array} \qquad \begin{array}{cc} 10 & 2 \\ \times\ 6 & \times\ 6 \\ \hline (60) & (12) \end{array} \qquad \begin{array}{cc} 10 & 4 \\ \times\ 7 & \times\ 7 \\ \hline (70) & (28) \end{array}$$

$$\begin{array}{c} 30 \\ +\ 24 \\ \hline (54 \text{ feet in all}) \end{array} \qquad \begin{array}{c} 60 \\ +\ 12 \\ \hline (72 \text{ feet in all}) \end{array} \qquad \begin{array}{c} 70 \\ +\ 28 \\ \hline (98 \text{ feet in all}) \end{array}$$

Here Is an Even Shorter Method

Day 1	*Day 2*	*Day 3*
Each trench is 10—8, or 18, feet long. He dug 3.	Each trench is 12 feet long. He dug 6.	Each trench is 14 feet long. He dug 7.

$$\begin{array}{c} 10 + 8 \\ \times\quad 3 \\ \hline (30 + 24) \end{array} \quad \begin{array}{c} 18 \\ \times\ 3 \\ \hline \begin{pmatrix} 24 \\ 30 \\ \hline 54 \end{pmatrix} \end{array} \begin{array}{l} 3 \times 8 \\ 3 \times 10 \\ \text{in all} \end{array} \quad \begin{array}{c} 12 \\ \times\ 6 \\ \hline \begin{pmatrix} 12 \\ 60 \\ \hline 72 \end{pmatrix} \end{array} \begin{array}{l} 6 \times 2 \\ 6 \times 10 \end{array} \quad \begin{array}{c} 14 \\ \times\ 7 \\ \hline \begin{pmatrix} 28 \\ 70 \\ \hline 98 \end{pmatrix} \end{array} \begin{array}{l} 7 \times 4 \\ 7 \times 10 \end{array}$$

Your Turn to Multiply

$$\text{1.} \quad \begin{array}{c} 12 \\ \times\ 8 \\ \hline \begin{pmatrix} 16 \\ 80 \\ \hline 96 \end{pmatrix} \end{array} \qquad \text{2.} \quad \begin{array}{c} 13 \\ \times\ 7 \\ \hline \begin{pmatrix} 21 \\ 70 \\ \hline 91 \end{pmatrix} \end{array} \qquad \text{3.} \quad \begin{array}{c} 17 \\ \times\ 6 \\ \hline \begin{pmatrix} 42 \\ 60 \\ \hline 102 \end{pmatrix} \end{array}$$

$$\text{4.} \quad \begin{array}{c} 15 \\ \times\ 4 \\ \hline \begin{pmatrix} 20 \\ 40 \\ \hline 60 \end{pmatrix} \end{array} \quad \text{5.} \quad \begin{array}{c} 19 \\ \times\ 9 \\ \hline \begin{pmatrix} 81 \\ 90 \\ \hline 171 \end{pmatrix} \end{array} \quad \text{6.} \quad \begin{array}{c} 16 \\ \times\ 5 \\ \hline \begin{pmatrix} 30 \\ 50 \\ \hline 80 \end{pmatrix} \end{array} \quad \text{7.} \quad \begin{array}{c} 18 \\ \times\ 8 \\ \hline \begin{pmatrix} 64 \\ 80 \\ \hline 144 \end{pmatrix} \end{array}$$

[SRA, 1974a, p. 102]

Teaching Instructions: Example 2

goal Development of estimation in multiplication

memo Rounding and estimating are used extensively throughout this program in all computation. These two skills are especially important in multiplication. Estimation **before** computation is one of the most effective ways to reinforce concepts of place value. It allows some sense to be made from the "magic" of partial products.

Independent learners are on their own. You'll have to decide about your other groups. The strugglers will need you. Use numberline diagrams again if the pupils have forgotten about rounding.

Student Activities: Example 2
(Desired Student Response)

1. "I paid about 50¢ for this souvenir from Virginia City." What does that statement really say?
   a   Does it tell exactly how much was paid?

   (Notice the word "about.")

   b   Does it tell if it cost more than 50¢? (No)
   c   Does it tell if it cost less than 50¢? (No)
   d   Would I say that if I really paid 25¢? 75¢? (No   No)
   e   Would I say that if I paid 40¢? 60¢? (No   No)
   f   Would I say that if I paid 45¢? 55¢? (Probably   Probably)
   g   Would I say that if I paid 48¢? 52¢? (Probably   Probably)
   h   What was probably the lowest price I would have paid to make that statement? the highest price? (55¢   45¢)

2. Key chains cost 36¢ apiece.
   About how much do 2 cost?
   (2×36 = ? Round 36 up to 40. 2×40 ?   80)
   Will the 2 cost *less* or more than 80¢? (Less)

3. There are 18 people in each bus. There are 6 buses. About how many people are there?
   (6×18 = ? Round 18 up to 20. 6×20 = ?   120)
   Are there *less* or more than 120 people? (Less)

4. 21 people can go on one tour. There are 8 tours planned for ten o'clock. About how many people can go on the ten o'clock tours?
   $\left(\begin{array}{l} 8 \times 21 \text{ is about } 8 \times 20. \\ 8 \times 20 = 160 \end{array}\right)$
   Is 8×21 *more* or less than 160? (More)

[SRA, 1974a, p. 104]

Diagnostic Assessment

Following are the teaching instructions and the test items for the first diagnostic assessment in this unit. As indicated above, the diagnostic assessments in this text are called "progress checks." The test in this example measures student mastery of the skill of multiplying a 2-digit factor by a 1-digit factor.

Teaching Instructions

The Progress Check is short, but it will signal the trouble spots.

$$69 \times 2$$

Incorrect student → responses
$$\left(\begin{matrix} 16 \\ 180 \\ 136 \end{matrix} \right.$$
) Fact errors

Addition error

$$58 \times 5$$

Incorrect student → responses
$$\left(\begin{matrix} 40 \\ 250 \\ 2540 \end{matrix} \right.$$
) Columns not aligned

Errors in multiplication facts mean more practice. Lined paper turned sideways will help place-value column alignment. Estimation will help catch gross errors.

If much additional work is needed, stop here. Complete mastery is not necessary, but a feeling of confidence is. Put your pupils to work making patterned practice sheets as suggested in activity 2. Ask your capable pupils to hlep you with peer-tutor work. Get involved with any supplemental materials you have available.

Diagnostic Test
(Desired Student Response)

Skill: Multiplying 2-digit by 1-digit number

Multiply:

1. 69	2. 58	3. 17	4. 74	5. 86	6. 45	7. 92
× 2	× 5	× 9	× 8	× 7	× 6	× 3
(138)	(290)	(153)	(592)	(602)	(270)	(276)

The student can score his own test using the correct answers provided on the "Pathfinder," (see Figure 9.1A, "Progress check, p. 106") Alternatively, the test answers can be removed from the Pathfinder, and the test can be scores by the teacher or another student [SRA, 1974].

The minimum pass level for this diagnostic test (progress check) is shown on Figure 9.1B. If the student answered six or more items correctly (0 or one wrong) he can proceed to Activities 1 or Survey 2. If the student missed three or more items, he should proceed to text page 98 if he took the progress check without completing the instruction on pages 98 through 105. If the student who missed three or more items on this progress check had completed this instruction, his learning problem should be diagnosed and appropriate remedial instruction should be prescribed. This remedial instruction can be selected from the learning activities referred to in Activities 1 of the Pathfinder. When the prescribed instruction has been completed, the student can take an alternate form of the progress check, which is provided in the teacher's guide.

Following is an example of one type of alternative prescriptive instruction provided in the curriculum materials. As indicated on side two of the Pathfinder (see Figure 9.1B), a wide variety of alternate learning activities is provided at various points throughout the chapter. The "activities" section of the Pathfinder refers the student to the alternative activities appropriate for that particular point in the instruction.

SHOWDOWN: A GAME OF STRATEGY

SKILLS NEEDED: Addition and multiplication of whole numbers
YOU WILL NEED: 2 markers
HOW TO PLAY: 2 can play

1. Each player places a marker on one of the corner squares marked START. Players take turns moving their marker one square at a time. They may move in any direction (horizontally, vertically, or diagonally).
2. After a player has moved, he multiplies the number in the square he came from by the number in the square he moved to. The product is his score for the move. For example, if he moves from the 8-square to the 6-square, his score is 8×6, or 48.
3. Each player keeps a record of his scores. However, he may *not* compute the sum of his scores on paper until the game is over.
4. The game is over when a player moves his marker to the SHOWDOWN square. At that time each player adds up his score. The player with the highest total score wins. (A player should not move to the SHOWDOWN square unless he thinks that his total score is greater than his opponent's.)
5. A player may not move to a square that already has a marker on it.
6. A player may not move to the same square more than twice in a game.

The Showdown board is reproduced on page 160 (SRA, 1974).

The postassessment measure, called the "check-out," for this unit contains 10 multiplication problems for each of three skills taught in the unit: (1) Multiplying 2-digit by 1-digit number, (2) multiplying 3-digit by 1-digit number, and (3) muliplying 2-digit by 2-digit number. The teaching instructions indicate that students are not expected to master the problems covering multiplying 2-digit by 2-digit numbers. In addition, the teaching instructions

START 1	4	12	15	8	15	9
5	3	9	10	7	6	12
13	8	2	3	5	11	3
14	6	9	SHOW-DOWN	4	7	16
4	11	4	2	3	9	11
9	8	6	8	10	2	6
8	13	9	15	12	5	1 START

suggest that administration of 5 of the 10 problems provided for each skill is sufficient to measure students' mastery. The additional five problems in each category can be used to recheck the progress of students who will be given additional instruction. These items can be used as alternate forms of the postassessment to measure mastery of the entire unit. As indicated above, alternate forms of both progress checks are provided for students who need reassessment on portions of the unit following remedial instruction.

The Pathfinder, shown in Figure 9.1, provides a space for each student who has performed successfully on the postassessment measure to indicate if he would like to serve as a tutor for other students who have not yet mastered this unit. When a student indicates that he wants to serve as a tutor, he places a small flag with his name on it on a box marked Chapter 5 on a "tutor board" which is displayed in

Personal Progress Folder   Name_____

Each column below lists things that you are learning to do in math. Choose the column that is marked with the same symbol as on the back of your book. When you know you can do one of the things on the list, write the date you learned it on the blank next to it. This is a good way to remind yourself of all the math ideas you've learned.

I know how to—

• tell the value of each digit in the numeral 999,999 and can read aloud or write all other numerals less than that _____

• estimate and find the sum of problems such as 9672 + 1358 + 169 _____

• estimate and find the differences of problems such as 7207 − 891 _____

• estimate and find the product of problems such as 98 × 76 and can show that I can change the order of the factors and still get the same answer _____

• estimate and find the answers to problems such as 7) 709 _____

• find the answer to word problems such as—
Fay collected 56 pop bottles on Monday, 12 on Tuesday, 24 on Wednesday, and 5 on Thursday. She couldn't find any more so she sold those she had. How many did she sell _____

• make a model to show $\frac{3}{4}$ and a model to show $\frac{2}{8}$ and compare their size, using one of the symbols <, >, or = _____

• find the answer to $\frac{3}{5} + \frac{2}{5}$ or $\frac{5}{7} - \frac{2}{7}$ and ny answers that are other names for one

• select examples of a sphere, cone, cylinder, cube, or rectangular prism _____

• use metric or customary units of measure to find the length of a piece of rope and tell how much it weighs _____

• use centimetres, metres, kilometres, inches, feet, yards, or miles as units of measure _____

• make a tally chart to show the results of a coin-toss experiment _____

Figure 9.2.

the classroom. A student who desires tutoring removes this flag and comes to ask for help.

In addition to completing the unit check-out, each student can record his progress in his "personal progress folder." Here he records the date on which he completed the unit and his score on the check-out. In addition, he can record the date on which he masters each of the objectives in the entire fourth grade curriculum. The segment of the personal progress folder in which the student records his mastery of the fourth grade objectives is shown in Figure 9.2.

The personal progress folder also indicates which units serve as prerequisites for subsequent units. For example, mastery of Units 2 and 3 are prerequisite for Unit 5. Mastery of Unit 5 is a prerequisite for Units 8 and 9. However, a student who has not mastered Unit 5 can work simultaneously on Unit 6, 4, 7 or 13, since successful performance in these units is not dependent upon mastery of Unit 5. If some students are having difficulty with Unit 5 and the teacher wishes to proceed with whole group instruction in mathematics, the students can work on one or more of the other unit sequences.

Science Research Associates Assessment Instruments

The final example surveys assessment instruments published by one corporation, SRA, which can be purchased by schools or individual classroom teachers for incorporation into the mastery curriculum.

Achievement Test Programs

Three of the achievement test programs are usually given on a school-wide, district-wide, or state-wide basis. The first program, called *Mastery: an evaluation tool* (MET), provides criterion-referenced information concerning the mastery of major curriculum objectives. The second program, called the *Achievement Series* (ACH), supplies norm-referenced data on major curriculum-related skill areas (clusters of objectives). The third program, called the *SRA Norm-Referenced/Criterion Referenced Testing Program* (NRT/CRT), makes available both norm-referenced and criterion-referenced information.

The DIA Assessment

The fourth assessment program, called *diagnosis®: an instructional aid* (DIA), is used in the classroom at the direction of the teacher. This program provides criterion-referenced information about individual student mastery of specific instructional objectives. A "Prescription Guide" references each objective to instruction in widely used basal texts and supplemental materials.

The DIA assessment is often used in conjunction with the school-wide or district-wide survey tests, such as MET or ACH. The survey test identifies potential areas of weakness. Then DIA is used in the classroom to identify the specific weaknesses and to locate appropriate prescriptions.

Tests from these SRA programs can be employed as the pre-assessment, diagnostic, and postassessment components of a mastery curriculum. The following are examples of actual uses of the SRA instruments.

Pre–Post Assessment. The MET permits the selection of locally relevant objectives and the construction of criterion-referenced tests customized to a school or district's curriculum. The MET program consists of two parallel sets of items for each objective; hence, a school can have two custom-built forms. Form A can be used for preassessment, and Form B can be used for postassessment.

For example, during the month of July, the teachers and curriculum specialists in District X selected the objectives they planned to emphasize during the coming school year. The list of objectives was sent to SRA, where three test items measuring each objective were selected from SRA's current item pool. The first version of the test of these objectives, Form A, was prepared using these items, and the test administration materials and answer sheets were printed. Within 7 weeks after the list of objectives was received by SRA, the Form A tests were completed and mailed to the schools. Form A served as a preassessment measure. This test was administered by the teachers, and the completed answer sheets were returned to SRA for scoring. SRA then scored the tests and returned the results to the schools in the form of individual student reports, classroom group reports and school- or district-wide summaries.

The student report indicated whether or not each student had mastered each objective. It also illustrated how well the student did on each of the three items measuring the objective. Overall test performance was also provided in terms of the number and percentage of objectives mastered. This report provided the teacher with information to identify objectives that needed attention, and appropriate instruction was provided.

Throughout the school year, the DIA was used by teachers in the classroom. Each objective in MET is correlated to the tests (Probes) in DIA: Hence, each teacher administered those Probes associated with the objectives that had not been mastered. In some instances, Probes were used to verify that the MET test data were accurate. In some cases, the Probes were used to do further diagnosis. Most often, however, the Probes were used by teachers to check mastery after instruction. Throughout, the Prescription Guide was used to locate appropriate instructional methods and materials.

At the end of the school year, SRA sent District X the Form B tests, which employed an alternate set of test items to measure the same objectives. SRA scored the tests and again provided reports which served as postassessment measures.

Annual Objective-Based Assessment.   District Y could not afford to purchase tests for both preassessment and postassessment. Instead, in March of the school year, teachers, administrators, and curriculum specialists chose objectives that posttested this year's curriculum and also selected objectives that pretested next year's curriculum. The list of objectives was sent to SRA where custom MET tests were prepared. When the tests were administered, SRA scored them and provided score reports that covered objectives for both years. Reports were given to this year's teachers for postassessment purposes. Duplicates of the same reports were set aside for next year's teachers for preassessment purposes. The DIA program was used throughout the school year, as in District X.

Pre—post comparisons are still possible in District Y because SRA alternated forms of MET for each grade. School-wide and district-wide pre—post comparisons were made year to year rather than at the beginning and end of each year.

Annual Assessment with Norms.   District Z used the DIA program in conjunction with the ACH. The ACH series provides the usual normative data for specific tests and subtests, but it also supplies information for major skill areas as measured by clusters of items (cluster analysis). Various Probes from DIA are correlated to the skill areas from ACH. In May, District Z administered ACH. Like District Y, SRA score reports were kept by current teachers with copies passed on to next year's teachers. In August, at a preschool workshop, teachers received Individual Skills Profiles (cluster analysis), which alerted them to possible skill weaknesses. Then, in September, DIA assessment measures were employed by teachers to diagnose specific problems, prescribe appropriate instruction, and recheck for mastery. The only difference between Districts Y and Z was the choice of survey assessment instruments.

The Best of Both Worlds.   Within the 1977 academic year, SRA published its NRT/CRT Program, which produces both objective-based and normative assessments of student performance. This program enables a school or district to use criterion-referenced preassessment or postassessment, while simultaneously obtaining normative information concerning student progress. Short forms of ACH have been developed that can be administered along with the MET tests. A school or district chooses its objectives, SRA develops the MET test, and SRA sends the school or district the MET test and the shortened ACH test. SRA then scores both tests, and provides results from both on the same set of reports. The teachers using the program obtain the MET correlation to their curriculum and an assessment of where the students stand on general content in relation to their peers. At the same time, criterion-referenced assessments can be made on a school- or district-wide basis without interrupting the continuity of the longitudinal norm-referenced assessment data base. The DIA program also can be used by teachers, as in the previous example.

An Example of Teacher Use. Among the SRA score reports that teachers find useful is the Individual Student Profile, or ISP. The ISP is designed to provide the maximum amount of diagnostic information appropriate for use with individual students.

The ISP from SRA's criterion-referenced program, MET, is illustrated in Figure 9.3. It provides the information needed to analyze each student's performance on each objective covered by the test and on each item measuring the objective. It also provides summary data for the test as a whole.

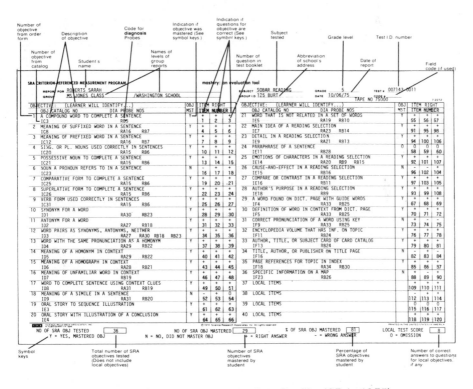

Figure 9.3. *Individual Student Profile (SRA, 1975).*

OBJECTIVE: (LEARNER WILL IDENTIFY...)		OBJ	ITEM RIGHT		
OBJ CATALOG NO	DIA PROBE NOS	MST	ITEM NUMBER		
21 WORD THAT IS NOT RELATED IN A SET OF WORDS		Y	+	+	+
IE5	RA19 RB10		55	56	57
22 MAIN IDEA OF A READING SELECTION		Y	+	+	+
IE7	_ RA23 RB14		91	95	98
23 DETAIL IN A READING SELECTION		Y	+	+	+
IE9	RA21 RB13		94	100	106
24 PARAPHRASE OF A SENTENCE		0	0	0	0
IE11	RB28		58	59	60
25 EMOTIONS OF CHARACTERS IN A READING SELECTION		Y	+	+	+
IE14	RA20 RB9 RB15		92	101	107
26 CAUSE-AND-EFFECT IN A READING SELECTION		N	-	-	+
IE15	RB16		96	102	104

Figure 9.4. *Excerpt from Individual Student Profile, produced in conjunction with SRA* Criterion-Referenced Program: An Evaluation Tool, The Guide to Mastery *(SRA, 1975).*

A portion of an ISP is pictured in Figure 9.4. The teacher can look at the 23rd objective, for example, and find out the following:

1. It covers *detail in a reading selection.*

2. The SRA objective number is IE9.

3. The corresponding DIA Probe numbers are RA21 and RB13.

4. The student mastered the objective—received a "Y."

5. The student answered all items correctly.

6. The items covering the objective were 94, 100, and 106.

Since mastery of the 23rd objective has been indicated, the student can proceed to the next objective.

The student omitted the 24th objective; the "O" indicates that the items covering that objective were not attempted by the student. Perhaps, during the testing, the teacher instructed the students to bypass items 58—60. If not, the student may have felt those items were too difficult; the teacher should clarify what happened by talking with the student.

Going on, the student mastered the 25th objective but did not master the 26th (*cause and effect*). The student incorrectly answered items 96 and 102. At this point, if the teacher has prepared further diagnostic materials or instructional activities, the student can be directed to go to them for further work. Or, the teacher can direct the student to probe RB16 from DIA for in-depth diagnosis and instructional prescriptions. In some instances, teachers find that an immediate follow-up to the MET data with DIA helps the teacher to confirm mastery and discover the underlying causes of learning

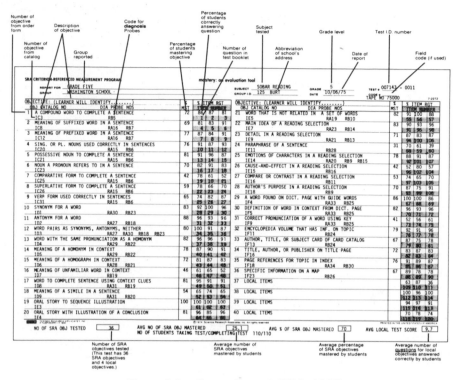

Figure 9.5. *Group Report (SRA, 1975).*

problems. MET tends to survey terminal learning objectives, and DIA often covers the specific corresponding instructional objectives.

The Group Report for the teacher's class is illustrated in Figure 9.5. That report indicates that the class had trouble with the 24th and 26th objectives. For example, only 42% of the class mastered the 26th objective. The students had particular problems with items 96 and 104, while 80% of the class got item 102 correct. When a sufficient number of students have trouble with a particular objective or item, the teacher has the option of employing group instruction in the remediation process.

SRA Learning Cycle. Realizing that the MET and DIA programs relate directly to instructional decisions, SRA also offers a management system for continuous-progress decision making. It is called the *SRA Learning Cycle.*

The Learning Cycle consists of continuous progress charts for students and groups of students, and an easy-to-use guide.

Figure 9.6 is an example from the guide presenting information

WORD IDENTIFICATION SKILLS

16. Phonics—Two Sounds of G

Objective: Orally given a word that begins with the sound /g/ or /j/, the learner
will identify a word that has the same initial hard or soft consonant
sound represented by the letter *g.*

Assessment Options:
I Formal
SRA *mastery* test objective 1B3
SRA *diagnosis* Probe RA-11
II Informal (sample)
A. Give each student a worksheet with rows of words beginning with either
the /g/ or /j/ sound. For example:
1. got   jump   gem   gamble
2. jelly   ginger   gobble   gap

B. Say a word twice that begins with the consonant sound you want to
test . . . "general" pause "general."

C. Ask the students to circle the words in row 1 that begin with the same
consonant sound they hear at the beginning of the word *general* . . . etc.

Learning Experiences:

Schoolhouse™ I; Word Attack	Reading Lab®Ia Power Builders	Reading Lab®Ib Power Builders	Reading Lab®Ic Power Builders	The SRA Skills Series: Phonics
Lime 17, 18	Green 2C, 5C, 8C, 11C	Lime 2C, 5C, 8C, 11C	Tan 2C, 5C, 8C, 11C	Unit 27

Figure 9.6.   *Example selected from* Learning Cycle Guide *(SRA, 1976).*

for a single learning objective. As can be seen from the example, the
following is provided:

1. Statement of the learning objective,
2. MET and DIA assessment options,
3. Informal assessment examples,
4. Page references to learning experiences that are available
from leading SRA supplemental materials.

A Final Note—The Mastery Criteria

In selecting the mastery criteria to be employed in its criterion-
referenced tests, SRA took into consideration the practical limitations that apply to administration of published tests in schools. The
cold, hard facts are that schools typically allocate less than 1% of the
materials of instruction budget to the purchase and scoring of assessment instruments.

If SRA were to design and publish a test that contained a representative number of items sufficient to sample the domain of each objective in the curriculum, the test would be too long and expensive. Most schools would not have allocated resources to their assessment budgets sufficient to enable them to purchase or administer such tests.

In view of these practical limitations, SRA adopted two separate approaches to setting mastery criteria, one for its criterion-referenced survey measures (MET) and the second for its in depth diagnostic measures (DIA), both of which were referred to above.

The MET tests attempt to strike a balance between an adequate number of objectives and an adequate number of items per objective, while meeting the practical requirements schools have for survey testing. The MET tests contain three multiple-choice items measuring each objective. SRA recommends that a student must correctly answer all three items to show mastery of a specific objective. This criterion was decided on after careful analysis of the chance factor involved in attaining mastery, and after an extensive consideration of overall test length. The chance factor is crucial since these tests will be used for preliminary and final identification of students mastery levels.

In Table 9.1, the probabilities of attaining mastery by chance alone are illustrated for one to five items per objective and various mastery criteria. The probability of attaining mastery by chance alone when the criterion is 3 out of 3 is .016. The probabilities for 4 out of 4 and 4 out of 5 are lower, but they would require increased test lengths of 33% and 67% respectively to cover the same number of objectives, while yielding very little increase in precision.

TABLE 9.1
Probability of Attaining Mastery by Chance Alone

Mastery criterion	Total number of items per objective[a]				
	1	2	3	4	5
1 or more correct	.250	.438	.578	.684	.764
2 or more correct	—	.063	.156	.262	.368
3 or more correct	—	—	.016	.051	.104
4 or more correct	—	—	—	.004	.016
5 correct	—	—	—	—	.001

[a]Each item has four choices (*SRA, 1975*).

For example, to cover 30 objectives with 5 items per objective the total test length would be 150 items and require for test administration three to four classroom periods. However, a 30 objective MET test would have only 90 items and require only two classroom periods. The 5 item version, with a criterion of 4 out of 5, would have the same chance probability of .016 as the recommended MET criterion of 3 out of 3. Note that a 90 item test with 5 items per objective would measure mastery of only 16 objectives. In the interest of economics, classroom interruption, and student fatigue, SRA decided on 3 items with a 3 out of 3 criterion.

As the second approach to setting mastery levels, SRA designed DIA with several different types of diagnostic tests (probes) intended to provide in-depth assessment of the causes of student learning strengths and weaknesses. These strengths and weaknesses have been identified, prior to the administration of the DIA probes, by survey tests, such as MET or the DIA survey, or in the course of the instruction.

DIA Probes contain various forms of test items, including multiple-choice, fill-in, and open-ended questions. The teacher selects the number and type of items administered to an individual student, based upon his or her judgment concerning the best approach to diagnosing that student's learning status. SRA suggests that the teacher employ an 80% mastery criterion with the DIA probes. However, the actual determination of the mastery criterion for each diagnostic test remains the responsibility of the individual classroom teacher.

Formative and Summative Mastery Model Curriculum Evaluation

As this brief description of currently available mastery model curricular materials indicates, sufficient instructional materials are now available to enable sophisticated formative and summative evaluation of the mastery model. Throughout this volume, the evaluative research conducted to date has been summarized and a critique provided.

As this review has demonstrated all too clearly, most of the research investigating mastery model implementations has employed one or perhaps two measures of student cognitive achievement and/or an all-too-brief student self-report affective consequence measure. Only one series of investigations (Okey & Ciesla, 1975) included a formal evaluation of the mastery teacher training materials. Only two investigations (Harrison, & Harrison, 1975; Lee *et al.*, 1971) incorporated observational measures of mastery teacher behavior. However, one major strength of this research is that, in contrast with research in some areas of education and psychology, most of these studies have been conducted in classroom rather than laboratory settings. The advantages of conducting mastery model implementation research in classroom and other natural settings far outweigh the disadvantages and should be continued in future research.

A major defect in the mastery model implementation research conducted to date has been the use of excessively simplistic research designs in the investigation of this highly complex, multidimensional process implemented over long time durations, having effects lasting for even greater time periods. The mastery model has demonstrated potential for producing positive cognitive and affective student consequences, as well as for increasing existing knowledge concerning the learning and instructional processes. Though complex longitudinal research is costly, these results indicate that it is warranted here.

The mastery implementation evaluation model developed by this author identifies the dimensions of the mastery implementation process that should be measured or otherwise taken into account in formative and summative evaluation of the model. The complete Torshen Mastery Implementation Evaluation Model (MIEM) is illustrated in Figure 9.7.

Research employing the MIEM to investigate mastery will utilize significantly more complex research designs than have been employed in this area. However, most models represent oversimplifications of the natural processes. Researchers employing MIEM should not hesitate to add additional dimensions or to increase the complexity of the dimensions included. One of the primary objectives of this model is to increase the consistency, and thus the comparability, of the information derived from mastery research. One cannot expect that all investigators will measure each of the dimensions in the MIEM. This evaluation model facilitates the collection, synthesis, and interpretation of data investigating subsets of the dimensions. Additionally, it is hoped that this model will encourage researchers to increase the number and type of dimensions measured in each investigation.

The diagram of the MIEM is, by and large, self-explanatory. The vertical component of the model enumerates the sources from which data are to be collected. The six basic data sources categories are as

DATA SOURCES

1. INSTRUCTION
   Content
   Method
   Evaluation
2. STUDENT
3. TEACHER(S)
4. CLASS GROUP(S)
5. SCHOOL
6. SCHOOL
   DISTRICT AND
   COMMUNITY

DATA COLLECTION METHOD(S)
DATA COLLECTION INSTRUMENT(S)
 SAMPLE
ADMINISTRATION DATE(S)
ADMINISTRATOR QUALIFICATIONS

OBJECTIVES

Domain
Mastery level
Selection procedures

PREASSESSMENT
INSTRUCTION
DIAGNOSTIC ASSESSMENT

Form 1
Form 2, etc.
Recycle

PRESCRIPTION

Remediation
Enrichment
Instructional sequence
 Prescription

POSTASSESSMENT

Initial measurement
Retention 1
Retention 2, etc.
Evidence re: generalizability
Relationship to long-term
 goal attainment

MASTERY IMPLEMENTATION
CONDITION
CONTROL CONDITION I,
CONTROL II, etc.

Mastery model components

Figure 9.7. *Torshen Mastery Implementation Evaluation Model.*

follows: (1) instruction, including content, method, and evaluation; (2) the student, representing each student participating in the research (the units of analysis should include the individual student, the classroom group, the school, and the school district); (3) the teacher(s); (4) the class group(s), including physical characteristics of the classroom, classroom management procedures, student grouping methods and classroom climate assessments; (5) the school, including the administration, available support services, and the origin and continuing perceptions of mastery model implementation, if any; (6) the school district and community.

The *instruction* category should include descriptions of the nature, level, and structure of the subject matter content. The type of instructional material should be recorded. Any specific technical equipment employed in the instructional process should be identified. The nature, variety, and implementation of prescriptive materials, including remedial and enrichment instruction, should be recorded in detail.

Data should also include the amount of instructional time allotted to each segment of the instruction and the proportion of the allotted instructional time that each student spends actively engaged in learning. Time actively devoted to learning outside of the classroom should also be recorded. The extent to which the teacher and/or the student determine the student's rate of progress (pace) through the instructional sequence should be measured.

The evaluation measures should be described in detail. This description should include the purposes for which the measures were developed, including the objectives the measures were designed to assess, if any. Mastery levels should be identified and the derivations of and justifications for these levels should be recorded. If alternate forms of a measure have been employed, evidence of the comparability of these forms should be recorded. Any other available information concerning the evaluation measures, such as examinations of the dimensionality of the measures, consistency of the structure of the measures across varied samples of individuals, inclusion of a specific measure .in a relevant multitrait–multimethod analysis, and so forth, should also be recorded. Any investigations of the relationship of a measure to other criteria, such as on-the-job performance or performance in more advanced related instruction, should be identified. (See Spady, 1977, and Spady & Mitchell, 1977, for a discussion of this topic.)

Examples of data to be included in the *student* category include cognitive, affective, and psychomotor entry characteristics. Crucial variables in this category are the extent and accuracy student's knowledge of the long-term goals and the objectives of the curriculum. The student's personal identification with these goals and objectives, his willingness to accept them as his own and his motivation and persistence allocated to achieving them are also included. Additional variables in this category are those involving the student role, including the nature and extent of student-initiated goals and activities, the definitions and frequency of occurrence of acceptable and unacceptable student behavior, and the extent of adaptability and flexibility of student learning methods and techniques.

Other student variables that may relate indirectly to the subject matter and method should also be measured, including students' perception of relationships to peers, teachers, and additional significant others, student perception of personal power over academic consequences, student long-term goals and their relationship to academic performance. In addition, factors such as student's age, sex, height, weight, sibling position, socioeconomic status, delinquency, and attendance record, physical and mental health, and so forth should be recorded.

Examples of data to be included in the *teacher* category are teacher's acceptance or rejection of the learning goals and objectives, the nature and extent of teacher planning and the teacher's own assessments of the subject matter and curriculum. The teacher's expectations concerning each student's performance and the teacher's affinity for or dislike of each student should be assessed. Teacher behavior, including proportion of instructional time devoted to lecture, discussion, seat work, small-group work, and individual contact with the student should be measured. In addition, teacher entry characteristics, such as age, sex, number of years of teaching experience, number of times and frequency of teaching present course, nature and duration of training, extent of in-service training, in-service training and other training relevant to mastery (if any), should be identified. The teacher's use of information obtained from evaluative procedures and the nature and effectiveness of the prescriptive teaching should be measured. The nature and effectiveness of the teacher's classroom management procedures and style should be measured. The teacher's knowledge of, attitude toward, and implementation of mastery procedures should be measured.

Examples of data collected in the *class group* category include classroom climate measures administered to both teachers and students. Student measures can assess whether the popularity center of the classroom is diffuse or clique-centered, whether the students feel they can be helpful to others or whether they perceive that they should look out only for themselves, and so forth. Teacher measures can assess whether the teacher creates a warm or cold atmosphere, whether the teacher is persistent or lax in discipline and in encouraging students to complete learning activities, whether the teacher is satisfied or dissatisfied with his or her position, whether the management and control are adequate or behavior problems are uncontrolled, and so forth.

The class group category should also measure the characteristics of the instructional space, including the amount of space provided per individual student and whether the available space is open or subdivided. The number of students per teacher should be identified. The availability and flexibility in the use of resources available per individual student within the classroom and outside of the classroom should be identified. Whether supplemental and basic instructional material are purchased or made by teachers or students, and the extent of teacher and student participation in selecting materials should be assessed.

In the school category, data should include information about the numbers, prescribed duties, and qualifications of administrators in the school, and about the power of the classroom teacher within that structure. The number and functions of the support services should be identified, including the number and assigned responsibilities of the faculty and staff. Both the availability and the actual use of these services should be measured. If at least one mastery model curriculum unit is being implemented in a school, then the origin of the decision to implement this model should be identified. The proportion of the curriculum in each classroom group devoted to mastery should be measured. For each administrator and teacher who comes into contact with the mastery curriculum, measures of that individual's knowledge of, attitude toward, and interest in mastery should be taken. Rewards available to staff and students for successfully implementing mastery should be identified.

The *school district and community* category should include an assessment of the extent to which school district personnel, parents and community members have accurate knowledge of the long-range learning goals employed in the school curriculum. Their perceptions of the school's learning goals, including their acceptance or rejection of the goals and their perception of the students' success in attaining highly valued learning outcomes should be measured. If the mastery model is implemented in a curriculum of a school within the district, perceptions of that curriculum held by parents, community leaders, and other community representatives should be assessed. If the school district personnel or community representatives have participated in developing the learning goals and initiating or maintaining the mastery curriculum, measurement of this process should be included. Any significant problems or major changes in attitude on the part of the initiators and later participants should be assessed. Socioeconomic status information and information concerning the distances students commute to school and the processes by which parents and/or administrators determine which students can attend that school should be included.

The variables identified in the above data source categories are intended as examples of the variables to be measured in mastery model implementation evaluation research. It is expected that researchers will add additional variables relevant to specific research investigations. Measures of each of the variables should be obtained in both mastery and comparable nonmastery curricula.

The horizontal components of the MIEM delineate categories of information relevant to data collection itself and to the six components of the mastery model. The first category, *data collection method*, requires the identification of the method or methods employed. It is recommended that multiple methods be employed, including test performance, nonparticipant observation, participant observation, and self-report. The data collection method should be identified for each variable measure.

The second category, *data collection instruments*, requires a listing of any and all instruments or other measures employed to assess each variable. The origin of the instrument, any relevant normative, criterion, or validation information, and the reason for selecting the instrument should be recorded.

The *sample* is the third data collection category. For each variable measured, the number and relevant characteristics of participating individuals should be identified. If a variable is measured at more than one point in time, individuals who participate in multiple measurements should be distinguished from those who participate less frequently or only once.

The fourth category, *administration dates*, requires the listing of each date on which each instrument is administered. The actual date of administration for each individual subject must be identified, even if that date varies considerably from the date of the majority of administrations of the instrument or from the planned administration schedule.

The fifth category, *administrator qualifications*, requires the listing of the relevant qualifications of the persons administering each measure of each variable on each administration date. Research personnel must be distinguished from personnel participating in the mastery model implementation. Each administrator's role in the mastery model implementation and/or the research must be identified. If an administrator is conducting the research to fulfill a requirement for completion of a Ph.D. degree or other degree, this fact should be identified, since much of the mastery research conducted to date has been both designed and administered by Ph.D. candidates. At present, a reasonable argument can be made for the proposition that the presence of a doctoral candidate, rather than the mastery model itself, accounted for the significant increases in student's cognitive performance reported in a substantial number of mastery model research investigations.

The next six categories represent the *six components of the mastery model*. Each of these categories requires the identification of the variables measured that are relevant to that particular component. Each of these categories must be completed, regardless of whether the instructional program being measured is considered a mastery condition, a special treatment condition, a nonmastery condition, or another form of control group.

The data should be organized so that a variable relevant to one or more of the six component categories is listed under the relevant category. For example, in the *objective category*, the objectives of the unit, sequence, or course should be identified in conjunction with the instruction data source category. The origin of the objectives should be identified in conjunction with the relevant category, teacher and/or student and/or school and/or community, and so forth. Teachers' and students' evaluation of the objectives, their attitudes towards the objectives, and the expectations concerning attainment of the objectives should be recorded in this category. The mastery levels implemented in the evaluation component of the instructional category should also be identified.

The domain of competence that each objective represents should be identified. In addition, the teacher's and each student's understanding of the meaning of each objective should be measured. The rationale for including the objective in this particular curriculum should be recorded and any evidence obtained in validation of this rationale should be included. The information relevant to the five other components should be organized in a similar fashion.

When this mastery implementation evaluation model is applied in research relevant to the mastery model, the significant dimensions of the implementation can be measured. The statistical technology and computer capacity needed to deal with the complex data collection and analysis procedures prescribed by the MIEM are now available.

The role and importance of each dimension and the variables within that dimension can be better understood when more of the significant dimensions of each implementation are measured. Furthermore, the use of a consistent categorization system will facilitate comparison and synthesis of the processes and results of distinct research investigations.

10

Problems and Potential

Although many of the processes and procedures included in the mastery approach to competency-based education are not new, implementing the entire mastery model is likely to require some fairly substantial changes in the typical educational program. Implementing a mastery program carries the risks and problems associated with making changes in established institutions, in general, and implementing educational innovations, in particular.

Administrative Problems

Administrative problems may be created when a mastery program is implemented. These problems can result from the very aspects of the mastery model that are among its strengths.

The mastery model permits varied and flexible grouping of students. This model also enables students to work toward diverse objectives using a wide range of instructional methods and materials. This diversity in the instructional program creates a need for extensive record keeping. When students are working toward different objectives using different instructional methods and materials, it is essential to keep a record of each student's instructional program.

It is also necessary to record the results of the various assessments of each student's progress. After the student has been in a mastery program for several years, his record could contain hundreds of pieces of information about his progress. Record-keeping procedures that highlight important information and do not require extensive amounts of teacher and student time must be used. The student progress folder included in the Mathematics Learning System (SRA, 1974) shown in Chapter 9 provides an example of an efficient record-keeping device that is not dependent upon the availability of computers or other equipment.

In using the records, each student's rights of privacy must be protected. Only qualified professionals and other persons directly affected by the records should have access to them. The records should be reviewed periodically, and inaccurate and inappropriate information should be removed. School personnel should receive assistance in interpreting the information in the records. Negative information should not receive excessive emphasis.

An additional problem created by increasing the diversity of the educational program involves guidance and placement. Many students may need assistance in planning the instructional programs that are most appropriate for them. Teachers assist the students in their classes in developing appropriate instructional programs. However, students may need assistance from a guidance specialist in order to select the curriculum and the course sequence most appropriate for them. Guidance and placement specialists may also be needed to administer and interpret postassessment, long-term retention and summative assessment measures. These specialists can also assist in establishing and maintaining complex daily schedules associated with extensive variations in the grouping of students.

Another source of potential problems is associated with the reward system of the mastery model. The model is designed to maximize the number of students attaining the performance levels defined as adequate for competence. The students' success in attaining these levels is intended to function as a reward for their efforts. Students' success is also intended to serve as the faculty's reward for their efforts in planning and preparation, in encouraging and motivating the students, in searching for methods and materials to meet each student's needs, in assessing students' performance and making appropriate modifications in the instructional program. Success of the students is also intended to reward students, faculty, and other persons for the time, effort, and cost involved in preparing and implementing the mastery program. However, students and teachers may be accustomed to receiving other rewards from prior educational programs.

In some educational programs, a class is considered to be well disciplined when each student works quietly in his seat. Discipline is considered less than adequate when students make noise and walk around the classroom. Much of the individual and group work in the mastery curriculum may require students to talk to each other and move around the classroom. Rewarding students who work quietly in their seats or imposing controls to keep students working quietly in their seats may not be appropriate when the instructional program requires students to communicate with each other and to use different learning areas of the classroom.

In some nonmastery educational programs, teachers do not revise an instructional program in accord with the needs and performance levels of specific groups of students. Once a teacher has prepared lessons and selected instructional materials, these plans are used repeatedly for several years. As a result, the teacher has time to devote to other professional activities, including serving on committees and pursuing research or other professional interests. Committee service and research produce their own rewards. The mastery curriculum requires substantial commitment of teacher time devoted to preparation and modification of the program to meet the individual student's needs. Practitioners implementing a mastery model curriculum may have less time to devote to other professional activities, at least in the beginning stages of the implementation. Practitioners need to receive appropriate rewards for the time and effort they are devoting to implementing the mastery process.

In some educational programs, many of the students spend a substantial amount of their time in activities other than those specified in the course curriculum. For some students, the primary rewards of schooling may come from the opportunities that school provides to get together with their friends, to read comic books and other nonacademic literature, or to daydream and sleep. Some students may need to devote more time to learning than they have in the past if they are to attain mastery. If the students are to devote the needed time, they may have to forego some of the rewards that their free time provided. Providing free time and social activities as a reward for mastery of educational objectives can encourage students to devote the necessary time to learning.

Neither students nor teachers ever want to look stupid. In some educational programs, a person looks stupid when he does not know an answer to a question or when he makes a mistake. Much of the evaluation in the mastery curriculum is aimed at measuring what students do not know and identifying the mistakes they have made.

The assessment procedures are also designed to identify weaknesses in the teaching methods and materials. These procedures produce recommendations that can help teachers improve the instructional program. The mastery assessment procedures can only be effective when teachers and students identify students' weaknesses and weaknesses in the instructional program. Students and teachers may need to be assured that they will not be considered stupid when weaknesses are identified.

In average-based educational programs, a few students in each class are evaluated as better than the other students. Some students may devote considerable time and effort toward being better than the other students. The mastery model places no limit on the number of students that can be considered successful. Students and teachers are encouraged to cooperate so that the maximum number of students can attain mastery. Teachers are encouraged to share with other instructors any instructional methods and materials they have found to be effective. Although competition will not be eliminated, cooperation may be increased. Teachers who were rewarded because their students were the highest achievers and students who were rewarded because they achieved better than all of their peers may find this type of reward to be less accessible in the mastery curriculum. However, these students and teachers may find other rewards, perhaps resulting from increased cooperation, meaningfulness, and diversity in the educational program or from the ability to progress further in a particular subject matter.

Finally, implementing a mastery program creates the administrative problems associated with starting any new program. The school faculty must be receptive and interested in making the change. The leadership must be supportive. And financial resources must be available, if needed.

According to Dennis Carmichael (1973, 1974), superintendent of a school district during the process of implementing mastery model curricula, the following administrative conditions are essential to successful implementation of the mastery model. (For additional consideration of this issue, refer to Campbell, 1969; Elmore, 1974.) Persons in the district must acknowledge that the existing educational programs can and should be improved. They must be willing to question, analyze, and evaluate the existing educational program and performances produced by that program.

Further, the school district needs a systematic management process which is capable of assessing student needs, analyzing the existing programs, selecting objectives, preparing instructional programs to accomplish these objectives, and monitoring and evaluating students' performance in these programs. When a mastery program is implemented, there is less need for a general supervisory staff and a greater need for staff trained in needs assessment, instructional analysis, program development and evaluation procedures. Preservice and in-service training programs should provide teachers with the needed skills. The management system should provide for free exchange of ideas among teachers, students, administrators, and the public.

Superintendent Carmichael found that effective leadership was crucial to the success of the mastery program. High level administrators should have knowledge and experience in a systematic management process. In each school building, the highest ranking administrator should subscribe to the district goals and objectives and be skilled in motivating teachers to implement the programs associated with these goals and objectives. The leadership should be able to involve parents, students, and teachers in the whole process of implementing mastery.

Teachers who were receptive to mastery met the following conditions. They were enthusiastic and viewed their work as satisfying and rewarding. They measured their success in terms of how well their students learned. They were aware of the learning process including differences in cognitive and affective processes. They saw the student as taking an active role. These teachers assumed the role of a director of individual learning. Instead of simply presenting information, they worked with students to find the best program for each student. The teachers were well informed and they participated in school and district planning. They viewed professional development positively and identified the areas in which they needed in-service training (Carmichael, 1974).

This description of administrative problems associated with implementing mastery applies to implementation on the district-wide basis. If mastery is to be implemented on a smaller scale, such as one school or one department within a school or one classroom, the conditions specified may be less dependent on the school system leadership.

Technical Problems

In addition to administrative problems, the mastery approach to competency-based education raises a number of technical problems.

The competency-based education process is based on definitions of performances students are expected to demonstrate as evidence that they have attained competence. Working definitions of competencies provide the basis for the objectives of the curriculum. Substantial amounts of educational resources are allocated to producing the performance levels that have been defined as adequate for competence. Mastery procedures can only be applied when a competence can be operationally defined and attainment can be measured.

Once a competence has been operationally defined and an educational program is designed to produce the prescribed levels of performance, substantial amounts of educational resources are allocated to producing the prescribed types and levels of performance. When the prescribed performances are judged to be of high priority, the instructional program may encourage the student to spend whatever time and effort is needed in order to master these performances. Since student time and educational resources are limited, the student may forego other instruction as the cost of attaining mastery of the objectives that have been judged to be crucial.

Allocating the resources the student needs to attain prescribed performance levels is efficient to the extent that the prescribed levels are, indeed, crucial for the student to attain and the performances prescribed do adequately represent the domain of competence that they have been operationally defined to represent. However, if the teachers themselves misunderstand the concepts and processes identified in the objectives, which they are responsible for teaching to the students, the curriculum does not implement the intended objectives (Herron, 1969). Furthermore, the content and crucial concepts must be understood and interpreted accurately by the teachers (Herron, 1969). If the performances are not crucial for the student to attain, if the prescribed mastery levels are inappropriate, if crucial aspects of the domain of competence have been omitted from the objectives, then allocating instructional resources to attaining the prescribed performance levels is inefficient and inaccurate. The effectiveness of the mastery process hinges on accurate implementation of the working definitions of performances prescribed as intended outcomes of the process.

Extensive research is needed to explore operational definitions of domains of competence and to evaluate the relevance and accuracy of various categories and levels of performance. At the present time, practitioners must rely heavily on their professional judgment as a basis for operationally defining competence and prescribing performance objectives. What objectives must be mastered if the student is to be successful in future courses, on the job, as a human being? Which objectives really make a difference to his future success? Of these crucial performances, which are most likely to be developed as a result of participating in planned instructional programs in school? Large scale longitudinal research is needed to provide the information needed to deal with these issues.

Mastery components also create technical problems associated with instructional methods and materials. In average-based instructional programs, most or all of the students are exposed to the same instruction. Because this instruction is usually more appropriate for some students than for others, students' individual differences create differences in the levels of performance that each student attains as a result of his exposure to the instruction.

Mastery programs require a greater repertoire of instructional possibilities than do average-based educational programs. Teachers and students need ready access to methods and materials appropriate for varied objectives, using varied approaches to instruction appropriate for students who enter the program with varied levels of competence. Alternative instructional methods and materials are also needed to remediate whatever learning difficulties may occur throughout the program. Often, one teacher must supervise the varied instruction occurring simultaneously in his class. Students who are using diverse instructional methods and materials must work side by side and compete for assistance from the teacher. Teachers may need in-service training and consulting assistance in developing and implementing appropriate classroom management.

Participants in a mastery program need to explore the instructional resources available to them and select the most appropriate methods and materials. The materials should be categorized by skill and topic so that alternative materials can be readily available. This process can be very time-consuming. Expert assistance may be needed. As is the case with definitions of competence and objective selection, practitioners must rely heavily on their professional judgments.

Practitioners must have ready access to results of research investigating the effectiveness of instructional methods and materials and the risks involved in using them. Preservice and in-service educational programs are needed to help practitioners incorporate the results of this research into their instructional programs. Services that evaluate available methods and materials and that design methods and materials to meet special needs should be available to practitioners.

Competency-based education in general, and mastery programs in particular, create numerous problems associated with measuring performance. The mastery approach to competency-based education includes the identification of specific levels of performance that students are expected to attain. Assessment procedures are needed to determine whether a student has attained the level of performance specified for him. Measurement procedures are also needed to identify each student's learning weaknesses so that appropriate instruction can be prescribed. In addition to providing information about each student's performance, measurement procedures are needed to evaluate the strengths and weaknesses of the curriculum.

Mastery programs employ measurement procedures that measure each student's performance and compare his performance with a standard of performance that has been defined as acceptable. Most available standardized, norm-referenced achievement tests were not designed to produce this information. These tests may be appropriate for measuring a range of important performances for students who perform close to the test mean. But they are not appropriate for measuring a range of important performances for students who perform considerably above or below the test mean. Mastery programs may require construction of tests that measure each student's progress toward attaining all of the relevant performances that a particular program is designed to produce.

Several problems arise in the process of constructing the performance-based assessment measures needed for mastery programs. In addition to general problems associated with criterion-referenced assessment, mastery programs often require the use of alternative forms of a test or other measure. One version of the test may be needed for initial diagnostic assessment. Several alternate forms may be needed for repeated diagnostic evaluation. Alternate forms or comparable measures may be needed for postassessment and assessment of retention. If the same form of a measure is administered to the same student more than one time, the student's prior experience with that measure may affect his performance. Creating alternative forms of measurement procedures requires access to a sample of equivalent assessment tasks, and the extent of task equivalence should be measured.

Mastery procedures use the student's performance on a series of assessment tasks as the standard for determining whether the student has been successful in the educational program. The relevance and representativeness of these tasks with respect to the objectives and competencies the tasks were designed to assess should be evaluated.

When the assessment task is the criterion or standard used to evaluate performance and when more than one task is used to evaluate a student's proficiency at various points in time, the reliability of the sample of tasks must be established.

If a student's performances in successive years are to be compared, measures used to evaluate his performance must be sufficiently comparable to permit these comparisons. Procedures are also needed to assess the performances of students who participate in different instructional programs aimed at producing similar or the same outcomes. To accomplish these various purposes, measures of performances specific to given instructional programs are needed. Additional measures that sample a wider range of the domain of performances will also be needed.

Normative procedures can also be used to give meaning to the results produced by mastery evaluation procedures. Students' performances can be ranked and interpreted according to their status in relation to their peers. However, comparisons of all students of a particular age group will probably be extremely difficult if the students are working toward different objectives, using different instructional materials, and devoting different amounts of time to various aspects of the instruction. Additional techniques will be needed to give meaning to the results produced by the evaluation procedures. One possible technique is simply to indicate the percentage of students in a given group who have achieved a given level of performance (Tyler, 1970).

Another potential problem results because mastery procedures are designed to identify for students and teachers the performances that will be measured as indicators of their success or failure. This encourages teachers to "teach to the test." It also encourages students to give special emphasis to the content that will be measured by the test. When the assessment procedures measure crucial aspects of the students' performance, knowledge of what will be measured provides guidance that helps students and teachers to focus on the essential aspects of the curriculum. However, if the tests measure insignificant or irrelevant aspects of students' performances, knowledge of what will be included in the test may guide students and teachers to focus upon the less important aspects of the instructional program. This potential problem emphasizes the importance of identifying and measuring crucial and relevant performances. Extensive research investigating the validity, dependability, interpretability, and generalizability of the criterion-referenced measures proposed for mastery programs is needed.

Advantages of Mastery

The advantages of mastery far outweigh the potential problems. And the advantages are numerous.

Mastery is a very logical process. The process begins by defining the outcome it intends to produce. Then instructional and assessment procedures designed to maximize the likelihood that each student will arrive at the desired outcome are selected. The prepared program is put into action, accompanied by assessment procedures designed to identify and correct its weaknesses while it is in progress. When the program has been completed, students' performances are compared with the intended outcomes. If the student has performed adequately, he proceeds to another unit or course. If a few students in a course have not performed adequately, they can begin additional instruction to correct their weaknesses, or other revisions in their instructional programs can be made. Major revisions in the curriculum can be made when most of the students who participated in the program did not perform adequately upon completion. Measures of students' performance can be used to evaluate the effectiveness of one instructional program, and the various aspects of the program, in comparison to other programs.

The processes involved in the mastery program are not new. Each has been subjected to extensive use in educational settings. None of these processes has been proven to be bad in and of itself.

The mastery processes structure educational programs to help most students in a group attain specific levels of performance. Mastery begins with the proposition that almost all students can learn the basic skills and knowledge contained in the curriculum. The skills and knowledge to be learned are divided into manageable segments and the segments are sequenced in a reasonable order. If some of the content covers prerequisites that are necessary for later learning, this content is taught first. Preassessments are conducted to determine whether the instruction is appropriate for each student's preparation, goals, and preferences. Each student's performance is evaluated frequently, and feedback is given to each student and his teachers. Students are told when their performance is accurate. When they make mistakes, their mistakes are identified quickly and remediation procedures are used if they are needed. Throughout the process, teachers, students, administrators, and other interested persons can participate in selecting the competencies, objectives, and instructional methods and materials they judge to be important for inclusion in the curriculum.

The mastery process provides a format for structuring instructional programs. This format enables those concerned with the educational process to participate actively in determining its direction. It encourages communication between students and teachers, administration, faculty, and other interested persons concerning the students' needs and the outcomes that educational programs should seek to attain. As these persons work together to assess students' needs, define competencies, and select objectives for the instructional program, they examine their own goals and objectives, their values and their feelings about school and schoolwork. This examination process can contribute to the continuous development of each person's self-knowledge. In addition, each person can help make the educational process more responsive to his own needs and goals through his participation.

The mastery format provides a structure for continuous planning and progress. Performances that are essential for students to attain are identified. Statements of the minimum levels of acceptable performance are included in educational objectives that are made known to students and faculty. Students continue learning until they have attained the acceptable levels of performance on these objectives. Whether students are working toward the same objectives using the same instruction or students in a group aim at varied objectives or use varied instructional procedures, the mastery evaluation procedures monitor each student's progress. The objectives, instructional program, and evaluation procedures are coordinated to keep each student working toward goals that are important for him.

While remediation programs are being conducted, every attempt is made to enable the student to continue his education. If the student's weakness is in a basic skill area, instructional procedures are selected that do not depend upon the basic skills not yet mastered. If, for example, a student is deficient in reading comprehension, this deficiency is identified. Time and resources can be allocated to help him improve his reading comprehension. Instructional programs that minimize dependence on reading comprehension can be selected for him. The student can continue working to improve his reading comprehension until he has reached an acceptable performance level or until the available instructional resources have been exhausted. He will not be confronted with instruction he has only the remotest chance of masterimg because he lacks the basic skills needed to comprehend it. The progress he makes will be evaluated and recognized. And the student will avoid much of the excessive criticism and negative evaluation that would come his way if he were expected to perform tasks for which he lacks the basic skills.

Educational resources can be more appropriately allocated when diagnostic evaluations have identified students' strengths and weaknesses as well as their needs, goals, and interests. In recent years, many students have entered advanced educational programs in universities and professional schools when they lack the basic prerequisites needed to perform adequately in these programs. When the students failed to perform adequately, many of the institutions added remediation programs to repair the students' basic skill deficiencies. Unfortunately, substantial amounts of educational resources and time were wasted before the students' deficiencies were identified. In addition, many students were forced to suffer the humiliation of failure in the very educational programs for which they had worked so hard to be admitted. Recognizing this, many institutions have instituted mastery procedures to increase the efficiency of their educational programs.

The mastery format is flexible enough to be applied in open, informal classrooms and in self-contained, formal classrooms, as well as in classrooms that fall between these two extremes. Many of the most ardent advocates of informal education and open classrooms have, in recent years, placed increased emphasis on the need for an underlying structure in this type of education. Brown University, for example, modified its curriculum to conform to the open classroom format. Within the last few years, Brown has returned to the more traditional structure.

Joseph Featherstone has influenced countless educators through his writings concerning the open classroom. He made the following observation in an introduction to his book, which included articles he had written for *The New Republic:*

> Many [of my articles] share an implicit theme: The necessity for establishing standards. By standards, I don't mean crudely mechanical check-lists or standardized national tests but rather a common conviction about what it means to do a good job [Featherstone, 1971].

The mastery components provide tools for identifying "what it means to do a good job," for monitoring the instructional process to determine whether it is doing a good job, and for repairing weaknesses in the educational program. If mastery procedures are used in conjunction with the open classroom techniques, they may help the participants incorporate the standards and structure they seek into the open classroom process.

Mastery components enable continuing research and development to be conducted. The issues of reliability and validity, relevance and generalizability of competencies and measurement instruments designed for the educational process can be investigated. Until rather recently, these questions were raised primarily in relation to evaluation. Many of the educational procedures in use today, and many of the processes included in a competency-based approach to mastery, are used because they appear reasonable. Common sense has served as a screen in selecting educational procedures. Continuing research and development will enable the collection of information concerning the accuracy of these commonsense judgments. The research and development process can help temper common sense with data.

The mastery procedures help educators and students identify specifically what they are learning in an educational program. If students are not learning what was intended for them, students and teachers know it. When they do learn, their progress is recognized. Progress can be positively reinforced and efforts towards progress can also be reinforced.

The mastery components provide tools for recognizing each student's progress. The performance of each student is viewed as successful when he attains mastery of the level of performance prescribed as acceptable. This evidence that the student has performed successfully can provide the basis for pride in his schoolwork, a view of himself as a competent learner, and continued persistence in academic tasks.

The mastery approach to competency-based education measures and recognizes each student's progress. Each student works on educational tasks that he has a reasonable chance of mastering. His progress toward mastery of the objectives is a major criterion used in determining evaluations of his performance. Remediation processes are available to him when he is having difficulty. In most cases, he has more than one opportunity to demonstrate his learning. Cooperating with other students does not endanger his own status when there is no limit on the number of students who can be considered successful. When emphasis on the process of averaging is diminished, evaluations that describe performance as less than successful are not prescribed for the half of the student population who perform below the average. Each student has an opportunity to have his progress recognized as acceptable even though the quality of the instruction may be less appropriate for him than it is for other students and he may require more learning time than his peers.

When a student faces challenging academic tasks and can succeed in mastering them, when the expectations concerning his performance are reasonable and realistic, and when the student knows that help is available when needed, the outlook is optimistic. Continuing academic progress results. If one goal is impossible to attain or otherwise nonproductive, a more appropriate goal can be selected. If one road leads to a dead end, he can blaze a new trail. There is always hope.

Bibliography

Abraham, F. J., & Newton, J. M. *The interview technique as a personalized system of instruction for economics: The Oregon experience.* Paper presented at the National Conference on Personalized Instruction in Higher Education, Washington, D.C., April, 1974.

Abrahamson, S., Denson, J. S., & Wolf, R. M. Effectiveness of a simulator in training anesthesiology residents. *Journal of Medical Education,* 1969, *44,* 515–519.

Adams, W. L. Why teachers say they fail pupils. *Educational Administration and Supervision,* 1932, *18,* 594–600.

Airasian, P. W. *Formative evaluation instruments: A construction and validation of tests to evaluate learning over short time periods.* Unpublished Ph.D. dissertation, University of Chicago, 1969.

Alberti, J. M. *Correlates of self-perception-in-school.* Paper presented to the American Education Research Association, New York, 1971.

Alvord, D. J. Relationships among pupil self concept, attitude toward national assessment of educational progress. *Dissertation Abstracts,* January, 1972, (32), No. 7, 3587.

Anastasi, A. *Psychological testing.* London: Macmillan, Collier-Macmillan, 1968.

Anderson, H. J. Correlation between academic achievement and teaching success. *Elementary School Journal,* 1931, *32,* 22–29.

Anderson, L. W. *Time and school learning.* Unpublished Ph.D. dissertation, University of Chicago, 1973.

Anderson, L. W. An empirical investigation of individual differences in time to learn. *Journal of Educational Psychology,* 1976, *68*(2), 226–233.

Anderson, L. W., & Block, J. H. Mastery Learning. In D. J. Treffinger, J. K. Davis, & R. E. Ripple (Eds.), *Handbook on educational psychology.* New York: Academic Press, forthcoming.

Anderson, L. W., Scott, C. C., & Hutlock, J., Jr. *The effects of a mastery learning program on selected cognitive, affective and ecological variables in grades 1 through 6.* Paper presented to the annual meeting of the American Educational Research Association, San Francisco, 1976.

Anderson, O. T., & Artman, R. A. A self-paced, independent study, introductory physics sequence—description and evaluation. *American Journal of Physics*, 1973, *41*, 12—18.

Anderson, R. C., Kulhavy, R. W., & Andre, T. Feedback procedures in programmed instruction. *Journal of Educational Psychology*, 1971, *62*, 148—156.

Arlin, M. N. The effects of formative evaluation on student performance. In H. F. Crombag & D. N. Degruijter (Eds.), *Contemporary issues in educational testing.* Paris: Mouton, 1974.

Asbury, C. A. Selected factors influencing over- and under-achievement in young school age children. *Review of Educational Research*, 1974, *44*(4), 409.

Atkinson, R. C. Computer-assisted instruction in initial reading. In *Proceedings of the 1967 Invitational Conference on Testing Problems.* Princeton: Educational Testing Service, 1968, 55—67. (a)

Atkinson, R. C. Computerized instruction and the learning process. *American Psychologist*, 1968, *23*, 225—239. (b)

Atkinson, R. C., & Wickens, T. D. Human memory and the concept of reinforcement. In R. Glaser (Ed.), *The nature of reinforcement.* New York: Academic Press, 1971.

Austin, S. M., & Gilbert, K. E. Student performance in a Keller Plan course in introductory electricity and magnetism. Mimeographed manuscript, Michigan State University, East Lansing, Michigan, undated.

Badwal, B. S. A study of the relationship between attitude towards school and achievement: Sex and grade level. *Dissertation Abstracts*, 1969, (30), 6-A, 2366.

Bailey, L. Contingency management in college foreign language instruction. In J. M. Johnston (Ed.), *Behavior research and technology in higher education.* Springfield, Illinois: Charles C Thomas, 1975.

Baley, D. *Cost-effectiveness of three methods of remedial instruction in mastery learning and the relationship between aptitude and achievement.* Unpublished Ph.D. dissertation, University of Southern California, 1972.

Ballow, F. W. Work of the Department of Educational Investigation and Measurement, Boston, Massachusetts. In *Standards and tests for the measurement of the efficiency of schools and school systems.* Fifteenth Yearbook of the National Society for the Study of Education, Part I. Bloomington, Illinois: Public School Publishing, 1916, 61—68.

Banas, C. "Sesame Street" rolls on with new objectives. *Chicago Tribune*, October 28, 1974, Sec. 3, p. 13.

Barr, A. S. *Wisconsin studies of the measurement and prediction of teacher effectiveness.* Madison: Dembar Publications, 1961.

Bass, B. M. Intrauniversity variation in grading practices. *Journal of Educational Psychology*, 1951, *42*, 366—368.

Baughman, E. E., & Dahlstrom, W. G. *Negro and White children: A psychological study in the rural south.* New York: Academic Press, 1968.

Battle, E. Motivational determinants of academic task persistence. *Journal of Personality and Social Psychology*, 1965, *2*, 209—218.

Beals, J. P. *An investigation of emotive perception among students in open space and conventional learning environments.* Unpublished Ph.D. dissertation, School of Education, University of Tennessee, 1972.

Beebe, J. D. *Self concept and achievement among elementary students in an experimental program.* Unpublished Ph.D. dissertation, University of North Dakota, 1972.

Beez, W. Influence of biased psychological reports on teacher behavior and pupil performance. In *Proceedings of the 76th Annual Convention of the American Psychological Association,* 1968, *3*, 605—606.

Bells, W. C. Reliability of repeated grading of essay type examinations. *Journal of Educational Psychology,* 1930, *21*, 48—52.

Benjamins, J. Changes in performance in relation to influences upon self conceptualization. *Journal of Abnormal and Social Psychology,* 1950, *45*, 473—480.

Berg, I. *Education and job: The great training robbery.* Boston: Beacon Press, 1971.

Berry, G. The Keller method in introductory philosophy courses: A preliminary report. In J. G. Sherman (Ed.), *PSI: 41 germinal papers.* Menlo Park, California: W. A. Banjamin, 1974.

Biehler, R. *Psychology applied to teaching.* Boston: Houghton Mifflin, 1974.

Bilby, R. W., Brookover, W. B., & Erickson, E. L. *Cognitions of self and student decision making.* Paper presented to the American Educational Research Association, Chicago, 1972.

Billings, D. B. PSI versus the lecture course in the principles of economics: A quasi-controlled experiment. In R. S. Ruskin & S. E. Bono (Eds.), *Personalized instruction in higher education.* Washington, D.C.: Center for Personalized Instruction, 1974.

Binder, D. M., Jones, J. G., & Strowig, R. W. Non-intellective self-report variables as predictors of scholastic achievement. *Journal of Education Research,* 1970, *63*, 364—366.

Blackburn, T., Semb, G., & Hopkins, B. The comparative effects of self-grading versus proctor grading on class efficiency and student performance. In J. M. Johnston (Ed.), *Behavior research and technology in higher education.* Springfield, Illinois: Charles C Thomas, 1975.

Bledsoe, J. C. Self concepts of children and their intelligence, achievements, interests, and anxiety. *Childhood Education,* 1967, *43*, 436—438.

Bledsoe, J. C., & Garrison, K. C. The self concepts of elementary school children in relation to their academic achievement, intelligence, interests, and manifest anxiety. USOE Cooperative Research Report No. 1008, University of Georgia, College of Education, 1962.

Block, J. H. *The effects of various levels of performance on selected cognitive, affective, and time variables.* Unpublished Ph.D. dissertation, University of Chicago, 1970.

Block, J. H. (Ed.). *Mastery learning: Theory and practice.* New York: Holt, Rinehart & Winston, 1971.

Block, J. H. Student learning and the setting of mastery performance standards. *Educational Horizons,* 1972, *50*, 183—191.

Block, J. H. *Mastery performance standards and student learning.* Unpublished paper, University of California, Santa Barbara, 1973. (a)

Block, J. H. Teachers, teaching and mastery learning. *Today's Education,* 1973, *63*(7), 30—36. (b)

Block, J. H. (Ed.). *Schools, society, and mastery learning.* New York: Holt, Rinehart & Winston, 1974.

Block, J. H., & Anderson, L. W. *Mastery learning in classroom instruction.* New York: Macmillan, 1975.

Block, J. H., & Burns, R. B. *Time in school learning: An instructional psychologist's perspecitve.* Paper presented at the annual meeting of the American Educational Research Association, Washington, D.C., 1975.

Block, J. H., & Burns, R. B. Mastery Learning. In F. N. Kerlinger (Ed.), *Review of research in education.* Vol. 4. Itasca, Illinois: F. E. Peacock Publishers, in press.

Block, J. H., & Tierney, M. An exploration of two correction procedures used in mastery learning approaches to instruction. *Journal of Educational Psychology,* 1974, *66,* 962–967.

Bloom, B. S. Thought processes in lectures and discussions. *Journal of General Education,* 1953, *7,* 160–169.

Bloom, B. S. Learning for mastery. *University of California Evaluation Comment,* 1968, *1,* No. 2.

Bloom, B. S. Individual differences in school achievement: A vanishing point? *Education at Chicago.* Department of Education, University of Chicago, Winter, 1971, 4–14. (a)

Bloom, B. S. Mastery learning and its implications for curriculum development. In E. W. Eisner (Ed.), *Confronting curriculum reform.* Boston: Little, Brown, 1971. (b)

Bloom, B. S. *An introduction to mastery learning theory.* Paper presented to the American Educational Research Association, New Orleans, Louisiana, 1973. (a)

Bloom, B. S. *Strategies to produce mastery learning in various cultural settings.* Paper presented to the American Educational Research Association, New Orleans, Louisiana, 1973. (b)

Bloom, B. S. An introduction to mastery learning theory. In J. H. Block (Ed.), *Schools, Society, and Mastery Learning.* New York: Holt, Rinehart & Winston, 1974. (a)

Bloom, B. S. Implications of the IEA studies for curriculum and instruction. *School Review,* 1974, *82*(3), 413–434. (b)

Bloom, B. S. *Human characteristics and instruction: A theory of school learning.* New York: McGraw-Hill, 1976.

Bloom, B. S., Engelhart, M. D., Furst, E. J., Hill, W. H., & Krathwohl, D. R. *Taxonomy of educational objectives. The classification of educational goals. Handbook I: Cognitive domain.* New York: David McKay, 1956.

Bloom, B. S., Hastings, J. T., & Madaus, G. F. *Handbook on formative and summative evaluation of student learning.* New York: McGraw-Hill, 1971.

Bobbitt, J. F. *The curriculum.* New York: Houghton Mifflin, 1918.

Bobbitt, J. F. *How to make a curriculum.* New York: Houghton Mifflin, 1924.

Bobbitt, J. F. *Curriculum of modern education.* New York: McGraw-Hill, 1941.

Bode, R. K., & Larsen, V. S. *SRA assessment survey technical report.* Chicago: Science Research Associates, 1974.

Bodwin, F. B. *The relationship between immature self-concept and certain educational disabilities.* Unpublished Ph.D. dissertation, Michigan State University, 1957.

Boehm, A. E., & White, M. A. Pupils' perceptions of school marks. *Elementary School Journal*, 1967, *67*, 237—240.

Borislow, B. Self-evaluation and academic achievement. *Journal of Counseling Psychology*, 1962, *9*, 246—254.

Bormuth, J. R. *On the theory of achievement test items.* Chicago: University of Chicago Press, 1970.

Bormuth, J. R. *Development of standards of reliability: Toward a rational criterion of passage performance.* Final Report, USDHEW, Project No. 9-0238. Chicago: University of Chicago, 1971.

Born, D. Exam performance and study behavior as a function of study unit size. In J. M. Johnston (Ed.), *Behavior research and technology in higher education.* Springfield, Illinois: Charles C Thomas, 1975.

Born, D. G., & Herbert, E. W. A further study of personalized instruction for students in large university classes. *Journal of Experimental Education*, 1971, *40*(1), 6—11.

Born, D. G., Gledhill, S. M., & Davis, M. L. Examination performance in lecture-discussion and personalized instruction courses. *Journal of Applied Behavior Analysis*, 1972, *5*, 33—43.

Born, D. G., & Whelan, P. Some descriptive characteristics of student performance in PSI and lecture courses. *Psychological Record*, 1973, *23*, 145—152.

Bowen, D., & Faissler, W. Entry level testing and the pattern of behavioral objectives in a Keller plan physics course. In J. M. Johnston (Ed.), *Behavior research and technology in higher education.* Springfield, Illinois: Charles C Thomas, 1975.

Bowen, L. S. Book review of Block, J. H. (Ed.), *Schools, Society, and Mastery Learning. The Education Forum*, 1975, *49*, 251—252.

Bower, E. M. Mental health in education, *Review of Educational Research*, 1962, *32*, 441—454.

Bowles, S., & Levin, H. M. The determinants of scholastic achievement—some recent evidence. *Journal of Human Resources*, 1968, *3*, 3—24.

Bracht, G. H., & Glass, G. V. The external validity of comparative experiments in educational and the social sciences. *American Educational Research Journal*, 1968, *5*, 437—474.

Braun, C. Teacher expectation: Sociopsychological dynamics. *Review of Educational Research.* Spring, 1976, *46*(2), 185—213.

Breland, N. S., & Smith, M. P. *A comparison of PSI and traditional methods of instruction for teaching introduction to psychology.* Paper presented at the National Conference on Personalized Instruction in Higher Education, 1974.

Breland, N. S., & Smith, M. P. *Cognitive and affective outcomes of PSI mastery programs as compared to traditional instruction.* Paper presented at the annual meeting of the American Educational Research Association, Washington, D.C. 1975.

Briggs, L. J. *Sequencing of instruction in relation to hierarchies of competence.* Pennsylvania: American Institutes for Research, 1968. (Available from Librarian, American Institutes for Research, 135 North Bellefield Avenue, Pittsburgh, Pennsylvania 15213.)

Brim, O. G., Goslin, D. A., Glass, D. C., & Goldberg, I. The use of standardized ability tests in American secondary schools and their impact on students, teachers and administrators. University of Pittsburgh, Coop Research Project No. 2334. New York: Russell Sage Foundation, 1965. (a)

Brim, O. G., Neulinger, J., & Glass, D. C. *Experiences and attitudes of American adults concerning standardized intelligence tests.* New York: Russell Sage Foundation, 1965. (b)

Brookover, W. B. Identification and analysis of elementary school social environment characteristics associated with differential school performance, socioeconomic status and racial composition of the schools controlled. USOE Coop Research Project. East Lansing, Michigan: Michigan State University, 1973.

Brookover, W. B., Erickson, E. L., & Joiner, L. M. Relation of self-concept to achievement in high school. USOE Project No. 2831. East Lansing, Michigan: Michigan State University, 1967. (a)

Brookover, W. B., Erickson, E. L., & Joiner, L. Self-concept of ability and school achievement. USOE Coop Research Project No. 2831. East Lansing, Michigan: Michigan State University, 1967. (b)

Brookover, W. B., LePere, J. M., Hamachek, D. E., Thomas, S., & Erickson, E. L. Self-concept of ability and school achievement. USOE Project No. 1636. East Lansing, Michigan: Michigan State University, 1965.

Brookover, W. B., Paterson, A., & Thomas, S. The relationship of self-images to achievement in junior high school subjects. Coop Research Project No. 845. East Lansing, Michigan: Michigan State University, 1962.

Brookover, W. B., Paterson, A., & Thomas, S. Self-concept of ability and school achievement. *Sociology of Education,* 1964, *37,* 271–278.

Brophy, J. E., & Good, T. Teachers' communications of differential expectations for children's classroom performance: Some behavioral data. *Journal of Educational Psychology,* 1970, *61,* 365–374.

Brophy, J. E., & Good, T. *Teacher-student relationships.* New York: Holt, Rinehart & Winston, 1974.

Brophy, J. E., Good, T., & Nedler, S. *Teaching in the preschool.* New York: Harper & Row, 1975.

Brown, J. L. The effects of revealing instructional objectives on the achievement level of selected eighth grade pupils in four predominantly black inner city schools (Ph.D. dissertation, Indiana University, 1970). *Dissertation Abstracts International,* 1971, *31,* 5869.

Brownfain, J. J. Stability of the self-concept as a dimension of personality. *Journal of Abnormal and Social Psychology,* 1952, *47,* 597–606.

Bruner, J. S. *The process of education.* Cambridge, Massachusetts: Harvard University Press, 1960.

Bruner, J. S. *The relevance of education.* New York: W. W. Norton, 1971.

Bryant, N. The effect of performance objectives on the achievement level of selected eighth science pupils in four predominantly black inner city public schools (Ph.D. dissertation, Indiana University, 1970). *Dissertation Abstracts International,* 1971, *31,* 5869.

Burrows, C. K., & Okey, J. R. *The effects of a mastery learning strategy on achievement.* Paper presented at the annual meeting of the American Educational Research Association, Washington, D.C., 1975.

Butler, R. A. Incentive conditions which influence visual exploration. *Journal of Experimental Psychology,* 1954, *48,* 19–23.

Cahen, L. *An experimental manipulation of the halo effect.* Unpublished Ph.D. dissertation, Stanford University, 1966.

Caldwell, E., & Harnett, R. Sex biases in college grading. *Journal of Educational Measurement,* 1967, *4,* 129—132.

Calhoun, J. F. *Elemental analysis of the Keller method of instruction.* Paper presented at the annual meeting of the American Psychological Association, Montreal, 1973.

Campbell, D. Reforms as experiments. *American Psychologist,* 1969, *24,* 409—429.

Campbell, D. T., & Stanley, J. C. Experimental and quasi-experimental designs for research on teaching. In N. L. Gage (Ed.), *Handbook of research on teaching.* Chicago: Rand McNally, 1963.

Campbell, P. B. School and self-concept. *Educational Leadership,* 1967, *24,* 510—513.

Caplin, M. D. Self-concept, level of aspiration, and academic achievement. *Journal of Negro Education,* 1968, *37,* 435—439.

Caplin, M. D. Relationship between self-concept and academic achievement. *Journal of Experimental Education,* 1969, *37,* 13—16.

Caponigri, R. S. *Capsulized mastery learning: An experimental and a correlational study of a mastery learning strategy.* Unpublished Ph.D. dissertation, Loyola University, 1972.

Carlson, J., & Minke, K. Fixed and ascending criteria for unit mastery learning. *Journal of Educational Psychology,* 1975, *67*(1), 96—101.

Carmichael, D. *Mastery learning: Its administrative implications.* Paper presented to the annual meeting of the American Educational Research Association, New Orleans, 1973.

Carmichael, D. Mastery learning: An educational innovation with administrative implications. In J. H. Block (Ed.), *Schools, society, and mastery learning.* New York: Holt, Rinehart & Winston, 1974.

Carroll, J. B. A model of school learning. *Teachers College Record,* 1963, *64,* 723—733. (a)

Carroll, J. B. Programmed instruction and student ability. *Journal of Programmed Instruction,* 1963, *2,* 7—11. (b)

Carroll, J. B. *Programmed self-instruction in Mandarin Chinese: Observations of student progress with an automated audiovisual device.* Wellesley, Massachusetts: Language Testing Fund, 1963. (c)

Carroll, J. B. School learning over the long haul. In J. D. Krumboltz (Ed.), *Learning and the educational process.* Chicago: Rand McNally, 1965.

Carroll, J. B. Problems of measurement related to the concept of learning for mastery. *Educational Horizons,* 1970, *48*(3), 71—80.

Carroll, J. B. Problems of measurement related to the concept of learning for mastery. In J. H. Block (Ed.), *Mastery learning: Theory and practice.* New York: Holt, Rinehart & Winston, 1971. Pp. 29—46.

Carroll, J. B. Importance of the time factor in learning. Paper presented at the annual meeting of the American Educational Research Association, New Orleans, 1973.

Carroll, J. B. *Rationality and irrationality in educational research.* Symposium at the annual meeting of the American Educational Research Association, Washington, D.C., 1975.

Carroll, J. B., & Spearitt, D. *A model for school learning.* Monograph No. 4. Cambridge, Massachusetts: Harvard University, Center for Research and Development of Educational Differences, 1967.

Carter, R. S. Non-intellectual variables involved in teachers' marks. *Journal of Educational Research,* 1953, *47,* 81–95.

Centi, P. Self-perception of students and motivation. *Catholic Education Review,* 1965, *63,* 307–319.

Charters, W. W. *Curriculum construction.* New York: Macmillan, 1923.

Chicago Board of Education. *Follow-up study of the 1976 High School graduates.* chicago: Department of Research and Evaluation, November, 1976.

Christmas, J. J. Self-concept and attitudes. In K. S. Miller & R. M. Dreger (Eds.), *Comparative studies of Blacks and Whites in the United States.* New York: Seminar Press, 1973.

Christoffersson, N. O. *The economics of time in learning.* Unpublished Ph.D. dissertation, University of Chicago, 1971.

Cioch, J. *Application of a mastery learning strategy in a quantity food laboratory course.* Unpublished Ph.D. dissertation, Pennsylvania State University, 1974.

Clark, J. P., & Thompson, S. D. *Competency tests and graduation requirements.* Reston, Virginia: National Association of Secondary School Principals, 1976.

Clinton, W. J. Center's new survey depicts rapid growth of PSI in the United States. *The Personalized System of Instruction Newsletter,* June, 1976, *4*(2), 1.

Cohen, H. L., Filipczak, J., & Bis, J. S. *Case I: An initial study of contingencies applicable to special education.* Silver Spring, Maryland: Education Facility Press, 1965.

Cohen, H. L., Goldiamond, I., Filipczak, J., & Pooley, R. *Training professionals in procedures for the establishment of educational environments: A report on the Case Training Institute (CTI).* Silver Spring, Maryland: Institute for Behavioral Research, 1968.

Coldeway, D. O., Santowski, M., O'Brien, R., & Lagowski, V. *A comparison of small group contingency management with the personalized system of instruction and the lecture system.* Paper presented at 2nd National Conference on Research and Technology in College and University Teaching, Georgia State University, Atlanta, 1974.

Cole, C., Martin, S., & Vincent, J. A comparison of two teaching formats at the college level. In J. M. Johnston (Ed.), *Behavior research and technology in higher education.* Springfield, Illinois: Charles C Thomas, 1975.

Coleman, J. S., Campbell, E. Q., Hobson, C. J., McPartland, J., Mood, A. M., Weinfeld, F. D., & York, R. L. *Equality of educational opportunity.* Final Report, USOE, Washington, D.C.: Government Printing Office, 1966, No. 38001.

Collins, K. M. *A strategy for mastery learning in Freshman Mathetmatics.* Unpublished study, Purdue University, Division of Mathematical Sciences, 1969.

Collins, K. M. *A strategy for mastery learning in modern mathematics.* Unpublished paper, Purdue University, 1970.

Combs, A. W. *The relationship of child perceptions to achievement and behavior in the early school years.* USOE Coop. Research No. 814. Washington, D.C.: U.S. Department of HEW, 1963.

Combs, A. W., & Taylor, C. The effect of the perception of mild degrees of threat on performance. *Journal of Abnormal and Social Psychology,* 1952, *47,* 420–424.

Combs, C. F. Perception of self and scholastic underachievement in the academically capable. *Personnel and Guidance Journal,* 1964, *43,* 47–51.

Conrad, C. J., Spencer, R. E., & Semb, G. *A counterbalanced comparison.* Paper presented at the annual meeting of the American Psychological Association, Washington, D.C., September, 1976.

Contreras, G. *Mastery learning: The relationship of different criterion levels and aptitude to achievement, retention, and attitude in a seventh grade geography unit.* Unpublished Ph.D. dissertation, University of Georgia, 1975.

Cook, J. M. Learning and retention by informing students of behavioral objectives and their place in the hierarchical learning sequence. (USOE Final Report). College Park, Maryland: University of Maryland, 1969. (ERIC Document Reproduction Service No. ED 036869).

Cooley, W. W., & Lohnes, P. R. *Evaluative inquiry in education.* New York: Irvington Publishers, in press.

Cooper, J. L., & Greiner, J. M. Contingency management in an introductory psychology course produces better retention. *Psychological Record,* 1971, *21,* 391–400.

Coopersmith, S. A method for determining types of self-esteem. *Journal of Abnormal and Social Psychology,* 1959, *59,* 87–94.

Coopersmith, S. *The antecedents of self-esteem.* San Francisco: W. H. Freeman, 1967.

Corey, J. R., McMichael, J. S., & Tremont, P. J. *Long-term effects of personalized instruction in an introductory psychology course.* Paper presented at the meeting of the Eastern Psychological Association, 1970.

Corey, J. R., & McMichael, J. S. Retention in a PSI introductory psychology course. In J. G. Sherman (Ed.), *PSI:41 germinal papers.* Menlo Park, California: W. A. Benjamin, 1974.

Cotler, S., & Palmer, R. J. Relationships among sex, sociometric, self and test anxiety factors and the academic achievement of elementary school children. *Psychology in the Schools,* 1970, *7,* 211–216.

Crandall, V. C., Katovsky, W., & Crandall, V. J. Children's beliefs in their own control of reinforcements in intellectual-academic achievement situations. *Child Development,* 1965, *36,* 91–109.

Crawford, W. J., Brophy, J. E., Evertson, C. M., Baum, M. C., & Anderson, L. M. *The student attribute study: Characteristics of students with differentially perceived ability levels and work habits.* Paper presented to the annual meeting of the American Educational Research Association, San Francisco, 1976.

Crittenden, W. B. The Edison project. An Evaluation of Phase I (Jan. 1971–July, 1972). Staff Development Center—Intermediate Level; Edison Junior High School (Multigrouped Nongraded Instructional Program). Mimeographed manuscript, July, 1972.

Cronbach, L. J. How can instruction be adapted to individual differences. In R. Gagné (Ed.), *Learning and Individual differences.* Columbus, Ohio: C. E. Merrill Books, 1967.

Cronbach, L. J. Test validation. In R. L. Thorndike (Ed.), *Educational measure-ment* (2nd ed.). Washington, D. C.: American Council on Education, 1971.

Cronbach, L. J. Book review of Block, J. H. (Ed.), *Mastery learning: Theory and practice. International Review of Education,* 1972, *18*(1), 250–252.

Cronbach, L. J., & Furby, L. How we should measure "change"—or should we? *Psychological Bulletin,* 1970, *74,* 68–80.

Cronbach, L. J., & Gleser, G. C. *Psychological tests and personnel decisions* (2nd ed.). Urbana, Illinois: University of Illinois Press, 1965.

Cronbach, L. J., Gleser, G. C., Nanda, H., & Rajaratnam, N. *The dependability of behavioral measurements: Theory of generalizability for scores and profiles.* New York: John Wiley & Sons, 1972.

Cronbach, L. J., & Snow, R. E. *Individual differences in learning ability as a function of instructional variables.* Final Report, USOE, Contract No. OEC4-6-061269-1217. Stanford, California: Stanford University, School of Education, 1969.

Cronbach, L. J., & Snow, R. E. *Aptitude and instructional methods.* New York: Irvington Press, forthcoming.

Cyrier, R., & Carpenter, J. L. *Experiences with a measure of self-concept in the Chicago schools.* Paper presented to the annual meeting of the American Educational Research Association, New Orleans, 1973.

Dalis, G. T. The effect of precise objectives upon student achievement in health education. *Journal of Experimental Education,* 1970, *39*(2), 20–23.

Davidson, H. H., & Lang, G. Children's perceptions of their teachers' feelings toward them related to self-perception, school environment and behavior. *Journal of Experimental Education,* 1960, *29,* 107–118.

Davies, C. S., & Semb, G. *Effects of progressive contract schedules on rates of course completion.* Paper presented at the annual meeting of the American Psychological Association, Washington, D.C., 1976.

Davies, I. K. *Competency based learning: Technology, management, and design.* New York: McGraw-Hill, 1973.

Davies, M. L. Mastery test proficiency requirement affects mastery test per-formance. In J. M. Johnston (Ed.), *Behavior research and technology in higher education.* Springfield, Illinois: Charles C Thomas, 1975.

DeCharms, R. Personal causation training in the schools. *Journal of Applied Social Psychology,* 1972, *2*(2), 95–113.

Deci, E. L. Intrinsic motivation, extrinsic reinforcement, and inequity. *Journal of Personality and Social Psychology,* 1972, *22*(1), 113–120.

DeGroat, A. F., & Thompson, G. G. A study of the distribution of teacher approval and disapproval among sixth-grade pupils. *Journal of Experimental Education,* 1949, *18,* 57–75.

Dempsey, R. A., & Smith, R. P. *Differential staffing.* Englewood Cliffs, New Jersey: Prentice-Hall, 1972.

Dexter, E. S. The effect of fatigue or boredom on teachers' marks. *Journal of Educational Research,* 1935, *28,* 664–667.

Diller, L. Conscious and unconscious self-attitudes after success and failure. *Journal of Personality,* 1954, *23,* 1–12.

Dittes, J. E. Effects of changes in self-esteem upon impulsiveness and delibera-tion in making judgments. *Journal of Abnormal and Social Psychology,* 1959, *58,* 348–356.

Doyle, W., Hancock, G., & Kifer, E. Teachers' perceptions: Do they make a difference? *Journal of the Association for the Study of Perception,* 1972, *7,* 21–30.

Duchastel, P. C., & Merrill, P. F. The effects of behavioral objectives on learning: A review of empirical studies. *Review of Educational Research,* 1973, *43*(1), 53–69.

Dweck, C. S. The role of expectations and attributions in the alleviation of learned helplessness. *Journal of Personality and Social Psychology,* 1975, *31,* 674–685.

Dyson, E. Study of ability grouping and the self-concept. *Journal of Educational Research,* 1967, *60,* 403–405.

Ebel, R. L. *Essentials of educational measurement.* Englewood Cliffs, New Jersey: Prentice-Hall, 1972.

Echelberger, E. *Relationships between personality traits and peer status.* Unpublished Ph.D. dissertation, University of Michigan, Ann Arbor, 1959.

Edwards, K. J., & Tuckman, B. W. *The effect of differential college experiences in developing the students' self and occupational-concepts: An application of discriminant analysis with longitudinal data.* Paper presented to the American Educational Research Association, New York, 1971.

Edwards-Penfold, D. M. The use of essays in selection at 11 Plus. Essay marking experiments: Shorter and longer essays. *British Journal of Educational Psychology,* 1956, *26,* 128–136.

Eisner, E. W. Instructional and expressive objectives; their formation and use in curriculum. In *Instructional Objectives.* American Educational Research Association Monograph on Curriculum Evaluation. Chicago: Rand McNally, 1969.

Elmore, R. F. *Planned variation experiments as policy analysis.* Paper presented to the annual meeting of the American Educational Research Association, Chicago, 1974.

Ely, D., & Hampton, J. *Predication of procrastination in a self-pacing instructional system.* Paper presented at the annual meeting of the American Educational Research Association, New Orleans, 1973.

Ely, D., & Minars, E. The effects of a large scale mastery environment on students' self-concept. *The Journal of Experimental Education,* 1973, *41*(4), 20–22.

Engel, M. The stability of the self-concept in adolescence. *Journal of Abnormal and Social Psychology,* 1959, *58,* 211–215.

Entwisle, D. *Expectations in mixed racial groups of children.* Paper presented at the annual meeting of the American Educational Research Association, 1973.

Erikson, E. H. Identity and the life cycle: Selected papers. *Psychological Issues,* 1959, *1.*

Erikson, E. H. *Childhood and society.* New York: Norton, 1963.

Estes, W. K. Learning theory and intelligence. *American Psychologist,* 1974, *29,* 740–749.

Evans, R. I. (Ed.). *Dialogue with Erik Erikson.* New York: Dutton, 1969.

Falstrom, P., & Abbott, R. *Aptitude and attribute interactions with personalized/unitized and lecture/midterm methods of instruction in elementary psychological statistics.* Paper presented at the annual meeting of the Western Psychological Association, Anaheim, California, 1973.

Farmer, J., Lachter, G., Blaustein, J., & Cole, B. The role of proctoring in personalized instruction. *Journal of Applied Behavior Analysis*, 1972, *5*, 401–404.

Feather, N. T. Effects of prior success and failure on expectations of success and subsequent performance. *Journal of Personality and Social Psychology*, 1966, *3*, 287–298.

Featherstone, J. *Schools where children learn*. New York: Liveright, 1971.

Fehlen, J. *A study of selected variables associated with mastery learning in a college mathematics course for prospective elementary teachers*. Unpublished Ph.D. dissertation, University of Minnesota, 1973.

Feldman, K. V., & Klausmeier, H. J. *The effects of a definition and a varying number of examples and non-examples on concept attainment*. Paper presented at the annual meeting of the American Educational Research Association, 1974.

Felker, D. W., Stanwyck, D. J., & Kay, R. S. The effects of a teacher program in self-concept enhancement on pupils' self-concept, anxiety, and intellectual achievement responsibility. *Journal of Educational Research*, 1973, *66*(10).

Ferster, C. B. Individual instruction in a large introductory psychology college course. *The Psychological Record*, 1968, *18*, 521–532.

Festinger, L. *A theory of cognitive dissonance*. Stanford, California: Stanford University Press, 1957.

Fiel, R. L., & Okey, J. R. The effects of formative evaluation and remediation on mastery of intellectual skills. *Journal of Educational Research*, 1974, *68*, 253–255.

Fink, M. B. Self-concept as it relates to academic achievement. *California Journal of Educational Research*, 1962, *13*, 57–62.

Finn, J. Expectations and the educational environment. *Review of Educational Research*, 1972, *42*, 387–410.

Finn, J. D. *A general model for multivariate analysis*. New York: Holt, Rinehart & Winston, 1974.

Flammer, G. H. Learning as the constant and time as the variable. *Engineering Education*, 1971, *61*, 511–514.

Flammer, G. H. Applied Motivation: A missing role in teaching. *Engineering Education*, 1972, *62*(6).

Fletcher, O. J., & Tyler, D. E. Teaching veterinary pathology by audiotutorial and learning for mastery methods. *Journal of the American Veterinary Medical Association*, 1972, *161*, 65–70.

Ford, W. S., & Muse, D. *Self-concept and students' future educational plans*. Paper presented to the American Educational Association, Chicago, 1972.

Foshay, A. W. *Toward a humane curriculum*. Paper presented to the annual meeting of the American Educational Research Association, Chicago, 1974.

Gage, N. L. *Teacher effectiveness and teacher education*. Palo Alto, California: Pacific Books, 1972.

Gagné, R. M. The acquisition of knowledge. *Psychological Review*, 1962, *69*, 355–365.

Gagné, R. M. *The conditions of learning*. New York: Holt, Rinehart & Winston, 1965.

Gagné, R. M. Learning hierarchies. *Educational Psychologist*, 1968, *6*, 1–9.

Gagné, R. M. Some new views of learning and instruction. In Don E. Hamachek (Ed.), *Human dynamics in psychology and education*. Boston: Allyn & Bacon, 1972.

Gagné, R. M., & Briggs, L. J. *Principles of instructional design.* New York: Holt, Rinehart & Winston, 1974.

Gagné, R. M., Mayor, J. R., Garstens, H. L., & Paradise, N. E. Factors in acquiring knowledge of a mathematical task. *Psychological Monographs,* 1962, *76*(7, Whole No. 526).

Gagné, R. M., & Paradise, N. E. Abilities and learning sets in knowledge acquisition. *Psychological Monographs,* 1961, *75*(14, Whole No. 518).

Galanter, E. (Ed.). *Automatic teaching: The state of the art.* New York: John Wiley & Sons, 1959.

Gallup, H. F. *The Introductory Psychology Course at Lafayette College, Easton, Pennsylvania: A description and tentative evaluation.* Paper presented to the Midwest Psychological Association Annual Meeting, April, 1969.

Geeslin, W. E., & Shavelson, R. J. An exploratory analysis of the representation of a mathematical structure in students' cognitive structures. *American Educational Research Journal,* 1975, *12*(1).

Gentile, J. R. *Educational psychology principles applied to educational psychology courses.* Paper presented at the annual meeting of the American Psychological Association, 1971.

Glaser, R. Instructional technology and the measurement of learning outcomes; some questions. *American Psychologist,* 1963, *18,* 519—521.

Glaser, R. A criterion-referenced test. In W. J. Popham (Ed.), *Criterion-referenced measurement.* New York: Holt, Rinehart & Winston, 1965. (a)

Glaser, R. (Ed.). *Teaching machines and programmed learning, II.* Washington, D.C.: National Education Association, 1965. (b)

Glaser, R. Adapting the elementary school curriculum to individual performance. In *Proceedings of the 1967 Invitational Conference on Testing Problems.* Princeton: Educational Testing Service, 1968, 3—36. (a)

Glaser, R. *Evaluation of instruction and changing educational models.* Los Angeles: Center for the Study of Evaluation of Instructional Programs, University of California, September 1968. (b)

Glaser, R. Individuals and learning: The new aptitudes. *Educational Researcher,* 1972, *1*(6), 5—13.

Glaser, R. Components of a psychology of instruction: Toward a science of design. *Review of Educational Research,* Winter, 1976, *46*(1), 1—24. (a)

Glaser, R. *Adaptive instruction: Individual diversity and learning.* New York: Holt, Rinehart and Winston, 1976. (b)

Glaser, R., & Nitko, A. J. Measurement in learning and instruction. In R. L. Thorndike (Ed.), *Educational Measurement* (2nd ed.), Washington, D.C.: American Council on Education, 1971. Pp. 625—670.

Glaser, R., & Resnick, L. Instructional psychology. *Annual Review of Psychology,* 1972, *23,* 207—276.

Glasnapp, D. *Causal analysis with a mastery learning paradigm.* Paper presented at the annual meeting of the American Educational Research Association, San Francisco, 1976.

Glasnapp, D., Poggio, J. P., & Ory, J. C. *Cognitive and affective consequences of mastery and non-mastery instructional strategies.* Paper presented at the annual meeting of the American Educational Research Association, Washington, D.C., 1975.

Glick, D. M., & Semb, G. *Effects of semester deadlines on student withdrawal.* Paper presented at the annual meeting of the American Psychological Association, Washington, D.C., 1976.

Glidewell, J. C., & Swallow, C. S. *The prevalence of maladjustment in elementary schools.* Chicago: University of Chicago, 1968.

Good, T. M., Biddle, B. J., & Brophy, J. E. *Teachers make a difference.* New York: Holt, Rinehart & Winston, 1975.

Good, T. M., & Dembo, M. Teacher expectations: Self-report data. *School Review,* 1973, *81,* 247–253.

Goodlad, J. I., & Anderson, R. H. *The nongraded elementary school.* New York: Harcourt, Brace and World, 1959.

Green, B. A. Physics teaching by the Keller Plan at MIT. *American Journal of Physics,* 1971, *39*(7).

Green, B. A. Fifteen reasons not to use the Keller Plan. In Sherman, J. G. (Ed.), *Personalized system of instruction.* Menlo Park, California: W. A. Benjamin, 1974. Pp. 117–119.

Green, T. M. Self-conceptions, physical fitness factors, school achievement and their interrelations with sixth-grade students. *Dissertation Abstracts,* December, 1971, (3) 6-A, 2713.

Greene, D., & Lepper, M. R. Intrinsic motivation: How to turn play into work. *Psychology Today,* September, 1974, 49–54.

Grobman, H. *Evaluation activities of curriculum projects.* AERA monograph series on curriculum evaluation, No. 2. Chicago: Rand McNanny, 1968.

Groff, P. Some criticisms of mastery learning. *Today's Education,* 1974, *63,* 88–91.

Gronlund, N. E. *Constructing achievement tests.* Englewood Cliffs, New Jersey: Prentice-Hall, 1968.

Gronlund, N. E. *Stating behavioral objectives for classroom instruction.* New York: Macmillan, 1970.

Gronlund, N. E. *Individualizing classroom instruction.* New York: Macmillan, 1974.

Guilford, J. P. *The nature of human intelligence.* New York: McGraw-Hill, 1967.

Hambleton, R. K. A review of testing and decision-making procedures for selected in individualized instructional programs, (ACT Technical Bulletin, No. 15). Iowa City, Iowa: The American College Testing Program, 1973.

Hamlish, E., & Gaier, E. L. Teacher-student personality similarities and marks. *School Review,* 1954, *62,* 265–273.

Hammer, B. Grade expectations, differential teacher comments, and student performance. *Journal of Educational Psychology,* 1972, *63,* 505–512.

Hanson, E. H. Do boys get a square deal in school? *Education,* 1959, *79,* 597.

Harlow, H. F. Mice, monkeys, men and motives. *Psychological Review,* 1953, *60,* 23–32.

Harnischfeger, A., & Wiley, D. Teaching-learning processes in elementary school: A synoptic view. Studies of Educative Processes, Report No. 9, University of Chicago, 1975.

Harris, C. W. (Ed.). *Problems in measuring change.* Madison, Wisconsin: University of Wisconsin Press, 1963.

Harris, C. W., Alkin, M. C., & Popham, W. J. (Eds.). *Problems in criterion-referenced measurement.* Los Angeles: UCLA Graduate School of Education, Center for the Study of Evaluation, 1974.

Harrison, M., & Harrison, F. *Mastery learning and quality of instruction.* Paper presented at the annual meeting of the American Educational Research Association, Washington, D.C., 1975.

Harrow, A. J. *A taxonomy of the psychomotor domain: A guide for developing behavioral objectives.* New York: David McKay, 1972.

Harshbarger, T. R. *Introductory statistics: A decision map.* New York: Macmillan, 1971.

Hartley, J. Programmed instruction 1954—1974: A review. *Programmed Learning and Educational Technology,* 1974, *11*(6), 278—291.

Hatcher, C. W., Felker, D., & Treffinger, D. J. *Prediction of upper grade reading achievement with measures of intelligence, divergent thinking, and self-concept.* Paper presented to the American Educational Research Association, Chicago, 1974.

Heider, F. *The psychology of interpersonal relations.* New York: Wiley, 1958.

Henderson, G. G. *An analysis of self-concept of academic ability as related to social-psychological variables, comprising school climate, in white and black elementary children within differential school settings.* Unpublished doctoral dissertation, Michigan State University, 1973.

Herron, M. D. *The nature of scientific inquiry as seen by selected philosophers, science teachers, and recent curricular materials.* Unpublished Ph.D. dissertation, University of Chicago, 1969.

Hills, J. R. Predictions of college grades for all public colleges of a state. *Journal of Educational Measurement,* 1964, *1*, 155—159.

Hills, J. R., Klock, J. A., & Bush, M. The use of academic prediction equations with subsequent classes. *American Educational Research Journal,* 1965, *2*, 203—206.

Hodgkinson, H. L. Improving education and work linkages. *Training and Development Journal,* July, 1976, *30*(7), 40—51.

Hoebrock, L. L., Koen, B. V., Roth, C. H., & Wagner, G. R. Theory of PSI evaluated for engineering education. *IEEE Transaction on Education,* 1972, *E-15*, No. 1.

Holland, J. L. Prediction of college grades from personality and aptitude variables. *Journal of Educational Psychology,* 1960, *51*, 245—254.

Hollander, E. P. Conformity, status, and idiosyncracy credit. *Psychological Review,* 1958, *65*(2).

Holman, M. G., & Docter, R. F. *Educational and psychological testing: A study of the industry and its practices.* New York: Russell Sage Foundation, 1972.

Horn, M. (Ed.). *The Wisconsin design for reading skill development.* Madison, Wisconsin: Wisconsin Research and Development Center for Cognitive Learning, 1972.

Horney, K. *Neurosis and human growth: The struggle toward self-realization.* New York: W. W. Norton, 1950.

Huck, S. W., & Long, S. D. The effect of behavioral objectives on student achievements. *Journal of Experimental Education,* 1973, *42*(1), 40—41.

Huff, S. Credentialing by tests or by degrees: Title VII of the Civil Rights Act and Griggs v. Duke Power Company. *Harvard Educational Review,* 1974, *44*(2), 246—269.

Hughes, D. An experimental investigation of the effects of pupil responding and teacher reacting on pupil achievement. *American Educational Research Journal,* 1973, *10*, 21—37.

Hughes, T. M. Relationship of coping strength to self-concept, school achievement, and general anxiety level in sixth grade pupils. *Journal of Experimental Education,* 1968, *37*, 59—64.

Hunt, E., Frost, N., & Lunneborg, C. Individual differences in cognition: A new approach to intelligence. In G. H. Bower (Ed.), *The psychology of learning and motivation* (Vol. 7). New York: Academic Press, 1973.

Hunt, J. McV. *Intelligence and experience.* New York: The Ronald Press, 1961.

Hursh, D., Wildgen, J., Minkin, B., Minkin, N., Sherman, J., & Wolf, M. Proctors' discussions of students' quiz performance with students. *In J. M. Johnston* (Ed.), *Behavior research and technology in higher education.* Springfield, Illinois: Charles C Thomas, 1975.

Husen, T. (Ed.). *International study of educational achievement in mathematics: A comparison of twelve countries* (Vols. I and II). New York: John Wiley & Sons, 1967.

Hutchins, R. M. *The learning society.* New York: Frederick A. Praeger, 1968.

Hymel, G. M. An investigation of John B. Carroll's model of school learning as a theoretical basis for the organizational structuring of schools. Final Report, NIE Project No. 3-1359, 1974.

Jamison, D., Fletcher, J. D., Suppes, P., & Atkinson, R. C. Cost and performance of computer-assisted instruction for compensatory education. In R. Radner & J. Froomkin (Eds.), *Education as an industry.* New York: Columbia University Press, 1973.

Jamison, D., Suppes, P., & Wells, S. The effectiveness of alternative instructional media: A survey. *Review of Educational Research,* 1974, *44,* No. 1.

Janeczko, R. The effect of instructional and general objectives on student self evaluation of psychomotor performance. *Journal of Industrial Teacher Training,* 1972, *9*(9), 14—21.

Jaynes, J. Hello, Teacher. . . . *Contemporary Psychology,* 1975, *20*(8), 629—631.

Jenkins, J. R., & Deno, S. L. Influence of knowledge and type of objectives on subject matter learning. *Journal of Educational Psychology,* 1971, *62*(1), 67—70.

Jensen, G. E. *The validation of aims for American democratic education.* Minneapolis: Burgess, 1950.

Johnston, J. M. (Ed.). *Behavior research and technology in higher education.* Springfield, Illinois: Charles C Thomas, 1975.

Johnston, J. M., & O'Neill, G. The analysis of performance criteria defining college grades as a determinate of college student academic performance. *Journal of Applied Behavior Analysis,* 1973, *6,* 261—268.

Johnston, J. M., & Pennypacker, H. S. A behavioral approach to college teaching. *American Psychologist,* 1971, *26,* 219—244.

Jones, E. L., Gordon, H. A., & Schechtman, G. *A strategy for academic success in a community college.* Unpublished manuscript, Olive-Harvey College, Chicago, 1975.

Jones, F. G. *The effects of mastery and aptitude on learning, retention, and time.* Unpublished Ph.D. dissertation, University of Georgia, 1974.

Jones, J. G., & Grieneeks, L. Measures of self-perception as predicators of scholastic achievement. *Journal of Educational Research,* 1970, *63,* 201—203.

Josephson, C. H. Do grades stimulate students to failure? *Chicago Schools Journal,* 1961, *43,* 122—127.

Judd, C. H. A look forward. In *The measurement of educational products.* Seventeenth yearbook of the National Society for the Study of Education, Part II. Bloomington, Illinois: Public School Publishing Company, 1918. Pp. 152—160.

Kappell, F. R. *Fron the world of college to the world of work.* New York: American Telephone and Telegraph Co., 1962.

Karlin, B. M. *The Keller method of instruction compared to the traditional method instruction in a Lafayette College history course.* Paper presented at the annual Psi Chi Colloquium, 1972.

Keller, F. S. Good-bye, Teacher. . . . *Journal of Applied Behavior Analysis,* 1968, *1,* 78–89.

Keller, F. S. Neglected rewards in the educational process. In S. R. Wilson & D. T. Tosti (Eds.), *Learning is getting easier.* San Rafael, California: Individual Learning Systems, 1972, 169–188.

Keller, F. S., & Sherman, J. G. *The Keller Plan handbook.* Menlo Park, California: W. A. Benjamin, 1974.

Kelley, E. G. A study of consistent discrepancies between instructor grades and test results. *Journal of Educational Psychology,* 1958, *49,* 328–334.

Kelly, H. H. Attribution in social interaction. In E. E. Jones, D. E. Kanouse, H. H. Kelley, R. E. Nisbett, S. Valins, & B. Weiner (Eds.), *Attribution: Perceiving the causes of behavior.* New Jersey: Geneva Learning Press, 1971.

Kersh, M. E. *A strategy for mastery learning in fifth-grade arithmetic.* Unpublished Ph.D. dissertation, University of Chicago, 1971.

Kester, S., & Letchworth, G. Communication of teacher expectations and their efforts on achievement and attitudes of secondary school students. *Journal of Educational Research,* 1972, *66,* 51–55.

Kifer, E. *The effects of school achievement on the affective traits of the learner.* Unpublished Ph.D. dissertation, University of Chicago, 1973.

Kim, H., *et al. A study of the Bloom strategies for mastery learning.* Seoul, Korea: Korean Institute for Research in the Behavioral Sciences, 1969.

Kim, H., *et al. The mastery learning project in the middle schools.* Seoul, Korea: Korean Institute for Research in the Behavioral Sciences, 1970.

Kim, H. Mastery learning in the Korean middle schools. *UNESCO Regional Office for Education in Asia,* September 1971, *6*(1), Sec. I, 55–60.

Kim, H., Cho, G., Park, J., & Park, M. An application of a new instructional model. Research Report No. 8. Seoul, Korea: Korean Educational Development Institute, 1974.

Kirby, B. C. Three error sources in college grades. *Journal of Experimental Education,* 1962, *31,* 213–218.

Klausmeier, H. J., Quilling, M. R., Sorenson, J. S., Way, R. S., & Glasrud, G. R. *Individually guided education and the multiunit elementary school (guidelines for implementation).* Madison, Wisconsin: Wisconsin Research and Development Center for Cognitive Learning, University of Wisconsin, 1971.

Klein, S. P., & Kosecoff, J. Issues and procedures in the development of criterion referenced tests. TM Report 26, ERIC Clearinghouse on Tests, Measurement and Evaluation. Princeton, New Jersey: Educational Testing Service, September, 1973.

Klopfer, L. E., & Champagne, A. B. *Formative evaluation of the* Individualized science program. Paper presented to the National Association for Research in Science Teaching, Chicago, 1974.

Knightly, J., & Sayre, J. Self-paced instruction for library science students. *Journal of Education for Librarianship,* Winter, 1972, 193–197.

Korman, A. K. Self-esteem as a moderator of the relationship between self-perceived abilities and vocational choice. *Journal of Applied Psychology,* 1967, *51,* 65–67.

Krathwohl, D. R. Stating objectives appropriately for program, for curriculum, and for instructional materials environment. *Journal of Teacher Education,* 1965, *12,* 83—92.

Krathwol, D. R., Bloom, B. S., & Masia, B. B. *Taxonomy of educational objectives. Handbook II: Affective domain.* New York: David McKay, 1965.

Kremer, B. J. Is coeducation unfair to boys? *Catholic School Journal,* 1965, *65,* 37—39.

Kueter, R. S. Instructional strategies: The effect of personality factors on recognition learning, using statements of behavioral objectives as opposed to no statements of behavioral objectives prior to instruction (Ph.D. dissertation, Indiana University, 1970). *Dissertation Abstracts International,* 1971, *31,* 539.

Kulik, J. A. PSI: A formative evaluation. In B. A. Green (Ed.), *Personalized instruction in higher education.* Washington, D.C.: Georgetown University, 1976.

Kulik, J. A., Kulik, C. J., & Carmichael, K. The Keller Plan in science teaching. *Science,* 1974, *183,* 379—383.

Kulik, J. A., Kulik, C. J., & Milholland, J. Evaluation of an individualized course in psychological statistics. In R. Ruskin, & S. Bono (Eds.), *Personalized instruction in higher education.* Washington, D.C.: Center for Personalized Instruction, 1974.

Lahaderne, H. M. *Adaptation to school settings: A study of children's attitudes and classroom behavior.* Unpublished Ph.D. dissertation, University of Chicago, 1967. (a)

Lahaderne, H. M. *Attitudinal and intellectual correlates of attention: A study of four sixth-grade classrooms.* Paper read at the annual meeting of the American Educational Research Association, New York, 1967. (b)

Landry, R. G. *Achievement and self-concept: A curvilinear relationship.* Paper presented to the annual meeting of the American Educational Research Association, Chicago, 1974.

Larkins, A. G., & Shaver, J. P. Hardnosed research and the evaluation of curriculum. Logan, Utah: Utah State University, College of Education, 1969 (Mimeo).

Larsen, V. S., & Aronson, R. *SRA Mathematics Learning System Field Verification Study Technical Report.* Chicago: Science Research Associates, October, 1973.

Larsen, V. S., Bode, R. K., & Morgan, J. M. *Growth and efficiency analysis (GAEA).* Chicago: Science Research Associates, January, 1975.

Lawson, T. E. Influence of instructional objectives on learning technical subject matter. *Journal of Industrial Teacher Education,* 1973, *10*(4), 5—14.

Lee, Y. D., *et al. Interaction improvement studies on the mastery learning project, Final report on mastery learning, April—November, 1971.* Educational Research Center, Seoul National University, November, 1971.

Lessinger, L. *Every kid a winner.* New York: Simon & Schuster, 1970.

Levin, T. *The effect of content-prerequisite and process-oriented experiences on application ability in the learning of probability.* Unpublished Ph.D. dissertation, University of Chicago, 1975.

Levine, H. G., & Forman, P. M. A study of retention of knowledge of neurosciences information. *Journal of Medical Education,* 1973, *48,* 867—869.

Lewin, K. *Field theory in social science.* New York: Harper & Row, 1951.

Lewis, P. *Significant others, self-concept of academic ability and achievement.* Unpublished Ph.D. dissertation, University of Chicago, 1974.

Lewis, W. A. Early prediction of college GPA using precollege grades. *Journal of Educational Measurement,* 1966, *3,* 35—36.

Lierley, P. *An application of Mastery Learning Theory to elementary school mathematics.* Unpublished paper, Department of Education, University of California, Santa Barbara, 1973.

Lindvall, C. M., & Cox, R. *Evaluation as a tool in curriculum development: The IPI evaluation program.* Chicago: Rand McNally, 1970.

Lippitt, R., & Gold, M. Classroom social structure as a mental health program. *Journal of Social Issues,* 1959, *15,* 40—49.

Livingston, S. A. Criterion-referenced applications of classical test theory. *Journal of Educational Measurement,* 1972, *9,* 13—26.

Lloyd, K. E. Contingency management in university courses. *Educational Technology,* 1971, *11,* 18—23.

Lloyd, K., & Knutzen, N. A self-paced programmed undergraduate course in the experimental analysis of behavior. *Journal of Applied Behavior Analysis,* 1969, *2,* 125—133.

Lobaugh, D. Girls and grades: Significant factor in evaluation. *Social Science and Mathematics,* 1947, *47,* 763—774.

Ludwig, D. J. Evidence of construct and criterion-related validity for the self-concept. *Journal of Social Psychology,* 1970, *80,* 213—223.

Ludwig, D. J., & Maehr, M. L. Changes in self-concept and stated behavioral preferences. *Child Development,* 1967, *38,* 453—467.

Luginbuhl, J. E. Role of choice and outcome on feelings of success and estimates of ability. *Journal of Personality and Social Psychology,* 1972, *22*(1), 121—127.

Lynch, M. D. *Evaluation of the validity of the items on the Piers Harris and Coopersmith measures.* Paper presented to the annual meeting of the American Psychological Association, Chicago, 1975.

Lynch, M. D. *Validation of the Kiddicon with construct measures.* Paper presented to the annual meeting of the American Psychological Association, Washington, D.C., 1976.

MacDonald-Ross, M. Behavioral objectives: A critical review. *Instructional Science,* 1973, *2,* 1—52.

Mackler, B. Grouping in the ghetto. *Education and Urban Society,* 1969, *2,* 80—96.

Madaus, G. F., Woods, E. M., & Nuttall, R. L. A causal model analysis of Bloom's Taxonomy. *American Educational Research Journal,* 1973, *10*(4), 253—262.

Mager, R. F. *Preparing instructional objectives.* Belmont, California: Fearon Publishers, 1962.

Mager, R. G. *Developing attitude toward learning.* Belmont, California: Fearon Publishers, 1968.

Mager, R. F. *Measuring instructional intent.* Belmont, California: Fearon Publishers, 1973.

Mager, R. F. *Goal analysis.* Belmont, California: Fearon Publishers, 1974.

Mager, R. F. *Preparing instructional objectives* (2nd ed.). Belmont, California: Fearon Publishers, 1975.

Mager, R. F., & Beach, K. M. *Developing vocational instruction.* Belmont, California: Fearon Publishers, 1967.

Mager, R. F., & Pipe, P. *Analyzing performance problems.* Belmont, California: Fearon Publishers, 1970.

Malott, R. (Ed.). Research and development in higher education: A technical report of some behavioral research at Western Michigan University. Kalamazoo, Michigan: Western Michigan University, 1971.

Manis, M. Personal adjustment, assumed similarity to parents, and inferred evaluations of the self. *Journal of Consulting Psychology,* 1958, *22,* 481–485.

Martin, R. A., & Pacheres, J. Good scholars not always the best. Cited in *Business Week,* Feb. 24, 1962, 77–78.

Marx, R. W., & Winne, P. H. *A validation study of self-concept in low SES black children with implications for educational programs.* Paper presented to the annual meeting of the American Educational Research Association, Chicago, 1974.

Mayer, R. E. Information processing variables in learning to solve problems, *Review of Educational Research,* 1975, *45,* No. 4.

Mayo, S. T. Mastery learning and mastery teaching. *NCME Measurement in Education,* 1970, *1,* 1–4.

Mayo, S. T., Hunt, R. C., & Tremmel, F. *A mastery approach to the evaluation of learning statistics.* Paper presented to the annual meeting of the National Council on Measurement in Education, Chicago, 1968.

McGuire, C., & Page, G. The assessment of clinical performance by oral and written simulations. In *Report to the faculty.* Chicago: University of Illinois, College of Medicine, Center for Educational Development, 1972–1973. Pp. 47–51.

McKeachie, W. J. The decline and fall of the laws of learning. *Educational Researcher,* 1974, *3*(3), 7–11.

McMichael, J. S., & Corey, J. R. Contingency management in an introductory psychology course produces better learning. *Journal of Applied Behavioral Analysis,* 1969, *2,* 79–83.

McNeil, J. D. Forces influencing curriculum. *Review of Educational Research,* 1969, *39,* 293–318.

Meichenbaum, D. H. *Cognitive factors in behavior modification: Modifying what clients say to themselves.* Paper presented to the Association for Advancement of Behavior Therapy, Washington, D.C., 1971.

Meichenbaum, D. H., Bowers, K. S., & Ross, R. R. Modification of classroom behavior of institutionalized female adolescent offenders. *Behavior Research and Therapy,* 1968, *6,* 343–353.

Meichenbaum, D. H., Bowers, K. S., & Ross, R. R. A behavioral analysis of teacher expectancy effect. *Journal of Personality and Social Psychology,* 1969, *13,* 306–316.

Meichenbaum, D. H., & Smart, I. Use of direct expectancy to modify academic performance and attitudes of college students. *Journal of Counseling Psychology,* 1971, *18,* 531–535.

Merrill, M. D., Barton, K., & Wood, L. E. Specific review in learning a hierarchical imaginary science. *Journal of Educational Psychology,* 1970, *61,* 102–109.

Meskauskas, J. A. Evaluation models for criterion-referenced testing: Views regarding mastery and standard-setting. *Review of Educational Research,* Winter, 1976, *46*(1), 133–158.

Meskauskas, J. A., & Webster, G. W. The American Board of Internal Medicine recertification examination process and results. *Annals of Internal Medicine,* 1975, *82,* 577–581.

Meyer, W. J., & Thompson, G. G. Sex differences in the distribution of teacher approval and disapproval among sixth-grade children. *Journal of Educational Psychology,* 1956, *47,* 385–396.

Miller, G. A., Galanter, E., & Pribram, K. H. *Plans and the structure of behavior.* New York: Holt, Rinehart & Winston, 1960.

Miller, S. *Measure, number and weight: A polemical statement of the college grading problem.* Ann Arbor, Michigan: Center of Research on Learning and Teaching, University of Michigan, 1967.

Millman, J. Passing scores and test lengths for domain-referenced measures. *Review of Educational Research,* 1973, *43,* 205–216.

Mitchell, J. V. Goal setting behavior as a function of self-acceptance, over- and under-achievement and related personality variables. *Journal of Educational Psychology,* 1959, *50*(3), 93–104.

Modu, C. C. *Affective consequences of cognitive changes.* Unpublished Ph.D. dissertation, University of Chicago, 1969.

Moore, J. W., Hauck, W. E., & Gagné, E. D. Acquisition retention, and transfer in an individualized college physics course. *Journal of Educational Psychology,* 1973, *64,* 335–340.

Moore, J. W., Mahan, M. J., & Ritts, A. C. Continuous progress concept of instruction with university students. *Psychological Reports,* 1969, *25,* 887–892.

Moore, L. M., & Baron, R. M. Effects of wage inequities on work attitudes and performance. *Journal of Experimental Social Psychology,* 1973, *9,* 1–16.

Morris, C., & Kimbrill, G. Performance and attitudinal effects of the Keller method in an introductory psychology course. *Psychological Record,* 1972, *22,* 523–530.

Morrison, H. C. *The practice of teaching in the secondary school.* Chicago: University of Chicago Press, 1926.

Morse, J., & Tillman, M. *Effects on achievement of possession of behavioral objectives and training concerning their use.* Paper presented at the annual meeting of the American Educational Research Association, 1972.

Morse, W. C. Self-concept in the school setting. *Childhood Education,* 1964, *41,* 195–198.

Morton, R. L. Influence of pupil conduct on teachers' marks. *Educational Research Bulletin,* 1932, *11,* 57–60.

Nance, D. *Limits: A mastery learning approach to a unit on limits of sequences and functions in a pre-calculus course and achievement in first semester calculus.* Unpublished Ph.D. dissertation, Michigan State University, 1974.

Naslund, R. A., Thorpe, L. P., & Lefever, D. W. *Achievement Series, Form E and F.* Chicago: Science Research Associates, 1971, 1972.

National Assessment of Educational Progress. *National Longitudinal Study of the High School Class of 1972. Tabular Summary of Student Questionnaire Data* (Vol. 1). U.S. Department of HEW No. 74-227A.

National Education Association. *Violations of human and civil rights: Tests and use of tests.* Report of the 10th National Conference on Civil Rights in Education. Washington, D.C.: National Educational Association, 1972.

National School Public Relations Association. *Individualization in schools: The challenge and the options.* "Project Plan," 1971.

Nazzaro, J. R., Todorov, J. C., & Nazzaro, J. N. Student ability and individualized instruction. *Journal of College Science Teaching*, December, 1972, 29–30.

Nedelsky, L. Absolute grading standards for objective tests. *Educational and Psychological Measurement*, 1954, *14*, 3–19.

Newman, F., Young, D., Ball, S., Smith, C., & Purtle, R. Initial attitude differences among successful, procrastinating and "withdrawn from course" students in a personalized system of statistics instruction. In J. Sherman (Ed.), *PSI: 41 germinal papers*. Menlo Park, California: W. A. Benjamin, 1974.

Oczelik, D. *Student involvement in the learning process.* Unpublished Ph.D. dissertation, University of Chicago, 1973.

Odell, C. W. High school marking systems. *School Review*, 1925, *33*, 346–354.

Okey, J. R. Altering teacher and pupil behavior with mastery teaching. *School Science and Mathematics*, 1974, *74*, 530–535.

Okey, J. R. Development of mastery teaching materials. Final Evaluation Report, USOE G-74-2990. Indiana University, 1975.

Okey, J. R. *The consequences of training teachers to use mastery learning.* Paper presented to the annual meeting of the American Educational Research Association, San Francisco, California, 1976.

Okey, J., & Ciesla, J. *Mastery teaching.* National Center for the Development of Training Materials in Teacher Education. Bloomington, Indiana: Indiana University, 1975.

O'Leary, K. D., & Becker, W. C. Behavior modification of an adjustment class: A token reinforcement program. *Exceptional Children*, 1967, *33*, 637–642.

Olson, D. R. *Towards a theory of instructional means.* Invited address presented to the American Educational Research Association, Chicago, 1974.

O'Neill, G., Johnston, J., Walters, W., & Rashed, J. The effects of quantity of assigned material on college student academic performance and study behavior. In J. M. Johnston (Ed.), *Behavior research and technology in higher education.* Springfield, Illinois: Charles C Thomas, 1975.

Oregon State Department of Education. *Minimum standards for Oregon public schools.*

Oswald, J. M., & Fletcher, J. D. *Some measured effects of specificity and cognitive level of explicit instructional objectives upon test performance among eleventh grade social science students.* Paper presented to the annual meeting of the American Educational Research Association, Minneapolis, 1970.

Ozehosky, R. J., & Clark, E. T. Children's self concepts and Kindergarten achievement. *Journal of Psychology*, 1970, *72(2)*, 185–192.

Page, E. B. Teacher comments and student performance. *Journal of Educational Psychology*, 1958, *49*, 173–181.

Palardy, J. What teachers believe—what children achieve. *Elementary School Journal*, 1969, *69*, 370–374.

Pallett, J. B. *Definition and predictions of success in the business world.* Unpublished Ph.D. dissertation, University of Iowa, 1965.

Paschal, B. J. Role of self concept in achievement. *Journal of Negro Education*, 1968, *37*, 392–396.

Pask, G., & Scott, B. *Uncertainty regulation in learning applied to procedures for teaching concepts of probability.* Chicago: System Research, 1972.

Pearson, W. *An attempt to design instructional techniques to accommodate individual differences in learning rates.* Unpublished Ph.D. dissertation, University of Chicago, 1973.

Peterson, R., Kroeker, L., & Torshen, K. P. Predicting clinical judgment for a primary grade apperception battery. *Journal of Personality Assessment*, 1976, *40*(4), 378–382.

Philippas, M. A., & Sommerfeldt, R. W. Keller vs. lecture method in general physics instruction. *American Journal of Physics*, 1972, *40*, 1300.

Phillips, B. Sex, social class and anxiety as sources of variation in school anxiety. *Journal of Educational Psychology*, 1962, *53*, 316–322.

Phillips, T., Drake, J., Quillen, M., Semb, S., & Semb, G. *Personalizing traditional instruction: An analysis of a peer grading procedure.* Paper presented at the annual meeting of the American Psychological Association, Washington, D.C., 1976.

Piaget, J. *The child's conception of number.* New York: Humanities Press, 1952. (a)

Piaget, J. *The origins of intelligence in children.* New York: International Universities Press, 1952. (b)

Piaget, J. *The construction of reality in the child.* New York: Basic Books, 1954.

Piatt, R. G. An investigation of the effect of the training of teachers in defining, writing and implementing educational behavioral objectives has on learner outcomes for students enrolled in a seventh grade mathematics program in the public schools. (Ph.D. dissertation, Lehigh University, 1969). *Dissertation Abstracts International*, 1970, *30*, 3352.

Piers, E. V., & Harris, E. B. Age and other correlates of self concept in children. *Journal of Educational Psychology*, 1964, *55*, 91–95.

Poggio, J. *Long-term cognitive retention resulting from the mastery learning paradigm.* Paper presented to the annual meeting of the American Educational Research Association, San Francisco, 1976.

Poggio, J. P., Glasnapp, D. R., & Ory, J. C. *The impact of test anxiety on formative and summative exam performance in the mastery learning model.* Paper presented at the annual meeting of the National Council on Measurement in Education, Washington, D.C., 1975.

Popham, W. J. (Ed.). *Criterion-referenced measurement.* Englewood Cliffs, New Jersey: Educational Technology Publishers, 1971.

Popham, W. J., *et al. Instructional objectives.* AERA monograph series on curriculum. Chicago: Rand McNally, 1969.

Popham, W. J., & Husek, T. R. Implications of criterion-referenced measurement. *Journal of Educational Measurement*, 1969, *6*, 1–9.

Posner, G. J., & Strike, K. A. A categorization scheme for principles of sequencing content. *Review of Educational Research*, in press.

Postlewait, S. N., & Hurst, R. N. *The audio-tutorial system incorporating minicourses and mastery.* Purdue University, Department of Biological Sciences, Lafayette, Indiana.

Postlewait, S. N., Novak, J. D., & Murray, H. *An integrated experience approach to learning with emphasis on independent study.* Minneapolis: Burgess Publishing, 1964.

Purkey, W. W., Graves, W., & Zellner, M. Self-perceptions of pupils in an experimental school. *Elementary School Journal*, 1970, *71*, 166–171.

Purves, A. C., & Levine, D. U. *Educational policy and international assessment:*

Implications of the IEA surveys of achievement. Berkeley: McCutchan, 1975.

Reppucci, N. E., & Saunders, J. T. Social psychology of behavior modification: Problems of implementation in natural settings. *The American Psychologist,* 1974, *29,* No. 9.

Resnick, L. B. (Ed.). *The nature of intelligence.* New York: John Wiley & Sons, 1977.

Resnick, L. B., Wang, M. C., & Kaplan, J. Task analysis in curriculum design: A hierarchically sequenced introductory mathematics curriculum. *Journal of Applied Behavior Analysis,* 1973, *6,* 679–710.

Reviere, M., & Haladyna, T. *Effects of learner variables on retention and two levels of cognitive material when learning for mastery.* Paper presented at the annual meeting of the American Educational Research Association, Chicago, 1974.

Reynolds, C., & Gentile, J. *Performance under traditional and mastery assessment procedures in relation to students' locus of control: A possible aptitude by treatment interaction.* Paper presented at the annual meeting of the American Educational Research Association, Washington, D.C., 1975.

Rice, M. *Variables in mastery learning in elementary social studies.* Unpublished manuscript, University of Georgia, 1973.

Robin, A. L., & Graham, M. Q. Academic responses and attitudes engendered by teacher versus student pacing in a personalized instruction course. In R. S. Ruskin & S. F. Bono (Eds.), *Personalized instruction in higher education.* Washington, D.C.: Center for Personalized Instruction, 1974.

Rohwer, W. D. Images and pictures in children's learning. *Psychological Bulletin,* 1970, *73,* 393–403. (a)

Rohwer, W. D. Mental elaboration and proficient learning. In J. P. Hill (Ed.), *Minnesota synposia on child psychology.* Minneapolis: University of Minnesota, 1970. Pp. 220–260. (b)

Rohwer, W. D. Learning, race and school success. *Review of Educational Research,* 1971, *41,* 191–210.

Romberg, T. A., & Harven, J. G. *Developing mathematical processes: Mathematics level one assessment manual.* Chicago: Rand McNally, 1972.

Romberg, T. A., Shepler, J., & King, I. *Mastery learning and retention.* Technical Report No. 151, Wisconsin Research and Development Center for Cognitive Learning. Madison, Wisconsin: University of Wisconsin, 1970.

Rosati, P. A comparison of the personalized system of instruction with the lecture method in teaching elementary dynamics. In J. M. Johnston (Ed.), *Behavior research and technology in higher education.* Springfield, Illinois: Charles C Thomas, 1975.

Rosenberg, M., & Simmons, R. G. *Black and White self-esteem: The urban school child.* The Arnold and Caroline Rose monograph series in sociology. Library of Congress No. 78 183124, Washington, D.C., 1971.

Rosenberg, M. *Society and the adolescent self-image.* Princeton, New Jersey: Princeton University Press, 1965.

Rosenshine, B. *Teaching behaviors and student achievement.* New York: Humanities Press, 1971.

Rosenshine, B. *Teacher competency research.* Paper presented to the annual meeting of the American Educational Research Association, Chicago, 1974.

Rosenshine, B., & Furst, N. Research on teacher performance criteria. In B. O.

Smith (Ed.), *Research in teacher education*. Englewood Cliffs, New Jersey: Prentice-Hall, 1971.

Rosenshine, B., & Furst, N. The use of direct observation to study teaching. In R. M. W. Travers, *Second handbook of research on teaching*. Chicago: Rand McNally, 1973.

Rosner, J. *A formative evaluation of the perceptual skills curriculum project*. Pittsburgh: University of Pittsburgh, Learning Research and Development Center, 1972.

Roth, C. H. Continuing effectiveness of personalized self-paced instruction in digital systems engineering. *Engineering Education*, 1973, *63*(6), 447–450.

Rothkopf, E. Z. Structural text features and the control of processes in learning from written materials. In R. O. Freedle, & J. B. Carroll (Eds.), *Language Comprehension and the Acquisition of Knowledge*, Washington, D.C.: Y. H. Winston & Sons, 1972.

Rothkopf, E. Z., & Kaplan, R. Exploration of the effect of density and specificity of instructional objectives on learning from text. *Journal of Educational Psychology*, 1972, *63*, 295–302.

Rotter, J. B. Generalized expectancies for internal versus external control of reinforcement. *Psychological Monographs*, 1966, *80*(Whole No. 609).

Rubovits, P. C., & Maehr, M. L. Pygmalion analyzed: Toward an explanation of the Rosenthal–Jacobson findings. *Journal of Personality and Social Psychology*, 1971, *19*, 197–203.

Rudnitsky, A. N., & Posner, G. H. *The effect of content sequence on student learning*. Paper presented to the annual meeting of the American Educational Research Association, San Francisco, 1976.

Ruskin, R. S. *The personalized system of instruction: An educational alternative*. Washington, D.C.: The American Association for Higher Education, 1974.

Ryan, B. A. PSI: *Keller's personalized system of instruction: An appraisal*. Paper presented to the annual meeting of the American Psychological Association, Washington, D.C., 1974.

Sanderson, H. *Roles of willingness to spend time and satisfaction with instruction in mastery learning: A step toward clarification*. Unpublished Ph.D. dissertation, State University of New York at Albany, 1973.

Schmuck, R. A., Luszki, M., & Epperson, D. C. Interpersonal relations and mental health in the classroom. *Mental Hygiene*, 1963, *47*(2), 289–299.

Schwab, J. J. Backtalk from abroad. *The University of Chicago Magazine*, 1974, *66*(5), 12–17.

Scriven, M. The methodology of evaluation. In R. W. Tyler, *et al.* (Eds.), *Perspectives on curriculum evaluation*. Chicago: Rand McNally, 1967.

Scriven, M. Problems and prospects for individualization. In H. Talmadge (Ed.), *Systems of individualized education*. Berkeley, California: McCutchan Publishing, 1975.

Sears, P. S. The effect of classroom conditions on the strength of achievement motive and work output of elementary school children. Coop Research Project No. OE 873, Stanford University, Stanford California, 1963.

Seligman, M. Fall into helplessness. *Psychology Today*, 1973, *7*(1), 43–48.

Seligman, M., & Maier, S. F. Failure to escape traumatic shock. *Journal of Experimental Psychology*, 1967, *74*, 1–9.

Semb, G. The effects of mastery criteria and assignment length on college student test performance. *Journal of Applied Behavior Analysis*, 1974, 7, 61—69.

Semb, G. An analysis of the effects of hour exams and student-answered study questions on test performance. In J. M. Johnston (Ed.), *Behavior research and technology in higher education.* Springfield, Illinois: Charles C Thomas, 1975.

Semb, G., Conyers, D., Spencer, R., & Sosa, J. An experimental comparison of four pacing contingencies. In J. M. Johnston (Ed.), *Behavior research and technology in higher education.* Springfield, Illinois: Charles C Thomas, 1975.

Setting Standard of Competence—The Minimum Pass Level. Chicago: University of Illinois, College of Medicine, The Evaluation Unit, Center for the Study of Medical Education, January, 1967.

Shavelson, R. J. Some aspects of the relationship between content structure and cognitive structure in physics instruction (Doctoral dissertation, Stanford University). Ann Arbor, Michigan: University Microfilms, 1971, 71—79, 759.

Shavelson, R. J. Some methods for examining content structure and cognitive structure in instruction. *Educational Psychologist*, 1974, *11*(2). (a)

Shavelson, R. J. Methods for examining representations of a subject-matter structure in a student's memory. *Journal of Research in Science Teaching*, 1974, *11*(3). (b)

Shavelson, R. J., & Stanton, G. C. Construct validations methodology and application to three measures of cognitive structure. *Journal of Educational Measurement*, 1975, *12*(2).

Shaw, M. C., & McCuen, J. T. The onset of academic underachievement in bright children. *Journal of Educational Psychology*, 1960, *51*, 103—108.

Sheppard, W. C., & MacDermot, H. J. Design and evaluation of a programmed course in introductory psychology. *Journal of Applied Analysis*, 1970, *3*, 5—11.

Sherman, J. G. (Ed.). *PSI: 41 germinal papers.* Menlo Park, California: W. A. Benjamin, 1974.

Silberman, M. L. Behavioral expression of teachers' attitudes toward elementary school students. *Journal of Educational Psychology*, 1969, *60*, 402—407.

Silberman, R., & Parker, B. Student attitudes and the Keller plan. *Journal of Chemical Education*, 1974, *51*, 393.

Simon, W. Expectancy effects in the scoring of vocabulary items: A study of scorer bias. *Journal of Educational Measurement*, 1969, *6*, 159—164.

Sink, D. L. Effects of training and revelation of objectives prior to reading a prose passage on eighth-grade student achievement at two different cognitive levels (Ph.D. dissertation, Indiana University, 1973). *Dissertation Abstracts International*, 1974, *34*, 4718.

Sjogren, D. D. Achievement as a function of study time. *American Educational Research Journal*, 1967, *4*, 337—343.

Skager, R. *Generating criterion referenced tests from objectives based assessment systems: Unsolved problems in test development, assembly and interpretation.* Paper presented at the annual AERA Meeting, New Orleans, 1973.

Skinner, B. F. The science of learning and the art of teaching. *Harvard Education Review*, 1954, *24*, 86—97.

Skinner, B. F. *The technology of teaching.* New York: Appleton-Century-Crofts, 1968.

Skinner, B. F. *Beyond freedom and dignity.* New York: Bantam-Vintage, 1971.

Sloggett, B. B. Use of group activities and team rewards to increase individual classroom productivity. In R. Ulrich, T. Stachnik, & J. Mabry (Eds.), *Control of human behavior* (Vol. VIII). Glenview, Illinois: Scott, Foresman, 1974.

Smith, E. R., & Tyler, R. W. *Appraising and recording student progress.* New York: Harper & Row, 1942.

Smith, J. K., Katims, M., & Steele, C. *Mastery learning and reading instruction.* Chicago: Board of Education, 1976 (unpublished paper).

Smith, J. K., & Wick, J. W. *Practical problems of attempting to implement a mastery learning program in a large city school system.* Paper presented to the annual meeting of the American Educational Research Association, San Francisco, 1976.

Snow, R. E. Representative and quasi-representative designs for research on teaching. *Review of Educational Research,* 1974, *44*(3), 265–291.

Snygg, D., & Combs, A. W. *Individual behavior.* New York: Harper and Brothers, 1949.

Soares, A. T., & Soares, L. M. *Interpersonal and self-perceptions of disadvantaged and advantaged high school students.* Paper presented to the annual meeting of the American Psychological Association, 1970.

Soares, L. M., & Soares, A. T. *A study of the interpersonal perceptions of disadvantaged children.* Paper presented to the annual meeting of the American Psychological Association, Washington, D.C., 1971.

Spady, W. G. Competency-based education: A bandwagon in search of a definition. *Educational Researcher,* 1977, *6*(1), 9–14.

Spady, W. G., & Mitchell, D. E. Competency based education: Organizational issues and implications. *Educational Researcher,* 1977, *6*(2), 9–15.

Spencer, R. E., Trask, T., & Semb, G. *A performance-based system for increasing unit size.* Paper presented to the annual meeting of the American Psychological Association, Washington, D.C., 1976.

SRA *Criterion-Referenced Program: An Evaluation Tool, The Guide to Mastery.* Los Angeles: The Regents of the University of California, 1974, 1975.

SRA *Diagnosis: An instructional aid.* Chicago: Science Research Associates, 1972, 1973, 1974.

SRA *Distar*[TM] *Arithmetic, Teacher's Guide.* Chicago: Science Research Associates, 1970.

SRA *Distar*[TM] *Arithmetic II.* Engelmann, S., & Carnine, D. Chicago: Science Research Associates, 1970.

SRA *Distar*[TM] *Arithmetic I, II. Behavioral objectives.* Chicago: Science Research Associates, 1971.

SRA *Learning Cycle Guide, Reading K-3.* Chicago: Science Research Associates, 1976.

SRA *Mathematics Learning System Text, Teacher's Guide, Level 4.* Chicago: Science Research Associates, 1974a.

SRA *Mathematics Learning System, Management Manual.* Chicago: Science Research Associates, 1974b.

SRA *Mathematics Learning System, Resource Box B.* Chicago: Science Research Associates, 1974c.

Staats, A. W. Language behavior therapy: A derivative of social behaviorism. *Behavior Therapy,* 1972, *3*, 165–192.

Staines, J. W. Self-picture as a factor in the classroom. *British Journal of Educational Psychology,* 1958, *28*, 97–111.

Stake, R. E. Objectives, priorities, and other judgment data. *Review of Educational Research*, 1970, *40*(2), 181–212.

Stanwyck, D. J., & Felker, D. W. *Intellectual achievement responsibility and anxiety as functional of self-concept of third to sixth grade boys and girls.* Paper presented to the American Educational Research Association, New York, 1971.

Stanwyck, D. J., & Felker, D. W. *Self-concept and anxiety in middle elementary school children: A developmental survey.* Paper presented to the annual meeting of the American Educational Research Association, Chicago, 1974.

Starch, D., & Elliott, E. C. Reliability of the grading of high school work in English. *School Review*, 1912, *20*, 442–457.

Starch, D., & Elliott, E. C. Reliability of grading work in mathematics. *School Review*, 1913, *21*, 254–295. (a)

Starch, D., & Elliott, E. C. Reliability of grading work in history. *School Review*, 1913, *21*, 676–681. (b)

Steiner, I. D. Self-perception and goal-setting behavior. *Journal of Personality*, 1957, *25*, 344–355.

Stephens, J. M. *The progress of schooling.* New York: Holt, Rinehart & Winston, 1967.

Stern, G. G., Stein, M. I., & Bloom, B. S. *Methods in personality assessment.* Glencoe, Illinois: Free Press, 1956.

Stice, J. E. Expansion of Keller Plan instruction in engineering and selected other disciplines: Final report. College of Engineering, The University of Texas at Austin, December, 1975.

Stringer, L. A., & Glidewill, J. C. *Early detection of emotional illnesses in school children: Final report.* Missouri: St. Louis County Health Department, 1967.

Strom, R. D., & Ray, W. Communication in the affective domain. *Theory into Practice*, 1971, *10*(4), 268–275.

Suchaniak, A. M., & Larsen, V. S. *1972–74 Field verification study of the SRA Mathematics Learning System.* Chicago: Science Research Associates, February, 1975.

Suchman, E. A. *Evaluative research: Principles and practice in public service and social action programs.* New York: Russell Sage Foundation, 1967.

Suppes, P. The uses of computers in education. *Scientific American*, 1966, *215*, 205–221.

Suppes, P. The place of theory in educational research. *Educational Researcher*, 1974, *3*(6), 3–10.

Suppes, P., Fletcher, J. D., Zanotti, M., Lorton, P. V., & Searle, B. W. Evaluation of computer-assisted instruction in elementary mathematics for hearing-impaired students. Technical Report No. 200, Institute for Mathematical Studies in the Social Sciences, Stanford University, March 17, 1973.

Suppes, P., & Groen, G. J. Some counting models for first grade performance data on simple addition facts (Tech. Rept. 90). Also in J. M. Scandura (Ed.), *Research in Mathematics Education.* Washington, D.C.: National Council of Teachers of Mathematics, 1967.

Suppes, P., & Morningstar, M. Computer-assisted instruction. *Science*, 1969, *166*, 343–350.

Suppes, P., & Morningstar, M. *Computer-assisted instruction at Stanford, 1966–68: Data, models, and evaluation of the arithmetic programs.* New York: Academic Press, 1972.

Sutterer, J., & Holloway, R. An analysis of student behavior with and without limiting contingencies. In J. M. Johnston (Ed.), *Behavior research and technology in higher education.* Springfield, Illinois: Charles C Thomas, 1975.

Talmadge, H. (Ed.). *Systems of individualized education.* Berkeley, California: McCutchan Publishing, 1975.

Taylor, D. D., Reid, J. C., Senhauser, D. A., & Shively, J. A. Use of minimum pass levels on pathology examinations. *Journal of Medical Education*, 1971, *46*, 876–881.

Tessler, R. C., & Schwartz, S. H. Help-seeking, self-esteem, and achievement motivation: An attributional analysis. *Journal of Personality and Social Psychology*, 1972, *21*(3), 318–326.

Thelen, H. A. *Classroom grouping for teachability.* New York: John Wiley & Sons, 1967.

Thorndike, E. L. The nature, purposes and general methods of measurements of educational products. In *The measurement of educational products.* Seventeenth Yearbook of the National Society for the Study of Education, Part II. Bloomington, Illinois: Public School Publishing, 1918.

Tiemann, P. W. *Student use of behaviorally-stated objectives to augment conventional and programmed revision of televised college economics lectures.* Paper presented to the annual meeting of the American Educational Research Association, Chicago, 1968.

Tiemann, P. W., & Markle, S. M. Remodeling a model: An elaborated hierarchy of types of learning. *Educational Psychologist*, 1973, *10*(3), 147–158.

Tobias, S. Achievement treatment interactions. *Review of Educational Research*, Winter, 1976, *46*(1), 61–74.

Torshen, K. P. *The relation of classroom evaluation to students' self concepts and mental health.* Unpublished Ph.D. dissertation, University of Chicago, 1969.

Torshen, K. P. The relation of classroom evaluation to students' self concepts. In J. H. Block (Ed.), *Mastery learning.* New York: Holt, Rinehart & Winston, 1971. P. 139. (a)

Torshen, K. P. The relation of classroom evaluation to students' self-concepts and mental health. In J. H. Block (Ed.), *Mastery learning.* New York: Holt, Rinehart & Winston, 1971. Pp. 140–141. (b)

Torshen, K. P. *The relationship of evaluations of students' cognitive performance to their self concept assessments and mental health status.* Paper presented to the American Educational Research Association, New Orleans, Louisiana, 1973.

Torshen, K. P. *Self concept: An examination of structure.* Presentation at the annual meeting of the American Educational Research Association, San Francisco, 1976.

Torshen, K. P., Peterson, R. A., & Kroeker, L. P. *Self-concept inventory for the primary grades.* Paper presented to the American Educational Research Association, Chicago, 1974.

Torshen, K. P., Kroeker, L., & Peterson, R. Primary self-concept inventory. In Orval, G. J. (Ed.), *Tests and measurements in child development: A handbook.* San Francisco: Jossey-Bass, 1976. (a)

Torshen, K. P., Kroeker, L., & Peterson, R. Self concept assessment in young children: Development of a self report, peer comparison measure. *Contemporary Educational Psychology*, in press.

Trabasso, T. Pay attention. *Psychology Today*, 1968, *2*, 30–36.

Trabasso, T., & Bower, G. H. *Attention in learning: Theory and research.* New York: John Wiley & Sons, 1968.

Troutt, G., Jr., & Jennings, B. *A competency base for curriculum development in preschool education.* Paper presented to the annual meeting of the American Educational Research Association, Chicago, 1974.

Tuchman, B. W., & Bierman, M. L. *Beyond Pygmalion: Galatea in the schools.* Paper presented to the American Educational Research Association, New York, 1971.

Tyler, B. Expectancy for eventual success as a factor in problem solving behavior. *Journal of Educational Psychology*, 1958, *49*, 166–172.

Tyler, L. E. *The psychology of human differences* (3rd ed.). New York: Appleton-Century-Crofts, 1965.

Tyler, R. W. *Basic principles of curriculum and instruction.* Chicago: University of Chicago Press, 1950.

Tyler, R. W. Assessing the process of education. *Phi Delta Kappa*, 1965, *47*, 13–16.

Tyler, R. W. The objectives and plans for a National Assessment of Educational Progress. *Journal of Educational Measurement*, 1966, *3*, 1–4.

Tyler, R. W. Changing concepts of educational evaluation. In R. Stake (Ed.), *Perspectives of curriculum evaluation.* American Educational Research Association Monograph Series on Curriculum Evaluation. Chicago: Rand McNally, 1967.

Tyler, R. W. Testing for accountability. *Nation's Schools.* December, 1970, *86*, 37–39.

Tyler, R. W., Gagné, R. M., & Scriven, M. (Eds.). *Perspectives of curriculum evaluation.* American Educational Research Association Monograph Series on Curriculum Evaluation. Chicago: Rand McNally, 1967.

Tyler, R. W., & Wolf, R. M. (Eds.). *Crucial issues in testing.* Berkeley, California: McCutchan Publishing, 1974.

Uhlinger, C. A., & Stephens, M. W. Relation of achievement motivation to academic achievement in students of superior ability. *Journal of Educational Psychology*, 1969, *51*(5), 259–266.

University of Illinois, College of Medicine, Center for Educational Development. *Report to the Faculty*, 1972–1973.

University of Illinois, College of Medicine. *Curriculum.* School of Basic Medical Sciences. Chicago: College of Medicine, University of Illinois, 1973. (a)

University of Illinois, College of Medicine. *Curriculum of the Abraham Lincoln School of Medicine of the University of Illinois College of Medicine.* Chicago: University of Illinois, College of Medicine, 1973. (b)

Vanyo, J. P., & Nicholson, S. J. A course in law and technology. *IEEE Transactions on Education*, 1975, E-18, *3*, 127–131.

Vinsonhaler, J. F., & Bass, R. K. A summary of ten major studies of CAI drill and practice. *Educational Technology*, 1972, 29–32.

Vygotsky, L. *Thought and language.* Cambridge, Massachusetts: MIT Press, 1962.

Walbesser, H. H., & Carter, H. Some methodological considerations of curriculum education research. *Educational Leadership*, 1968, *26*, 53–64.

Walen, S. R. *Personalized instruction using the oral interview technique—preliminary report on near-zero procrastination problems.* Paper presented at the MIT Conference on the Keller plan, Cambridge, Massachusetts, 1971.

Walker, D. F., & Schaffarzick, J. Comparing curricula. *Review of Educational Research*, 1974, *44*(1), 83–111.

Ware, A. *A comparison of two mastery learning strategies for teaching geographic concepts.* Unpublished Ph.D. dissertation, University of Washington, 1975.

Washburne, C. W. Educational measurements as a key to individualizing instruction and promotion. *Journal of Educational Research*, 1922, *5*, 195–206.

Wattenberg, W. W., & Clifford, C. Relations of self-concepts to beginning achievement in reading. *Child Development*, 1964, *25*, 461–467.

Wesler, J. R., Lamar, C. H., & Wilsam, N. J. An examplary program in comparative anatomy utilizing learning for mastery minicourses and multi-media instruction. *British Journal of Medical Education*, 1972.

Welsh, W. W., & Walberg, H. J. A national experiment in curriculum evaluation. *American Educational Research Journal*, 1972, *9*, 373–383.

Wentling, T. L. Mastery versus non-mastery instruction with varying test item feedback instruments. *Journal of Educational Psychology*, 1973, *65*, 1, 50–58.

Westbury, I. Curriculum evaluation. *Review of Educational Research*, 1970, *40*(2), 239–260.

Westbury, I. Conventional classrooms, "open" classrooms, and the technology of teaching. (Privately printed). University of Chicago, 1972.

White, K., & Allen, R. Art counseling in an educational setting: Self-concept change among pre-adolescent boys. *Journal of School Psychology*, 1971, *9*(2), 218–225.

White, R. T. Research into learning hierarchies. *Review of Educational Research*, 1973, *43*(3), 361–375.

White, R. T. The validation of a learning hierarchy. *American Education Research Journal*, 1974, *11*(2), 121–136.

White, R. W. Motivation reconsidered: The concept of competence. *Psychological Review*, 1959, *66*, 297–333.

White, R. W. Competence and the psychosexual stages of development. In M. Jones (Ed.), *Nebraska Symposium of Motivation.* Lincoln: University of Nebraska Press, 1960, 97–141.

White, R. W. Ego and reality in psychoanalytic theory: A proposal regarding independent ego energies. *Psychological Issues*, 1963, *3* (No. 3, Monograph 11).

White, S. H. *Social implications of the definition of intelligence.* Paper presented at the annual meeting of the American Educational Research Association, Chicago, 1974.

Whitehurst, C., & Whitehurst, G. Forced excellence versus "free choice" of grades in undergraduate instruction. In J. M. Johnston (Ed.), *Behavior research and technology in higher education.* Springfield, Illinois: Charles C Thomas, 1975.

Wiley, D. E., & Harnischfeger, A. Explosion of a myth: Quantity of schooling and exposure to instruction, major educational vehicles. *Educational Researcher*, 1974, *3*(4), 7–12.

Williams, R. L., & Cole, S. Self-concept and school adjustment. *Personnel and Guidance Journal*, 1968, *46*, 478–481.

Willis, S. *Formation of teachers' expectations of students' academic performance.* Unpublished Ph.D. dissertation, University of Texas at Austin, 1972.

Wilson, J. W., Cahen, L. S., & Begle, E. G. *NLSMA reports* (Vols. 1–25).

Stanford University: The Board of Trustees of Leland Stanford Junior University, 1968–1972.

Wilson, S. R., & Tosti, D. T. *Learning is getting easier.* San Rafael, California: Individual Learning Systems, 1972.

Winkler, D. R. Time and learning: An economic analysis. Paper presented at the annual meeting of the American Educational Research Association, Washington, D.C., 1975.

Witters, D. R., & Kent, G. W. Teaching without lecture—evidence in the case for individualized instruction. *The Psychological Record,* 1972, *22,* 169–175.

Womer, F. B. *What is national assessment.* Ann Arbor, Michigan: National Assessment of Educational Progress, 1970.

Wood, D. A. *Test construction.* Columbus, Ohio: Merrill, 1961.

Woods, S. S., Resnick, L. B., & Groen, G. J. An experimental test of five process models for subtraction. *Journal of Educational Psychology,* 1975, *67,* 17–21.

Wyckoff, D. *A study of mastery learning and its effects on achievement of sixth grade social studies students.* Unpublished Ph.D. dissertation, Georgia State University, 1974.

Wylie, R. C. *The self-concept.* Lincoln, Nebraska: University of Nebraska Press, 1961.

Wyne, M. D., White, K. P., & Coop, R. H. *The Black self.* Englewood Cliffs, New Jersey: Prentice-Hall, 1974.

Yando, R. M., & Kagan, J. The effect of teacher tempo on the child. *Child Development,* 1968, *39,* 27–34.

Yeager, J. L., & Kissel, M. A. *An investigation of the relationship between selected student characteristics and time required to achieve unit mastery.* Working Paper No. 46, University of Pittsburgh, Learning Research and Development Center, 1969.

Zeaman, D., & House, B. J. The role of attention in retardate discrimination learning. In N. R. Ellis (Ed.), *Handbook of mental deficiency.* New York: McGraw-Hill, 1963.

Zeaman, D., & House, B. J. The relation of I.Q. and Learning. In R. M. Gagné (Ed.), *Individual differences.* Columbus, Ohio: Charles E. Merrill Books, 1967.

Index

A

Average-based methods, 9–18, 182,
185
  historical perspective, 9–13
  deficiencies, 4–5, 13–17, 21–22,
    130–131

C

Competency-based education, 19–27
  defined, 17–19
  implementation considerations,
    24–27, 184–186
  program goals, 19–20, 24, 105,
    143–145
    issues in planning, 20–21,
      184–185
  selection and allocation of
    instruction, 22–23
  selection of evaluation procedures,
    23
Criterion-referenced evaluation, 123,
  162–167, 186–187

D

Domains of competence, 29–37,
  108–110

classification of, 30, 177
  arts of learning, 34
  humane curriculum, 30–32
  taxonomies, 29–30, 32–33, 108,
    110
  defined, 29

M

Mastery model, 41–139, 143–177
  administrative considerations,
    179–183
  appropriate application, 44–46, 48
  components, 41–45
    diagnostic assessment, 43,
      116–117, 122–126, 149,
      150–151, 162–168
    instruction, 43, 112–122, 148,
      155–185
    objectives, 29–30, 42, 77–78, 100,
      103–105, 145–147, 148,
      150–151, 162–170, 177, 184
      affective, 147
      classification of, 29–30
      definition of, 29, 145
      format, 103–105, 145
      objective-referenced postassess-
        ment, 57–67, 78, 104
      role in learning process, 104–105

objectives (*continued*)
  sequencing, 107–112, 116–117
preassessment, 42–43, 85–86,
    106–107, 111–112, 150–155,
    163–164, 180
  effective measures, 106
  prerequisite skills, 107–111
prescription, 43–44, 126–134, 149
    152–153, 158–160, 167–168
  enrichment, 44
  flow chart, 128–129
  relocation, 43
  remediation, 43, 126–127
  sample prescription form, 133
postassessment, 44, 63, 69–71,
    134–139, 150–153, 159–162,
    162–168, 186–187
  the chance factor, 168–170
  record-keeping, 161, 167,
    179–180
  reinforcement and grading,
    135–139
  reward system, 180–182
  test length, 169
curriculum implementations
  Chicago Public Schools, 59,
    69–70, 78–79
  Distar, 67, 145
  Lorain, Ohio, 58–59, 68, 77, 79,
    81, 82
  Mastery Teaching, 77, 80–81, 82
  Mathematics Learning Systems,
    57–58, 78–81, 149–162
  evaluation of, 57–58, 67, 78,
    79–80, 81
  examples, 149–162
  PSI, 66, 68, 80, 83
  Seoul, Korea, 60–61, 83
  University of Illinois College of
    Medicine, 61–62, 146–147,
    148–149
defined, 37, 41
historical perspective, 46–47, 48–51,
    53–54

implementation manuals, 143
Mastery implementation evaluation
    model, 171–178
research investigations
  affective outcomes, 75–101
    critique, 76, 101
    parents' attitudes, 79–80
    student perceptions, 80–84,
      89–90
    teachers' attitudes toward the
      curriculum, 78–79
    teachers' expectations, 76–78,
      84–90
  cognitive outcomes, 55–74
    critique, 73, 119, 125–126,
      170–171
    entry skills, relation to post-
      assessment performance,
      51–53, 72
    norm-referenced assessment,
      61–71
    objective-referenced postassess-
      ment criteria, 57–67, 162–168
    retention, 71
  Cooley and Lohnes multivariate
    evaluation model, 73–74
technical considerations, 183–187
Minimum pass level, 23, 42, 105, 117,
    123–126, 135–136, 146,
    167–170, 186–187

N

Norm-referenced evaluation, 67–71,
    123, 162, 164–167, 186–187

S

School performance model, 51–53
Student motivation, 95–100, 115
Student self-concept, 82–83, 85,
    90–95, 97–98, 115
Impact model, 92–93

A
B
C
D
E
F
G
H
I
J